COMPARATIVE EUROPEAN POLITICS

General Editors: Hans Daalder and Ken Newton

Editorial Board: Brian Barry, Franz Lehner,
Arend Lijphart, Seymour Martin Lipset, Mogens Pedersen,
Giovanni Sartori, Rei Shiratori,
Vincent Wright

Electoral Systems and Party Systems

COMPARATIVE EUROPEAN POLITICS

Comparative European Politics is a series for students and teachers of political science and related disciplines, published in association with the European Consortium for Political Research. Each volume will provide an up-to-date survey of the current state of knowledge and research on an issue of major significance in European government and politics.

Electoral Systems and Party Systems

A Study of Twenty-Seven Democracies 1945–1990

AREND LIJPHART

in collaboration with

Don Aitkin
Asher Arian
Thomas C. Bruneau
Pradeep K. Chhibber
Ivor Crewe
Wilfried Dewachter
A.-P. Frognier
William P. Irvine
W. Keith Jackson
Gary C. Jacobson
Markku Laakso
John C. Lane
Rafael López Pintor
Thomas T. Mackie

George Th. Mavrogordatos
Sten S. Nilson
Dieter Nohlen
Cornelius O'Leary
Jean-Luc Parodi
Mogens N. Pedersen
Anton Pelinka
Bo Särlvik
Yasunori Sone
Alberto Spreafico
Björn S. Stefánsson
Jürg Steiner
Jan Verhoef
Rafael Villegas Antillón

OXFORD UNIVERSITY PRESS
1994

Oxford University Press, Walton Street, Oxford OX2 6DP

Oxford New York Toronto
Delhi Bombay Calcutta Madras Karachi
Kuala Lumpur Singapore Hong Kong Tokyo
Nairobi Dar es Salaam Cape Town
Melbourne Auckland Madrid
and associated companies in
Berlin Ibadan

Oxford is a trade mark of Oxford University Press

Published in the United States
by Oxford University Press Inc., New York

British Library Cataloguing in Publication Data
Data available

Library of Congress Cataloging in Publication Data
Lijphart, Arend.
Electoral systems and party systems : a study of twenty-seven
democracies, 1945–1990 / Arend Lijphart ; in collaboration with Don
Aitkin . . . [et al.].
— (Comparative European politics)
Includes bibliographical references.
1. Elections. 2. Political parties. 3. Comparative government.
I. Aitkin, Don. II. Title. III. Series.
JF1001.L54 1994 324.6'3—dc20 93–16032
ISBN 0–19–827347–9

1 3 5 7 9 10 8 6 4 2

Typeset by Graphicraft Typesetters Ltd., Hong Kong
Printed in Great Britain
on acid-free paper by
Bookcraft (Bath) Ltd.,
Midsomer Norton, Avon

Acknowledgements

This book owes more to the advice and assistance of other scholars than any other book I have written. First of all, I want to express my deep gratitude to my team of collaborators whose names appear on the title-page: experts on each of the twenty-seven countries—and, in Thomas T. Mackie's case, on all of these countries—who provided me with important data, interpretations, and feedback on the rules and operation of the electoral systems in their countries. My goal in recruiting this advisory team was to combine the advantage of collaborative input with the advantage of single-authored output. I believe that this approach has been very fruitful, and I can recommend it to other comparativists.

The Central Library of the University of California, San Diego, has also made an important contribution to this project by systematically acquiring copies of either the official election statistics or the most authoritative election data for all of my twenty-seven democracies from 1945 on. I am especially grateful to the three librarians who worked tirelessly to organize this collection (which has become the Lijphart Elections Archive in the Central University Library): Renata G. Coates, Anita R. Schiller, and Terry M. Vrable.

In addition to my collaborators, many other scholars have given me extremely helpful advice and constructive criticisms, and I want to give them my heartfelt thanks as well: Clive Bean, Nathaniel L. Beck, André Blais, David Butler, Gary W. Cox, Markus M. L. Crepaz, Panayote E. Dimitras, Jörgen Elklit, André Eschet, Michael Gallagher, Bernard N. Grofman, Colin A. Hughes, Mark P. Jones, Sadafumi Kawato, Ashok Lahiri, Alain Lancelot, Malcolm Mackerras, Alan D. McRobie, Steven R. Reed, Philip G. Roeder, Richard Rose, Prannoy Roy, Rainer-Olaf Schultze, Rei Shiratori, Matthew S. Shugart, Kaare Strom, Rein Taagepera, Michael F. Thies, and Fernand Walch.

I also want to state my appreciation to Oxford University Press editors Tim Barton and Henry Hardy for their assistance, encouragement, and patience. This project was started while I held Guggenheim and German Marshall Fund Fellowships, and I gratefully acknowledge the financial assistance that they provided.

In view of the unusual degree to which I have relied on the advice and assistance from my team of collaborators and many other scholars, I must make the conventional statement of exclusive responsibility with special emphasis: I was the final authority on all matters of fact, analysis, organization, and interpretation, and blame for any errors is mine alone.

A. L.

Contents

Tables

Notes on the Author and the Collaborators

AREND LIJPHART is Professor of Political Science at the University of California, San Diego. He is the author of *The Politics of Accommodation*, *Democracy in Plural Societies*, and *Democracies*, editor of *Parliamentary versus Presidential Government*, and co-editor of *Choosing an Electoral System*, and *Electoral Laws and their Political Consequences*.

DON AITKIN is Vice-Chancellor of the University of Canberra and a former Head of the Department of Political Science in the Institute of Advanced Studies of the Australian National University. His many publications include *Stability and Change in Australian Politics*, *Australian Political Institutions*, and *Surveys of Australian Political Science*.

ASHER ARIAN is Distinguished Professor in the Ph.D. Program in Political Science at the Graduate School and University Center of the City University of New York; he is also Professor of Political Science at the University of Haifa. He is the author of *Politics in Israel*, *The Choosing People*, *Ideological Change in Israel*, and other books.

THOMAS C. BRUNEAU is Professor of Political Science at the Naval Postgraduate School in Monterey, California. He has written or co-authored *Politics and Nationhood: Post-Revolutionary Portugal*, *Politics in Contemporary Portugal*, *Portugal in Development*, and other works on Portuguese as well as Brazilian politics.

PRADEEP K. CHHIBBER is Assistant Professor of Political Science at the Ohio State University. He has written on Indian electoral behaviour and has co-ordinated several national post-election and general-attitude surveys in India.

IVOR CREWE is Professor of Government at the University of Essex. His many writings on British and comparative politics include *The British Electorate, 1963–1987*, *British Parliamentary*

Constituencies, Electoral Change in Western Democracies, Party Identification and Beyond, and *Élites in Western Democracy*.

WILFRIED DEWACHTER is Professor of Political Science at the Catholic University of Leuven (Louvain), Belgium. His major books are *De wetgevende verkiezingen als proces van machtsvorming in het Belgisch politiek bestel, Politiek in België: Geprofileerde machtsverhoudingen, Besluitvorming in politiek België*, and many other studies of Belgian politics, elections, and campaign costs.

A.-P. FROGNIER is Professor of Political Science at the Catholic University of Louvain in Louvain-la-Neuve, Belgium. He is the co-author of *Votes, clivages socio-politiques et développement régional en Belgique* and the author of many other studies of the politics of Belgium and Luxembourg.

WILLIAM P. IRVINE is Professor of Political Science at Queen's University in Kingston, Ontario. He has written *Does Canada Need a New Electoral System?* and other studies of Canadian elections, election rules, and electoral behaviour.

W. KEITH JACKSON is Professor of Political Science at the University of Canterbury, Christchurch, New Zealand. His most important publications on New Zealand politics and government are *The New Zealand Legislative Council, New Zealand: Politics of Change*, and *The Dilemma of Parliament*.

GARY C. JACOBSON is Professor of Political Science at the University of California, San Diego. His many writings on the US Congress and on Congressional elections include *Money in Congressional Elections, The Politics of Congressional Elections*, and *The Electoral Origins of Divided Government*.

MARKKU LAAKSO is both a political and a medical scientist and, in the latter capacity, he is affiliated with the University of Kuopio, Finland. He is the co-inventor of the 'effective number of political parties', the most widely used measure of multipartism, and he is the author of a series of studies of the cube law, electoral thresholds, and other aspects of electoral systems.

JOHN C. LANE is Professor Emeritus of Political Science at the State University of New York in Buffalo. In addition to his expertise on German politics, he has a special interest in Malta and he has collected a large machine-readable data set on the Maltese lower house elections from 1921 to 1987.

RAFAEL LÓPEZ PINTOR is Professor of Sociology at the Universidad Autónoma in Madrid. He is the author of *La opinión pública española del franquismo al democracia* and many other publications on public opinion and voting behaviour in Spain as well as in Latin America. He also serves as an electoral consultant to the United Nations.

THOMAS T. MACKIE is Senior Lecturer in Politics at the University of Strathclyde, Glasgow. He is the co-author of *The International Almanac of Electoral History*, the third edition of which appeared in 1991, of the three *Europe Votes* volumes, covering the European Parliament elections in 1979, 1984, and 1989, and other books such as *Electoral Change*.

GEORGE TH. MAVROGORDATOS is Professor of Political Science at the University of Athens. His writings include *Stillborn Republic: Social Coalitions and Party Strategies in Greece, 1922–1936* and *Rise of the Green Sun: The Greek Elections of 1981*.

STEN S. NILSON is Professor Emeritus of Political Science at the University of Oslo. He is the author of *Histoire et sciences politiques*, *Knut Hamsun und die Politik*, and *Knut Hamsun: un aigle dans la tempête*, as well as many other studies of Norwegian and comparative politics.

DIETER NOHLEN is Professor of Political Science at the Ruprecht-Karls-University in Heidelberg. He is an expert on elections and electoral systems with an emphasis on Germany, Latin America, and world-wide comparisons. His many books include *Wahlen in Deutschland*, *Wahlsysteme der Welt*, *Wahlrecht und Parteiensystem*, *Elections and Electoral Systems*, *La Reforma electoral en América Latina*, and *Enciclopedia electoral de América Latina y del Caribe*.

CORNELIUS O'LEARY is Professor of Political Science at Queen's University in Belfast. He is the author of *Irish Elections, 1918–77: Parties, Voters and Proportional Representation* and other studies of Irish politics as well as books on British and Northern Ireland politics.

JEAN-LUC PARODI is Professor of Political Science at the Institut d'Études Politiques in Paris and Secretary-General of the French Political Science Association. He is the author of *Les Rapports entre le législatif et l'exécutif sous la Ve République, 1958–1962*, and co-author of several books including *War Will Not Take Place: The*

French Parliamentary Elections, March 1978 and *Le Député français.*

MOGENS N. PEDERSEN is Professor of Political Science and Dean of Social Sciences at Odense University. He has served as editor of the *European Journal of Political Research* for more than a decade. His books include *The Professionalization of Legislatures: A Comparative Study of Political Recruitment in Denmark and Norway, Lawyers in Politics: The Danish Folketing and American Legislatures,* and *The Dynamics of European Party Systems.*

ANTON PELINKA is Professor of Political Science at the University of Innsbruck. He is the author of *Demokratie und Verfassung in Österreich, Social Democratic Parties in Europe,* and other books, and he also co-edited *The Austrian Party System.*

BO SÄRLVIK is Professor of Political Science at the University of Göteborg. He has written *Opinionsbildningen vid folkomröstningen 1957, Decade of Dealignment: The Conservative Victory of 1979,* and other works on Swedish and British electoral politics.

YASUNORI SONE is Professor of Political Science and Policy Management at Keio University in Tokyo. He is the author of *Contemporary Political Analysis* and *Political Economy of Decision-Making,* and co-editor of *Political Dynamics in Contemporary Japan, Contemporary Democratic Theories,* and other books.

ALBERTO SPREAFICO was Professor of Political Science at the University of Florence until his death in August 1991. His best-known works are the major co-edited volumes *Elezione e comportamento politico in Italia* and *Vent'anni di elezione in Italia (1968–1987);* some of his later writings focus on parties and elections in Spain and Latin America.

BJÖRN S. STEFÁNSSON is a political scientist and public policy expert working free-lance in Reykjavik. He is the author of *Tjodfelagid og troun tess* and *Hjariki.* His most recent publication on voting procedures is 'Borda's Method Applied: The Right to Make a Proposal' in the 1991 volume of *Quantity.*

JÜRG STEINER is Professor of Political Science at the University of Berne, Switzerland, and at the University of North Carolina, Chapel Hill. His publications include *Amicable Agreement Versus Majority*

Rule: Conflict Resolution in Switzerland, European Democracies, and the co-authored volume *A Theory of Political Decision Modes: Intraparty Decision Making in Switzerland*.

JAN VERHOEF is a political scientist who has studied Dutch electoral systems, especially in the pre-PR period. After serving at the University of Leiden and the Ministry of Housing, Physical Planning, and the Environment in The Hague, he now heads the Verhoef Management Consultancy.

RAFAEL VILLEGAS ANTILLÓN is President of the Supreme Elections Tribunal of Costa Rica in San José. He is the author of *El Tribunal Supremo de Elecciones y el registro civil de Costa Rica: análisis jurídico-estructural y técnico* and related works.

Abbreviations

FPTP	first-past-the-post (plurality formula)
LR	largest remainders
LSq	least-squares index
LV	limited vote
PR	proportional representation
SNTV	single non-transferable vote
STV	single transferable vote

1

Introduction: Goals and Methods

EXCEPT in very small communities, democracy necessarily means *representative* democracy in which elected officials make decisions on behalf of the people. How are these representatives elected? This indispensable task in representative democracies is performed by the electoral system—the set of methods for translating the citizens' votes into representatives' seats. Thus the electoral system is the most fundamental element of representative democracy.

The aim of this book is to analyse the operation and the political consequences of electoral systems, especially the degree of proportionality of their translation of votes into seats and their effects on party systems. My emphasis will be on the electoral systems that have been used in the world's most successful democracies—that is, those that have been in existence for a long time—most of which are European democracies. I shall describe the electoral systems in terms of their three most basic properties: the electoral formula (such as plurality, the different forms of proportional representation, and so on), the district magnitude (the number of representatives elected per district), and the electoral threshold (the minimum support that a party needs to obtain in order to be represented). These three elements, which will be defined more precisely later on, together with the size of the representative body, will be shown to have major consequences, especially for proportionality but also for party systems.

The number of electoral systems is, in principle, infinite; the number of systems that democratic engineers and reformers have proposed is much smaller; and the number that have been in actual use is smaller still. I shall try to show that there is neither as much variation in electoral systems nor as much complexity as is often assumed. In particular, systems of proportional representation—to which I shall henceforth refer as PR—are often thought of as inherently complicated; newspaper articles reporting on PR elections almost automatically call the PR system being used a 'complex form of PR'! In fact, with only a few exceptions, PR systems can be classified and described in relatively simple and straightforward terms. One of the reasons for the unnecessary confusion surrounding electoral systems is that both electoral engineers and students of electoral systems have used confused terminologies—with the same term sometimes being used for different practices and the same practice referred to by different terms. I shall try to clarify and simplify the basic terms, and I shall present the principal properties of the various electoral systems in clearly defined categories so as to facilitate comparisons among them as well as the systematic testing of their political consequences.[1]

WHICH ELECTORAL SYSTEMS?

This analysis covers the electoral systems used in twenty-seven democracies from 1945 to 1990—that is, those used in the vast majority of the free and democratic parliamentary elections (at the national level in countries larger than mini-states) that have ever been conducted. Of the twenty-seven democracies, twenty-four are the world's most durable democracies with a history of free elections without major interruptions since 1945 or shortly thereafter. They are the four most populous countries of Western Europe (the United Kingdom, France, Germany, and Italy), the five Nordic states (Sweden, Norway, Denmark, Finland, and Iceland), the three Benelux states (The Netherlands, Belgium, and Luxembourg), four other smaller democracies (Ireland, Austria, Switzerland, and Malta), and eight countries outside Europe (the United States, Canada, Costa Rica, Israel, India, Japan, Australia, and New Zealand).

To these I added Spain, Portugal, and Greece, although they do not qualify under the criterion of long-term and uninterrupted democracy.[2] On the other hand, they have been democratic since the mid-1970s and are generally judged to be stable and consolidated democracies; moreover, it seems appropriate to consider them alongside the other West European democracies. Malta is another somewhat doubtful case for inclusion since it did not become independent until 1964, but it did conduct free universal-suffrage elections as an internally self-governing territory from 1947. It also offers the advantage of providing a second example, in addition to Ireland, of the unusual single transferable vote (STV) form of PR. Finally, a practical advantage of including Malta as well as Spain, Portugal, and Greece is that their election data are available in the *International Almanac of Electoral History*, the handbook that serves as the major source of election data for this study.[3]

As the year in which the Second World War ended, 1945 is a conventional starting-point for studies in the social sciences. It is especially appropriate for this study because, prior to 1945, many of the countries listed above were not democratic or democratic for only a short period (such as Germany, Italy, and Japan), not yet independent (India and Israel), or did not have fully democratic elections with universal suffrage since women did not have the right to vote (France and Belgium). Of course, even after 1945, two of our countries continued to have serious restrictions on the right to vote: the United States until the passage of the Voting Rights Act in 1965 and Switzerland until the adoption of women's voting rights in 1971. Most of our countries conducted elections in 1945 or 1946; for the others, the starting-point is the first election after 1945 followed by an uninterrupted period of regular free elections lasting until the end of 1990.

The year 1990 was chosen as the end of the period under analysis for practical reasons—the availability of accurate and comparable election data. However, three elections held before the end of 1990—the November 1989 election in India and the December 1990 elections in Germany and Denmark—could not be included because the necessary election information was still missing when the data analysis had passed a critical point. There may also be some symbolic significance in ending the analysis just prior to the 1990 all-German election because this was an election in a partly new and different country and, even more significantly, it marked the end of the post-Second World War era.

The electoral systems to be analysed are those for national lower-house elections (or, in the case of unicameral parliaments, the elections of the one chamber) in the countries and the period indicated. This means that all other national (upper-house and presidential) and all subnational elections are excluded, even when they are direct, popular elections. The only exception is that, for the twelve members of the European Community, the elections to the

European Parliament are included. For the purpose of this analysis, I am treating the European Parliament as a set of national
mini-parliaments. This does not represent a correct view of the
actual operation of the European Parliament, but it *is* an accurate
interpretation of the way it is elected—by twelve different electoral systems that are generally much more closely related to the
twelve national parliamentary electoral systems than they are to
each other. Vernon Bogdanor writes that even the third cycle of
European elections, held in 1989, again 'proved to be, as in 1979
and 1984, primarily an arena for a set of national contests'.[4] And
Hermann Schmitt cites survey data showing that most voters continue to think of the parties competing for election to the European Parliament as national parties, and that they would also 'prefer
to have parties in the European Parliament structured along national rather than on political-ideological lines'.[5]

    In addition to enriching the data base for this study, the inclusion
of the Euro-elections has two special advantages. First, it provides
examples of the election of relatively small representative bodies:
all of the twelve countries have European Parliament delegations
that are considerably smaller than the lower or only chambers
of their national parliaments. Second, it offers good opportunities
for controlled comparison, because for most countries the electoral systems for the national parliaments and for the national
mini-parliaments in the European Parliament resemble each other
closely but are not completely identical.

    Table 1.1 lists the 350 parliamentary and 34 Euro-elections that
form the empirical basis of this comparative study. In almost all
cases, all the votes cast and all seats at stake in an election are
included in the analysis. However, I made a few exceptions to this
general rule in order to make the comparisons of votes and seats
as accurate as possible. For instance, I excluded all uncontested
seats for which no votes were cast or recorded (mainly in countries with majoritarian election systems but also in Ireland and
Switzerland) and seats filled by indirect election (the West Berlin
representatives in the Bundestag and in the European Parliament).
In order not to confuse the effects of different electoral systems,
I excluded the few STV districts (both votes and seats) from British elections, which have been mainly plurality elections: the four
two-member and three-member STV districts in the 1945 parliamentary election and the Northern Ireland three-member STV

TABLE 1.1. National legislative (lower or only house) elections and European Parliament elections in 27 democracies, 1945–90

Country	National elections		European elections		Total	Exclusions
	Number	Years	Number	Years		
Australia (AUL)	19	1946–90	—	—	19	Uncontested seats
Austria (AUT)	14	1945–90	—	—	14	—
Belgium (BEL)	15	1946–87	3	1979–89	18	—
Canada (CAN)	15	1945–88	—	—	15	Uncontested seats
Costa Rica (CR)	10	1953–90	—	—	10	—
Denmark (DEN)	19	1945–88	3	1979–89	22	Faroes, Greenland
Finland (FIN)	13	1945–87	—	—	13	—
France (FRA)	14	1945–88	3	1979–89	17	Overseas departments and territories, Algeria
Germany (GER)	11	1949–87	3	1979–89	14	West Berlin
Greece (GRE)	7	1974–90	3	1981–89	10	—
Iceland (ICE)	14	1946–87	—	—	14	—
India (IND)	8	1952–84	—	—	8	Uncontested seats
Ireland (IRE)	14	1948–89	3	1979–89	17	Uncontested seats
Israel (ISR)	12	1949–88	—	—	12	—
Italy (ITA)	11	1946–87	3	1979–89	14	—
Japan (JPN)	18	1946–90	—	—	18	The two seats left unfilled in the 1946 election
Luxembourg (LUX)	10	1945–89	3	1979–89	13	The 1948 and 1951 partial elections were treated as one election

TABLE 1.1. (Cont.)

Country	National elections		European elections		Total	Exclusions
	Number	Years	Number	Years		
Malta (MAL)	11	1947–87	—	—	11	—
Netherlands (NET)	14	1946–89	3	1979–89	17	—
New Zealand (NZ)	16	1946–90	—	—	16	—
Norway (NOR)	12	1945–89	—	—	12	—
Portugal (POR)	7	1975–87	2	1987–89	9	Citizens living abroad
Spain (SPA)	5	1977–89	2	1987–89	7	—
Sweden (SWE)	14	1948–88	—	—	14	—
Switzerland (SWI)	11	1947–87	—	—	11	Uncontested seats
United Kingdom (UK)	13	1945–87	3	1979–89	16	Four STV districts (1945), the Northern Ireland STV district (Euro-elections), and uncontested seats
United States (US)	23	1946–90	—	—	23	Non-voting representatives of the District of Columbia, Puerto Rico, etc.
TOTAL	350		34		384	

district used for the 1979, 1984, and 1989 Euro-elections. I also followed the usual scholarly conventions of focusing on metropolitan France only (excluding the delegates from the overseas departments and territories) and analysing Denmark without the Faroes and Greenland. A few more details of this kind are provided in Table 1.1.

BASIC METHODOLOGY

In contrast with Douglas W. Rae's classic study, in which elections serve as the units of analysis,[6] my cases are seventy *electoral systems*, defined as sets of essentially unchanged election rules under which one or more successive elections are conducted. Elections held under the same electoral system are regarded as repeated observations of the operation of a single electoral system. For instance, Finland provides only one electoral system under which its thirteen parliamentary elections were held, whereas Germany provides six different electoral systems, four Bundestag and two European Parliament systems, that guided its total of fourteen elections.

My variables are the basic characteristics of electoral systems, measures of disproportionality, and measures of multipartism and of the production of majority parties. I follow two basic multivariate approaches. One is a comparable-cases strategy that concentrates on within-country variations when more than one electoral system is used in the same country; this permits the examination of the effect of changing one aspect of an electoral system while the system remains the same in other respects. Additionally, the effect of small changes *within* electoral systems—changes that are not sufficiently important to signify changes *of* the electoral system—will be examined.

The second basic strategy relies on a cross-sectional research design in which cross-tabulations as well as multiple correlation and regression are applied to the seventy electoral systems. However, what is an advantage for the first strategy—having attractive comparable cases in the form of more than one electoral system in the same country—presents somewhat of a problem for the second strategy, because it means that some of the cases are not completely independent. For this reason, I shall also present an analysis of fifty-three, instead of seventy, cases by combining those electoral systems in the same country where such a combination is at all possible and justifiable.

A different but at least equally crucial aspect of my research strategy was the combination of a collaborative project with, as its product, a single-authored book. Experts on, and usually in, each of the twenty-seven countries, supplied me with vital information, interpretation, and feedback on the rules and operation of their countries' electoral systems. My goal was to find the optimal mix of the pooled wisdom provided by joint scholarship with the consistency of having one author and researcher-in-chief.

Finally, a major methodological goal of this book is to promote replication. As the following chapters will repeatedly show, a host of important decisions must be made with regard to classification, measurement, and other methodological matters. I shall always explicitly defend my choices, and, in many instances, I shall also show the results that would have been yielded if different measures and methods had been used. But I want to make it as easy as possible for my readers to reanalyse the data according to the alternatives that *they* prefer. For this purpose, all of the basic data are easily available. The detailed characteristics of the seventy electoral systems are given in the tables of Chapter 2. The measures of disproportionality and multipartism for the same seventy electoral systems are listed in Appendix B. If readers want to do a more thorough replication, they can obtain the disproportionality and multipartism measures for each of the 384 elections from the author.[7] Finally, all of the raw election data may be found in a few easily accessible sources: the *International Almanac of Electoral History* together with the 1989 and 1990 updates in the *European Journal of Political Research* (for all of the countries except India and Costa Rica) and the two volumes *Europe Votes 2* and *Europe Votes 3* (for the European Parliament elections).[8] Appendix C contains a list of corrections and clarifications concerning these data as well as the election figures for India and Costa Rica.

OVERVIEW AND PREVIEW

Chapter 2 will give a detailed description and classification of the seventy electoral systems. It will also highlight general patterns (such as the high frequency of the use of list PR and of the d'Hondt formula) and general trends (such as the increasing use of more proportional methods and the increasing use of two-tier districting systems). Chapter 3 will examine the concepts of electoral disproportionality, multipartism, and majority-party generation, and will discuss the advantages and disadvantages of the different operational measures that have been proposed. How to measure disproportionality presents the most serious problem, but I shall show not only that my preferred measure—Michael Gallagher's least-squares index—offers a good solution, but also that values of the different measures advocated by other scholars correlate highly with those of the least-squares measure.

The next three chapters examine the relationships between the electoral system variables, disproportionality, multipartism, and majority-party generation. Chapter 4 does so by examining within-country variation, and Chapter 5 by means of a cross-sectional design. Chapter 6 extends the analysis by examining the potential explanatory power of four additional elements of electoral systems: ballot structure, malapportionment, presidentialism, and *apparentement*. My main conclusions will be that, of the five dependent variables, disproportionality is the one that can be explained best in terms of the electoral system characteristics, and that the strongest explanation of the various dependent variables is provided by what I shall call the 'effective threshold', a combination of district magnitude and electoral thresholds. The effect of the electoral system on multipartism is more modest but still very important, and the explanatory power of the other electoral system variables—the electoral formula, assembly size, *apparentement*, ballot structure, and presidentialism—is also more modest but, again, not at all negligible. Chapter 7 will conclude by examining some of the practical lessons that electoral engineers and reformers can learn from my findings.

2

Electoral Systems: Types, Patterns, Trends

THE foremost purpose of this book is to analyse the political effects of electoral systems. The first step that needs to be taken towards that goal is the description and classification of the electoral systems. This is usually done in terms of the different 'dimensions' of electoral systems—a practice that I shall also adopt for the description of the seventy electoral systems of our twenty-seven countries between 1945 and 1990 in the bulk of this chapter. The last three sections will deal with the empirical relations between the dimensions and with general patterns and trends in the development of electoral systems.

DIMENSIONS OF ELECTORAL SYSTEMS

There is broad agreement among electoral system experts that the two most important dimensions of electoral systems, with major consequences for the proportionality of election outcomes and for party systems, are the electoral formula and the district magnitude.[1] Three main types of electoral formulas and a large number of subtypes within each of these are usually distinguished: majoritarian formulas (with plurality, two-ballot systems, and the alternative vote as the main subtypes), PR (classified further into largest remainders, highest averages, and single transferable vote formulas), and semi-proportional systems (such as the cumulative vote and the limited vote). The purpose of the introduction of PR in many countries was to achieve greater proportionality and better minority representation than the earlier majoritarian electoral methods had produced.

District magnitude is defined as the number of representatives elected in a district (constituency). One of the best-known findings of Douglas W. Rae's 1967 study *The Political Consequences of Electoral Laws*—the first systematic comparative analysis of the effects of electoral systems on disproportionality and multipartism, which has been a major source of inspiration for this book—was the extremely strong influence of district magnitude.[2] Rae modestly attributes this proposition to James Hogan who wrote in 1945: 'the decisive point in P.R. is the size [magnitude] of the constituencies: the larger the constituency, that is, the greater the number of members which it elects, the more closely will the result approximate to proportionality.'[3] And twenty years earlier, George Horwill had already referred to district magnitude as 'the all-important factor'.[4]

In PR systems, proportionality—and the chances for small parties to gain representation—are necessarily very limited when there are only two or three representatives per district, but increase dramatically when magnitude increases. In countries with multi-member districts, district magnitude tends to vary; in this study, therefore, magnitude will usually refer to the *average* district magnitude. It can be calculated very simply by dividing the total number of seats in the legislature (to which I shall henceforth refer as the assembly size) by the number of districts. Because of the importance of this dimension, all three variables—average magnitude, number of districts, and assembly size—will be listed for each electoral system in the tables in this chapter that provide the basic information on our seventy electoral systems. As will be discussed shortly, assembly size is also an important factor in its own right.

One complication with regard to magnitude is that there may be two, or even more, levels of districts; for instance, a country with PR elections may be divided into, say, ten or twenty electoral districts, but may also have a national district that is superimposed on the lower-level districts. This type of system, for which Rae has coined the term 'complex districting',[5] will be explained in due course.

Another important dimension of electoral systems is the electoral threshold, that is, a minimum level of support which a party needs in order to gain representation. If the electoral law provides for such a threshold, it is usually applied at the national level (indicated by N in the tables), but it may also be imposed at the district (D), or at an in-between, regional (R) level, and the minimum may be defined in terms of a certain number of votes, a percentage of the votes, or some other criterion such as the winning of at least one seat in a lower-level district in order to be eligible for seats in the higher-level district.

Not all electoral systems have such legal thresholds—in fact, most do not—but, as Rein Taagepera and Matthew S. Shugart have pointed out, even in the absence of an explicit legal threshold, an actual threshold is implied by the other two dimensions of the electoral system, especially by district magnitude.[6] Low magnitudes have the same effect as high thresholds: both limit proportionality and the opportunities for small parties to win seats; as magnitudes increase and thresholds decrease, proportionality and the chances for small parties improve. In other words, legal thresholds and district magnitudes can be seen as two sides of the same coin. Accordingly, I shall often treat these two dimensions as one variable. All magnitudes and legal thresholds can be converted into a single operational indicator: the effective threshold, stated in terms of a percentage of the total national vote. How the effective threshold is calculated will be explained later.

The fourth major dimension on which this study will focus is assembly size—that is, the total number of seats in the legislature. Rae calls attention to this 'generally neglected variable', but he does not enter it into his empirical analysis.[7] Its effect has not been studied systematically by other electoral system analysts either, perhaps because they have tended to see it as a factor external to the electoral system, that is, as merely a characteristic of legislatures elected according to particular electoral systems rather than as a characteristic of electoral systems as such. However, if electoral systems are defined as methods of translating votes into seats, the total numbers of seats available for this translation appears to be an integral and legitimate part of the systems of translation.

In any case, there can be no doubt that assembly size can have a strong influence on proportionality and on the degree of multipartism. For instance, if four parties win 41, 29, 17, and 13 per cent of the national vote in a PR election—to use the example that I shall also use in Appendix A to illustrate the operation of different PR formulas—there is no way in which the allocation of seats can be handled with a high degree of proportionality if the election is to a mini-legislature with only five seats; the chances of a proportional allocation improve considerably for a ten-member legislature; and perfect proportionality could be achieved, at least in principle, for a 100-member legislative body. Of course, the same pattern theoretically applies to non-PR systems as well, but since these systems do not even aim at proportionality, the hypothesis that assembly size may have a significant additional effect on their degree of disproportionality may seem less plausible. Nevertheless, Taagepera has found that, in plurality elections, the degree of disproportionality does tend to increase, all other factors being equal, as the size of the legislature decreases.[8] In short, there is ample theoretical justification to include assembly size as one of the important dimensions of electoral systems.

As already stated in the previous chapter, I define an electoral system as a set of essentially unchanged election rules under which one or more successive elections are conducted in a particular democracy. This definition can now be refined by stating it in terms of the four major dimensions of electoral systems: if there is a significant change on one or more of the four dimensions, this means that a new electoral system must be distinguished. A further refinement is needed in order to define precisely what counts as significant change. The electoral formula is a discrete variable; hence any change in the formula can be recognized easily and will be regarded as a significant change. In two-tier districting systems, the criterion will be a change in formula at what I shall define later as the decisive tier. However, since the other three dimensions are continuous variables, exact cut-off points have to be specified.

For all three, I propose a 20 per cent criterion: 20 per cent or greater change in district magnitude (in two-tiered districting systems, the magnitude at the more important upper level will be counted), 20 per cent or more change in the national legal threshold (or the adoption of such a threshold where none existed before), and 20 per cent or greater change in assembly size. For instance, a change in legal threshold from 5 to 6 or more, in district magnitude from 10 to 12 or more, or in assembly size from 200 to 240 or more (or the other way around) will be regarded as changes that create a different electoral system.[9] This criterion is necessarily arbitrary; cut-off points anywhere between 10 per cent and 25 per cent would also be reasonable and legitimate. By selecting the relatively high value of 20 per cent, I am deliberately opting to err on the side of caution: in particular, I want to avoid artificially inflating the number of cases (electoral systems) for the analysis by creating two or more cases that are too strongly alike and that really should be treated as a single case. Chapters 4 and 5 will examine, respectively, the effects of changes within electoral systems and of changes in a smaller set of cases generated by combining relatively similar cases; in other words, these analyses will first relax and then tighten the 20 per cent criterion, and will therefore provide a check of whether 20 per cent is too strict or too lenient as the cut-off point.

FOUR OTHER ELECTORAL SYSTEM VARIABLES

The above four dimensions provide the framework for the description and classification of the seventy electoral systems in this chapter and will also be the main independent variables in the analysis of the effects of these electoral systems in Chapters 4 and 5. In addition, I shall pay some attention to four minor, but not necessarily negligible, aspects of electoral systems and test their political consequences: ballot structure, malapportionment, the difference between legislative elections in parliamentary and in presidential systems, and the possibility of linked lists.

First, ballot structure is one of Rae's three basic dimensions of electoral systems along with formula and magnitude. (Rae does not consider thresholds and assembly size.) Ballot structure can be either categorical, if the voter can give his or her vote to one party only, which is the case in most electoral systems, or ordinal if the voter can divide his or her vote among two or more parties. (The term 'ordinal ballot structure' is somewhat misleading because it includes, but is not limited to, systems in which voters rank order two or more parties.) Rae hypothesizes that ordinal ballots, by allowing vote dispersion, may encourage multipartism, but finds that his evidence (for twenty countries in the period from 1945 to 1964) contradicts his hypothesis.[10] However, since the hypothesis is not implausible, it is worth retesting it against the much broader empirical evidence of our seventy electoral systems.

Second, in his recent analysis of the proportional or disproportional effects of different electoral formulas, Michael Gallagher rightly warns his readers that other dimensions of electoral systems may also affect the degree of proportionality of election outcomes: in addition to district magnitude and thresholds (he does not mention the factor of assembly size), he points to 'the possibility of malapportionment'.[11] In single-member district systems, malapportionment means that the districts have substantially unequal voting populations; malapportioned multi-member districts have magnitudes that are not commensurate with their voting populations. Obviously, malapportionment may systematically favour one or more parties and therefore contribute to electoral disproportionality. Malapportionment often takes the form of rural or regional overrepresentation. It has not been a serious problem in most of our long-term democracies during the post-Second World War era, but its possible influence is also worth testing.

Third, Shugart has shown that presidential systems can have an important effect on legislative elections if presidential elections are by plurality and if legislative elections are held at the same time: large parties have an advantage in presidential races since smaller parties do not have much of a chance to have one of their candidates elected, and this advantage tends to carry over into the legislative elections.[12] Hence, presidentialism tends to discourage multipartism. Because our set of countries includes only two presidential systems (the United States and Costa Rica), it does not offer an optimal opportunity to test this hypothesis, but semi-presidential systems (France, Finland, and Portugal) and parliamentary systems with directly elected presidents (Austria, Iceland, and Ireland) may be hypothesized to have similar effects.

The fourth variable that I shall examine pertains especially to PR systems in which voters choose among competing party lists. In several of these, parties are allowed formally to link or connect their lists, which means that their combined vote total will be used in the initial allocation of seats. A set of such inter-party connected lists is usually referred to by the French term *apparentement*. As Andrew McLaren Carstairs has pointed out, since almost all electoral systems, including PR, in practice favour the larger parties to some extent, 'the question of whether or not *apparentement* is permitted can be of great importance to the smaller parties'.[13] Several other electoral systems have features that are functionally equivalent to *apparentement*. Along with ballot structure, malapportionment, and presidentialism, it will be tested in Chapter 6.

MAJORITARIAN ELECTION SYSTEMS

Table 2.1 lists the twelve majoritarian election systems that have operated in seven of our countries during the 1945–90 period. Six of these countries used only majoritarian electoral systems, and the basic facts concerning their entire electoral system history is contained in the table: Canada, New Zealand, and the United States used the same system throughout the period, and Australia, India, and the United Kingdom, while undergoing a significant change on one dimension, stayed within the confines of majoritarianism. France is the only country in the table with only two (of its six) electoral systems in Table 2.1.

When countries have used two or more systems, they are numbered in chronological order; for instance, IND1 is the first system used in India in the 1952 and 1957 elections, and IND2 is the Indian system for the elections from 1962 to 1984; and the two French systems are labelled FRA3 and FRA6 because two non-majoritarian systems occurred before FRA3 and again between FRA3 and FRA6. For countries with European Parliament elections (all of which took place at the end of our period, between 1979 and 1989), these Euro-election systems are identified by their chronological numbers and also, for the sake of maximum clarity, by the letter 'E'. For example, UK1 is the system for House of Commons elections and UK2E the system for electing British representatives to the European Parliament. I shall use the same conventions in the tables for PR and other electoral systems later on in this chapter. Furthermore, all of these tables will also list the number of elections in each electoral system and the time-span during which these elections took place (in the second column).

Two further general conventions will be used in order to make these tables as clear and informative as possible. One is that all integers indicate exact and unchanging numbers; all other numbers indicate averages. For instance, the district magnitudes of 1 in Table 2.1 mean that in these electoral systems all districts in all elections were, without exception, single-member districts, whereas the three district magnitudes of 1.00 indicate the use of some, but very few, two-member or multi-member districts. Second, it is noted which entries indicate approximations. An example is the plurality

TABLE 2.1. Twelve majoritarian electoral systems, in decreasing order of district magnitude, 1945–90

Electoral system[a]	Number and years of elections	Electoral formula	District magnitude[b]	Number of districts	Assembly size	Legal threshold N/R/D[c] (%)	Effective threshold (%)
IND1	2: 1952–7	Plurality	1.21	396	480.50	—	35[d]
CAN	15: 1945–88	Plurality	1.00	267.07	268.27	—	35[d]
US	23: 1946–90	Plurality[d]	1.00	433.83	435.17	—	35[d]
UK1	13: 1945–87	Plurality	1.00	631.69	632.85	—	35[d]
IND2	6: 1962–84	Plurality	1	522.00	522.00	—	35[d]
NZ	16: 1946–90	Plurality	1	85.69	85.69	—	35[d]
UK2E	3: 1979–89	Plurality	1	78	78	—	35[d]
FRA3	7: 1958–81	Majority-Plurality	1	470.14	470.14	12[d] (D)	35[d]
FRA6	1: 1988	Majority-Plurality	1	555	555	17[d] (D)	35[d]
AUL1	1: 1946	Alternative vote	1	74	74	—	35[d]
AUL2	15: 1949–83	Alternative vote	1	122.20	122.20	—	35[d]
AUL3	3: 1984–90	Alternative vote	1	148	148	—	35[d]

Notes:
[a] See description of electoral systems on pp. 13–14, 16.
[b] See description of integers used on p. 16.
[c] See description of level at which the threshold is applied on p. 11.
[d] Approximation.

formula for US House of Representatives elections; this has indeed been the usual formula, but the majority-runoff method has also been used (in Louisiana, where the first stage of the election is referred to as the 'non-partisan primary', and in Georgia). All values of the effective threshold in Table 2.1 are also indicated as approximations; the reasons for using these approximations and the definition of the term 'effective threshold' will be given later on during the discussion of PR systems. (It is also worth recalling the exclusions specified in Table 1.1; in particular, the numbers of districts and the assembly sizes are based on contested seats only.)

Of the many majoritarian formulas that exist in theory, Table 2.1 shows that only three have been in actual use in our set of countries between 1945 and 1990: plurality, majority-plurality, and the alternative vote.[14] The plurality formula—often also called the first-past-the-post (FPTP) or relative majority method—stipulates that, in single-member districts, voters can cast one vote each and that the candidate with the most votes wins. (In two-member districts, voters have two votes and the two candidates with the most votes win; and so on.) Five countries have used plurality and have used it almost without exceptions: Canada, India, New Zealand, the United Kingdom, and the United States.[15]

The French Fifth Republic provides the only instance of the two-ballot majority-plurality formula. Here the rule is that a majority (that is, an absolute majority—more than half of the valid votes) is required for election on the first ballot; if the first ballot does not produce a winner, a second ballot is conducted and the candidate with the most votes wins, even if he or she wins only a plurality of the votes. The second ballot can have more than two candidates, but the usual second-ballot pattern in France is a contest between two principal candidates, because the weakest candidates are forced to withdraw and other candidates may withdraw voluntarily in favour of stronger candidates of allied parties. However, the majority-plurality formula should be distinguished from the majority-runoff in which the second round of the election is restricted to the top two candidates from the first round; it may therefore be characterized as the majority-majority formula, in contrast with the French majority-plurality method. The majority-runoff has not been used in our set of countries for legislative elections (with the small exception of some US Congressional elections, noted above), but it is used for direct presidential elections in France, Portugal, and Austria.[16]

Australia is the only country that has used the alternative vote. Voters are asked to list the candidates in order of their preference. If a candidate receives an absolute majority of first preferences, he or she is elected; if not, the weakest candidate is eliminated, and his or her ballots are redistributed among the remaining candidates according to these ballots' second preferences; this process continues until a majority winner emerges. As a simple example, let us assume that there are four candidates (*A*, *B*, *C*, and *D*) receiving, respectively, 41, 29, 17, and 13 per cent of the voters' first preferences; since no candidate has received a majority of the first preferences, candidate *D* is eliminated. Let us further assume that the second preferences on *D*'s ballots are for *C*; this means that, after the second round of counting, *C* now has 30 per cent of the vote, *A* 41 per cent, and *B* 29 per cent. *B* is therefore eliminated next, and in the third round of counting, the contest is between *A* and *C*—one of whom will be the winner. The alternative vote, which in Australia is usually referred to as 'preferential voting', may be thought of as a refinement of the majority-runoff formula in the sense that weak candidates are eliminated one at a time (instead of all but the top two candidates at the same time) and that voters do not have to go to the polls twice.[17]

The plurality systems are listed first in Table 2.1 (followed by majority-plurality and alternative vote) and, within the plurality group, the systems are listed in decreasing order of district magnitude. The most striking characteristic of these magnitudes is that, with the exception of the first Indian system, they are either exactly 1 or very close to 1; that is, single-member districts have been the rule and two-member or larger multi-member districts very infrequent exceptions. The only instance of substantial numbers of larger than single-member districts occurred in the 1952 and 1957 Indian elections: slightly more than a third of the seats were in two-member districts (and in one three-member district in 1952). The next on the list is Canada, which had two two-member districts in the nine elections from 1945 to 1968, yielding an average district magnitude for all fifteen elections of slightly less than 1.005, rounded to 1.00 in Table 2.1. The United States had between one and three two-member districts in the Congressional elections from 1946 to 1968—as well as one eight-member district in 1962 (the state of Alabama)—for an overall average magnitude of 1.003.[18] And the United Kingdom had fifteen two-member districts in 1945, yielding an average magnitude of 1.002 for all of its post-war parliamentary elections.

As the foregoing already implies, it is also striking that all larger than single-member districts were abolished everywhere: in the United Kingdom after the 1945 election, in India after 1957, and both in Canada and in the United States after 1968. From 1970 on, only single-member districts survived.

All majoritarian systems make it difficult for small parties to gain representation (unless they are geographically concentrated), because they need to win majorities or pluralities of the vote in electoral districts. For this reason, all majoritarian systems tend to systematically favour the larger parties, to produce disproportional election outcomes, and to discourage multipartism.[19] District magnitudes larger than 1 tend to reinforce these tendencies; at the extreme, a single at-large (nation-wide) district would, assuming strict party-line voting, give all legislative seats to the plurality or majority party. For instance, if the 435 members of the US House of Representatives were elected in one 435-member district, with each voter having 435 votes and casting these votes for either 435 Democratic or 435 Republican candidates, the House would end up consisting of either 435 Democrats or 435 Republicans. It is therefore a very important characteristic of the majoritarian systems in Table 2.1 that they are largely single-member district systems. Single-member districts do not make majoritarian systems into proportional ones, but they do limit the degree of disproportionality. The exact degrees of disproportionality and of the discouragement of multipartism that remains will be analysed in Chapters 4 and 5.

Given the prevalence of single-member districts, the number of districts in all majoritarian election systems is large—in fact, equal or almost equal to the assembly size in most cases. In most countries, the size of the assembly has remained very stable, especially in the United States where a membership of 435 Representatives was maintained throughout the period with the exception of the two elections after the admission of Hawaii and Alaska when it was temporarily raised to 437. At the other extreme, Australia's House of Representatives doubled in size from 1946 to the late 1980s. France's National Assembly was expanded by about 17 per cent from the 1981 two-ballot election to the 1986 PR contest, and the larger size was retained when the double-ballot was readopted for the 1988 election.

Finally, since majoritarian election systems are inherently unfavourable for small parties, they do not need—and generally do not use—legal thresholds. The one exception, as Table 2.1 shows, is the threshold that French election law has set for access to the second ballot. In 1958 and 1962, candidates with less than 5 per cent of the district vote in the first round were barred from the second ballot; this was raised to 10 per cent of the eligible electorate (approximately 13 per cent of the valid votes) for the next three elections and to 12.5 per cent, again of the eligible voters (about 17 per cent of the valid votes), before the 1978 election. However, both in France and in the other majoritarian systems, parties need many more votes in order to get elected to the legislature in significant numbers and not to be severely underrepresented. For this reason, I estimate the 'effective threshold'—a term to be defined more precisely in the next section—for all majoritarian systems to be about 35 per cent.

PR: SINGLE-TIER DISTRICTING AND D'HONDT

PR systems are the most common type of electoral systems: fifty-two of our total of seventy—almost three-fourths—unambiguously fit this category. Moreover, as I shall show later, the remaining six non-PR and non-majoritarian systems (in Japan, Greece, and France) are closer to PR than to majoritarian systems and five (in Japan and Greece) can be interpreted as PR systems. I shall present the fifty-two straightforward PR systems in four tables, two for the single-tier and two for the two-tier systems.

Table 2.2 lists the systems that, within the PR family, are the most common: those using one-tier districting and the d'Hondt formula. What was said about the majoritarian formulas also applies to PR formulas: many more have been invented—and even more can be imagined—than are in actual use. In addition to the most frequently used d'Hondt formula, only six PR formulas (and a few that closely resemble these) have been used in all of the PR systems during the 1945–90 period: modified Sainte-Laguë (which,

TABLE 2.2. Twenty-one PR systems with d'Hondt formula and single-tier districting, in increasing order of district magnitude, 1945–90

Electoral system[a]	Number and years of elections	Electoral formula	District magnitude[b]	Number of districts	Assembly size	Legal threshold N/R/D[c] (%)	Effective threshold (%)
FRA1	3: 1945–Nov. 1946	d'Hondt	5.19	102	529.33	—	12.9
FRA5	1: 1986	d'Hondt	5.79	96	556	5(D)	11.7
LUX2E	3: 1979–89	d'Hondt	6	1	6	—	11.3
SPA1	5: 1977–89	d'Hondt	6.73	52	350	3(D)	10.2
NOR1	2: 1945–9	d'Hondt	7.50	20	150	—	9.2
SWI	11: 1947–87	d'Hondt	8.20	23.91	195.55	—	8.5
SWE1	1: 1948	d'Hondt	8.21	28	230	—	8.5
BEL2E	3: 1979–89	d'Hondt	12.00	2	24	—	5.9
POR1	7: 1975–87	d'Hondt	12.40	20	248.00	—	5.7
FIN	13: 1945–87	d'Hondt	13.21	15.15	200	—	5.4
LUX1	10: 1945–89	d'Hondt	14.02	4	56.10	—	5.1
DEN4E	3: 1979–89	d'Hondt	15.33	1	15.33	—	4.7
POR2E	2: 1987–9	d'Hondt	24	1	24	—	3.0
NET3E	3: 1979–89	d'Hondt	25	1	25	4(N)	4
SPA2E	2: 1987–9	d'Hondt	60	1	60	—	1.2
GER4E	2: 1979–84	d'Hondt	78	1	78	5(N)	5
FRA4E	3: 1979–89	d'Hondt	81	1	81	5(N)	5
NET1	3: 1946–52	d'Hondt	100	1	100	1(N)	1
ISR1	1: 1949	d'Hondt	120	1	120	—	0.6
ISR3	5: 1973–88	d'Hondt	120	1	120	1(N)	1
NET2	11: 1956–89	d'Hondt	150	1	150	0.67(N)	0.67

Notes:

[a] See description of electorate systems on pp. 13–14, 16.

[b] See description of integers used on p. 16.

[c] See description of level at which the threshold is applied on p. 11.

like d'Hondt, is a highest averages or divisor system), four largest remainders or quota systems (using the Hare, Droop, and two Imperiali quotas), and the single transferable vote (STV, which always uses the Droop quota). The highest averages and largest remainders (LR) systems are list PR systems in which voters vote for lists of candidates (although they may also be able to express a preference for one or more candidates within their preferred list), in contrast with STV in which they cast a preferential vote for individual candidates.

Among the highest averages formulas, the d'Hondt method (which uses the divisor series 1, 2, 3, 4, etc.) is the least proportional and systematically favours the larger parties. It contrasts with the pure Sainte-Laguë formula (using the odd-integer divisor series 1, 3, 5, 7, etc.) which approximates proportionality very closely and treats large and small parties in a perfectly even-handed way. In practice, the Sainte-Laguë formula is used only in a modified form in which the first divisor is raised from 1 to 1.4, thereby making it harder for small parties to gain their first seats—and hence reducing the proportionality of the election result to some extent.[20]

The oldest and best known of the LR systems uses the Hare quota, which is the total number of valid votes cast (V) divided by the district magnitude (M, the number of seats available in the district): V/M.[21] Parties are given as many seats as they have won quotas, and any remaining seats are given to the parties with the largest remainders of votes. The Hare quota is impartial as between small and large parties and tends to yield closely proportional results. Less proportional outcomes are produced by the Droop quota which divides the votes by $M + 1$, the normal Imperiali quota which uses $M + 2$, and the reinforced Imperiali quota which uses $M + 3$ as the denominator. The use of these lower quotas means that there will be fewer remaining seats to be allocated—and hence also more wastage of remaining votes, which is especially harmful to the smaller parties and results in a decrease in proportionality. The Imperiali quotas are so low that there will often not be any remaining seats. Whenever the quota is lowered to such an extent that all seats can be assigned without the use of remaining votes, the outcome becomes exactly the same as that of the d'Hondt formula.[22]

STV is a preferential rather than a list system but, if voters cast mainly party-line votes or if most of the inter-party cross-over votes offset each other—a simplifying but not unrealistic assumption—its results can be compared to those of LR. All STV systems need to select a quota that elects a candidate and, in principle, any of the quotas discussed above could be used. In practice, however, STV systems invariably use the Droop quota.

To sum up, as far as their effects on the proportionality of the electoral outcome and on multipartism are concerned, the differences cut across the broad categories of divisor, quota, and STV systems. The d'Hondt and LR-Imperiali systems are the least proportional and systematically favour the larger parties; modified Sainte-Laguë, LR-Droop, and STV form an intermediate category; and LR-Hare is the most proportional formula. These tendencies are explained in greater detail in Appendix A, which also provides more detailed descriptions and examples of the operation of the different formulas.

By definition, PR requires multi-member districts, that is, a district magnitude of at least 2 seats.[23] In order to achieve a minimum of proportionality, however, the magnitude should be considerably larger than 2 and, as argued in the beginning of this chapter, magnitude impacts the degree of proportionality and the chances for small parties very strongly. Table 2.2 presents the twenty-one d'Hondt single-tier districting systems in increasing order of magnitude. The smallest average magnitude among these systems is above 5 seats, in the immediate post-war French elections, but magnitudes vary greatly—up to 150 seats in the Netherlands since 1956. About half have the maximum magnitude allowed by their assembly size: a single at-large (nation-wide) district. This means that they combine the least proportional formula with the most proportional magnitude. In the case of Luxembourg's Euro-elections, the magnitude is still only 6 seats, since only a total of 6 seats are available in this 'assembly'—the smallest assembly size among all of our electoral systems. However, the other ten systems with at-large elections also have the largest magnitudes (and are all listed in the bottom half of the table); six of these are systems for Euro-elections, and the other four are the extremely large-magnitude Dutch and Israeli election systems. The number of districts in the other systems range widely, from 2 to 102.

The large magnitudes are partly offset again by the use of legal thresholds. Eight of the electoral systems shown in Table 2.2 have such thresholds, but the majority do not. However, as already indicated in the beginning of this chapter, even in the absence of an explicit legal threshold, the district magnitude and the electoral formula, especially magnitude, effectively imply a barrier to smaller parties. For instance, in a small district with a magnitude of 5 seats (like the average district in France in 1945–6), it is easy to see that one-fifth of the votes is sufficient for winning a seat, but that this is very unlikely or even impossible with only one-tenth of the votes. It is more difficult, however, to find the exact equivalent: for a given average district magnitude, what is the effective threshold at the national level?

EFFECTIVE THRESHOLDS

There are three problems in determining the effective threshold. First, the threshold implied by district magnitude is not one specific percentage but a range of possibilities between the so-called thresholds of representation and exclusion. The threshold of representation (or inclusion) is the minimum percentage of the vote that can earn a party a seat under the most favourable circumstances; the threshold of exclusion is the maximum percentage of the vote that, under the most unfavourable conditions, may be insufficient for a party to win a seat. Another way of portraying these two thresholds is as a lower and an upper threshold: if a party passes the lower threshold, it becomes possible for it to win a seat; when it passes the upper threshold, it is guaranteed to win a seat.

Plurality single-member district systems can provide the simplest illustration of these thresholds. Assume such a district in which five candidates compete. The lower threshold is 20 per cent because a candidate can win with slightly more than this vote percentage in the most favourable situation of the other four candidates evenly splitting the other votes (each receiving just under 20 per cent of the vote). The higher threshold is 50 per cent in the most unfavourable situation of our candidate being faced by one very strong candidate; now only 50 per cent plus one vote guarantees election. A simple PR illustration is the following: a three-member district, three parties, and the d'Hondt formula.

The lower threshold is 20 per cent since it is possible for a party to win a seat with just over this percentage of the vote if the other two parties are kind enough to split the rest of the votes evenly, each receiving just below 40 per cent of the vote (or to receive just below 60 per cent and just below 20 per cent respectively). The higher threshold is 25 per cent: by exceeding this percentage slightly, a party will win a seat even in the most unfavourable case of one of the other parties garnering all of the other votes, that is, almost 75 per cent.

In addition to the problem of determining the exact threshold in the range between the upper and lower thresholds, there are two additional problems. One is that, while these thresholds are largely determined by the district magnitude, they are also influenced to some extent by the electoral formula and the number of political parties that compete. Second, both the magnitude and the number of parties may vary considerably from district to district.

In order to deal with these problems, I shall follow Taagepera and Shugart's lead, although my final solution will be slightly different from theirs.[24] They suggest a series of useful and reasonable approximations: that the number of parties be assumed to be about the same as the district magnitude, that the average magnitude for the system as a whole be used, that the formulas also be roughly averaged, and, most importantly, that the effective threshold be assumed to be half-way between the upper and the lower thresholds. Under the first of these assumptions, the upper threshold is almost the same for all formulas: it is equal to or slightly below the Droop quota, that is (expressed as a percentage), $100\%/(M + 1)$.

Unfortunately, the lower threshold varies much more for the different formulas. Taagepera and Shugart pick the lower threshold for the LR-Hare formula: $100\%/Mp$ (where p is the number of parties). This yields too low an estimate for three reasons. One is that the LR-Hare threshold of representation is not only the lowest of all of the formulas but much lower than the others, especially d'Hondt. Second, the low LR-Hare threshold occurs only in the highly exceptional situation of all parties having very small remainders, which allows a small party to win a seat with a fraction of a Hare quota; for instance, in a district with 10 seats and 10 parties and a vote distribution of 91 per cent for one big party and about 1 per cent for the other 9 small parties, one of these small parties can win a seat with just above 1 per cent of the vote. The more normal situation is for the average remainder to be half of a Hare quota—and therefore also for the lower threshold to be one-half the Hare quota: $100\%/2M$. Third, since LR-Hare is itself an unusual formula, it makes more sense to use the lower threshold of the most common formula, namely d'Hondt. As it happens, the d'Hondt lower threshold is only slightly higher than the more normal LR-Hare threshold just estimated.[25]

This $100\%/2M$ threshold therefore appears to be the natural candidate to be used for the average lower threshold. The effective threshold now becomes the mean of the upper threshold—$100\%/(M+1)$—and the lower threshold—$100\%/2M$—or:

$$T_{\text{eff}} = \frac{50\%}{(M+1)} + \frac{50\%}{2M}.$$

It should be noted that the Taagepera–Shugart effective threshold, based on the same Droop quota that I use but on the much lower LR-Hare threshold of representation, turns out to be appreciably lower than my effective threshold: after some more streamlining, Taagepera and Shugart arrive at the attractively simple effective threshold of $50\%/M$. It is worth noting further that their effective threshold is the same as my lower threshold (the threshold of representation).

In order to determine which of the two alternatives offers the closest equivalent to the formal thresholds imposed by electoral laws, I compared two groups of PR systems. The first group consists of the twenty systems that have clear legal thresholds, independent of the values of their district magnitudes and independent of any assumptions about whether the lower or middle thresholds should be chosen as the effective thresholds.[26] The second group consists of thirty-seven systems whose effective thresholds are inferred entirely or partly from district magnitudes or where assuming a low threshold, like the threshold of representation, versus a middle threshold makes a difference in the calculations (as in the Belgian and first Austrian systems to be discussed later). In the first group, I regressed the percentage of disproportionality (using the least-squares index, my principal measure of disproportionality to be explained in the next chapter) on the effective threshold, and I found a regression coefficient of 0.42; this means that for every percentage increase in the effective threshold, disproportionality increased by 0.42 per cent. I repeated this operation for the second group using alternatively the lower Taagepera–Shugart threshold and my effective threshold. The regression coefficients were 0.50 and 0.40 respectively—showing that the latter measure is the closer equivalent. When the electoral formula (d'Hondt and LR-Imperiali versus all other formulas) and assembly size (logged) were also entered into the equations, the regression coefficient was 0.42 in the first group and 0.54 and 0.42 respectively in the second group—confirming the better equivalence of my measure of effective magnitude.[27]

Another way of judging the two alternative measures of effective threshold is to examine which one yields the higher correlations with the various measures of disproportionality and multipartism for all fifty-seven PR systems and for our universe of electoral systems. Here my findings are that it does not make a great deal of difference whether the Taagepera–Shugart measure or my measure is used (see Chapter 5). One plausible explanation of the relatively strong relationships between the Taagepera–Shugart threshold and multipartism is that small parties may be encouraged not just by the prospect of being proportionally represented but by the hope of gaining any representation at all, even if it is well below full proportionality.

Three further comments on effective thresholds are in order. One is that neither the Taagepera–Shugart nor my effective threshold works well for plurality and majority systems. For $M = 1$, both equations yield the value of 50 per cent—which is obviously the upper threshold, above which victory is guaranteed, instead of an average between upper and lower thresholds. As in the case of PR systems, it is much easier to determine the upper than the lower threshold because the latter is strongly influenced by the number of candidates in the race. If we assume a relatively small number of candidates, say four of five, the lower threshold is about 20 to 25 per cent—yielding an effective threshold, half-way between the upper and lower limits, of about 35 per cent. This rough but reasonable estimate is used for all of the majoritarian systems in Table 2.1—including the early Indian system with the slightly higher M of 1.21, and also including the Australian majority system where my assumption is that candidate with 35 per cent of the first preferences has a reasonable chance of being elected with the help of second preferences transferred from weaker candidates.[28] However, in order to emphasize the roughness of this estimate, it is given as a round number without decimals.[29]

The second comment concerns the effective thresholds in PR systems: in some cases, these can be given with a high degree of precision (particularly when there is a national legal threshold expressed in percentage terms), but when they have to be calculated from average district magnitudes or on the basis of other criteria (of which some examples will be discussed shortly), they are also rather rough estimates. Hence—in contrast with average district magnitudes, numbers of districts, and assembly sizes, which can all be determined very accurately—the values of the effective thresholds are given to only a single decimal place. The one exception is the Dutch electoral system since 1956 (at the bottom of Table 2.2) in which the national legal threshold, and therefore also the effective threshold, is exactly two-thirds of 1 per cent.

Finally, it is worth re-emphasizing that all effective thresholds except national legal thresholds are not only rough estimates but also midpoints in a range between no representation and full representation. Hence, falling short of such an effective threshold does not necessarily entail getting no representation at all—as it does when the threshold is a national legal barrier—but being substantially underrepresented.[30]

In Table 2.2, the effective threshold for each system is the larger of the value computed from the average magnitude and the legal threshold, if any. The two district-level thresholds are applied in districts with such a low average magnitude that the national effective threshold is actually higher. In the 1986 French case, the 5 per cent district threshold was meaningless in the 93, out of the total of 96, districts with magnitudes of about 14 or fewer seats. In the Spanish parliamentary election system, the 3 per cent district threshold becomes effective only for district magnitudes above about 24 seats: of the 52 districts, only Barcelona and Madrid have greater magnitudes. Similarly, the national effective threshold has been much higher than the district-level legal threshold in the two French majority-plurality systems (see Table 2.1 above). The legal threshold here is the minimum vote in the first round that entitles a candidate to compete in the second round.[31]

The six national legal thresholds in Table 2.2 are all higher than the effective thresholds implied by the district magnitudes, although in the Dutch and Israeli cases, the legal threshold does not raise

the barrier a great deal. The two Israeli systems near the bottom
of Table 2.2 provide a good example: the 1 per cent legal threshold adopted after the 1949 election did raise the effective threshold, but only from 0.6 to 1 per cent.[32] The French and German
Euro-election systems are examples of a much stronger boost from
an implied threshold of only around 1 per cent to a legal threshold
of 5 per cent.

PR: SINGLE-TIER DISTRICTING AND NON-D'HONDT FORMULAS

The other single-tier districting systems—those that do not use the
d'Hondt formula—are presented in Table 2.3. The fact that there
are only eleven systems in this table, compared with twenty-one
in Table 2.2, is a good indication of the popularity of the least
proportional d'Hondt method. And fewer than half of the non-
d'Hondt systems use the most proportional LR-Hare formula. (For
its Euro-elections, Greece has used a procedure not quite identical with, but closely akin to, LR-Hare.)[33] On the other hand, the
district magnitudes of these non-d'Hondt systems, while display-
ing almost the same range as those using d'Hondt, are by and
large appreciably lower. The lowest are in the four STV systems;
one important reason is that, in these preferential systems, high
magnitudes are impractical because these entail large numbers of
candidates—which impose heavy burdens on the voters who have
to rank order these candidates. We find the highest magnitudes, as
before, in the systems with at-large elections.

The systems are listed in increasing order of district magnitude.
Because most of them do not have legal thresholds, all but one of
the effective thresholds shown in the table are in decreasing order.
The one exception is the system for the 1989 German Euro-election:
Germany switched from the d'Hondt to the LR-Hare formula but
maintained the relatively high 5 per cent national threshold.

PR: TWO-TIER DISTRICTING SYSTEMS

The remaining twenty-one PR systems are somewhat more complicated, mainly because they use two tiers of districts but also

TABLE 2.3. Eleven PR systems with non-d'Hondt formulas and single-tier districting, in increasing order of district magnitude, 1945–90

Electoral system[a]	Number and years of elections	Electoral formula	District magnitude[b]	Number of districts	Assembly size	Legal threshold N/R/D[c] (%)	Effective threshold (%)
IRE1	14: 1948–89	STV	3.75	40.50	152.00	—	17.2
IRE2E	3: 1979–89	STV	3.75	4	15	—	17.2
MAL1	5: 1947–55	STV	5	8	40	—	13.3
MAL2	5: 1962–81	STV	5.10	11.20	57.00	—	13.1
CR1	2: 1953–8	LR-Hare	6.43	7	45	—	10.6
NOR2	9: 1953–85	Modified Sainte-Laguë	7.80	19.56	152.44	—	8.9
CR2	8: 1962–90	LR-Hare	8.14	7	57	—	8.5
SWE2	6: 1952–68	Modified Sainte-Laguë	8.27	28	231.67	—	8.4
GRE3E	3: 1981–9	LR-Hare[d]	24	1	24	—	3.0
GER6E	1: 1989	LR-Hare	78	1	78	5(N)	5
ISR2	6: 1951–69	LR-Hare	120	1	120	1(N)	1

Notes:
[a] See description of electorate systems on pp. 13–14, 16.
[b] See description of integers used on p. 16.
[c] See description of level at which the threshold is applied on p. 11.
[d] Approximation.

because many of them have legal thresholds that are not easy to translate into effective thresholds. The basic rationale for two-tier districting is to combine the advantage of reasonably close voter-representative contact offered by smaller districts with the advantage of greater proportionality and minority representation offered by larger districts.[34]

Two types of two-tier methods can be distinguished: remainder-transfer and adjustment-seats systems. The first is used by the seven electoral systems in Table 2.4. In the lower-tier districts, one of the LR formulas is applied, but instead of allocating the remaining seats to the parties with the highest remainders of votes in these districts, all remaining votes and seats are transferred to, and allocated in, higher-tier districts. The fourteen systems shown in Table 2.5 belong to the second type: here the districts at the lower level are used for the initial allocation of seats, but the final allocation takes place at the higher level on the basis of all of the votes cast in all of the lower-tier districts that together make up the higher-tier district. Most commonly, a certain number of adjustment seats are provided at the higher level in order to even out the disproportionalities that may have occurred at the lower level. (The numbers of these adjustment seats can be calculated easily by subtracting the total of the lower-tier seats—the number of districts times the average magnitude at the lower level—from the total number of seats, i.e., the assembly size.)[35]

The tables report the basic characteristics for both tiers, with the more important higher level listed first. In fact, with regard to the proportionality of the election outcome and the opportunities for small parties, the upper level is the *decisive* level. The one exception concerns the electoral formula in remainder-transfer systems. Here the formula at the lower level predominates: no higher-tier formula is able to favour systematically the larger over the smaller parties, since the parties with the highest totals of remaining votes are not necessarily the largest parties. What is of crucial importance for the proportionality of the outcome is how many seats will be available at the higher level—which is determined by the lower-tier formula. Only LR-Hare at the lower level produces a sufficient number of remaining seats for full proportionality. The seven remainder-transfer systems exhibit the entire range of LR formulas: in decreasing order of proportionality, LR-Hare, LR-Droop, partly LR-Droop and partly normal LR-Imperiali

TABLE 2.4. Seven PR systems with two-tier districting and remainder transfers, in decreasing order of effective threshold, 1945–90

Electoral system[a]	Number and years of elections	Tier	Electoral formula[b]	District magnitude[c]	Number of districts	Assembly size	Legal threshold N/R/D[d] (%)	Effective threshold (%)
AUT1	8: 1945–70	H	d'Hondt	41.25	4	165	SR[e](R)	8.5
		L	LR-Droop	6.60	25			
GRE5	3: June 1989–90	H[f]	LR-Hare[f]	22.15	13	300[f]	–	3.3
		L	LR-Droop	5.14	56			
AUT2	6: 1971–90	H	d'Hondt	91.50	2	183	SR(R)	2.6
		L	LR-Hare	20.33	9			
ITA2	2: 1948–53	H	LR-Hare	582.00	1	582.00	SR(N)	2.4
		L	Reinforced LR-Imperiali	18.77	31			
ITA3	8: 1958–87	H	LR-Hare	625.75	1	625.75	SR(N)	2.0
		L	LR-Imperiali	19.55	32			
ITA4E	3: 1979–89	H	LR-Hare	81	1	81	–	0.9
		L	LR-Hare	16.20	5			
ITA1	1: 1946	H	LR-Hare	556	1	556	–	0.1
		L	LR-Droop/ Imperiali	17.94	31			

Notes:

[a] See description of electoral systems on pp. 13–14, 16.

[b] The lower-tier formulas are italicized because they are the decisive formulas in these two-tier districting systems.

[c] See description of integers used on p. 16.

[d] See description of level at which the threshold is applied on p. 11.

[e] SR means special rules (as explained on pp. 38–9).

[f] Approximations; the GRE5 assembly size includes 12 seats allocated separately in a third, national, tier.

TABLE 2.5. Thirteen PR systems with two-tier districting and adjustment seats, in decreasing order of effective threshold, 1945–90

Electoral system[a]	Number and years of elections	Tier	Electoral formula	District magnitude[b]	Number of districts	Assembly size	Legal threshold N/R/D[c] (%)	Effective threshold (%)
ICE1	5: 1946–June 1959	H	d'Hondt	52	1	52	SR[d](N)	8.7
		L	Plurality/d'Hondt	1.46	28			
ICE2	9: Oct. 1959–87	H	d'Hondt	60.33	1	60.33	SR(N)	5.8
		L	d'Hondt[e]	6.14	8			
GER1	1: 1949	H	d'Hondt	36.55	11	402	5(R)	5
		L	Plurality	1	240			
GER2	1: 1953	H	d'Hondt	54.11	9	487	5(N)	5
		L	Plurality	1	242			
GER3	8: 1957–83	H	d'Hondt	496.88	1	496.88	5(N)	5
		L	Plurality	1	247.75			
GER5	1: 1987	H	LR-Hare	497	1	497	5(N)	5
		L	Plurality	1	248			
BEL1	15: 1946–87	H	d'Hondt	23.48	9	211.33	SR(R)	4.8
		L	LR-Hare	7.04	30			

SWE3	7: 1970–88	H	Modified Sainte-Laguë	349.29	1	349.29	4(N)	4
		L	Modified Sainte-Laguë	11.07	28			
NOR3	1: 1989	H	Modified Sainte-Laguë	165	1	165	4(N)	4
		L	Modified Sainte-Laguë	8.26	19			
DEN2	3: Sept. 1953–60	H	LR-Hare	175	1	175	2.6^e(N)	2.6
		L	Modified Sainte-Laguë	5.87	23			
DEN3	12: 1964–88	H	LR-Hare	175	1	175	2 (N)	2
		L	Modified Sainte-Laguë	7.30	18.50			
DEN1	4: 1945– Apr. 1953	H	LR-Hare	148.50	1	148.50	SR(N)	1.6
		L	d'Hondt	4.83	23			
MAL3	1: 1987	H	LR-Hare[e]	69	1	69	—	1.1
		L	STV	5	13			

Notes:

[a] See description of electoral systems on pp. 13–14, 16.
[b] See description of integers used on p. 16.
[c] See description of level at which the threshold is applied on p. 11.
[d] SR means special rules (as explained on pp. 38–9).
[e] Approximation.

(in the smaller and larger districts respectively in the first post-war Italian election), normal LR-Imperiali, and reinforced LR-Imperiali—with only two countries, Italy and Austria, providing instances of all of these formulas.[36]

In the adjustment-seats systems, the higher-tier formulas are decisive. Like the decisive formulas in the remainder-transfer systems, they range from the least proportional to the most proportional methods. Most are divisor methods (d'Hondt in Germany and Iceland, and modified Sainte-Laguë in Sweden and Norway) but LR-Hare has also been used fairly frequently (in Germany since 1987 and in all Danish parliamentary elections). Malta introduced a contingent higher tier before the 1987 election: if the party winning a majority of the first preference votes does not win a majority of the lower-tier seats, it receives a sufficient number of upper-level adjustment seats to ensure it a parliamentary majority. This provision became operative in the 1987 election when the Nationalist Party had to be awarded four adjustment seats to turn its narrow national vote majority into a majority of parliamentary seats. This method does not fit any of the standard PR formulas, but it comes closer to LR-Hare than to any of the other methods.[37]

In keeping with the basic rationale of two-tier districting, the district magnitudes at the lower level are fairly small, usually less than 10 seats; Italy and, since 1971, Austria are the major exceptions. Germany has taken the idea of small lower-tier districts, providing close voter–representative contact, to its logical extreme by adopting single-member districts at the lower level. The other side of the coin, however, is that this requires a relatively large number of upper-tier seats for the purpose of proportional adjustment.[38] In all of the two-tier systems (assuming that, in the adjustment-seats systems, there are enough adjustment seats), the effects of small magnitude at the lower level are overridden at the higher level. At the upper level, the district magnitudes are all sizeable, ranging from a minimum of well over 20 seats to the huge national district of more than 600 seats in recent Italian elections. In about two-thirds of the two-tier systems, the upper-tier district is a national at-large district.

Without legal thresholds, such large upper-tier districts offer from very good to near-perfect proportionality and excellent opportunities for even very small parties. Four of these systems have indeed operated without legal thresholds. In the case of the 1946

Italian upper-tier district of 556 seats, this yields the lowest effective threshold—only 0.1 per cent—of any of our electoral systems.
It is therefore not surprising that most of the two-tier systems
do have legal thresholds. These tend to be more complex than the
thresholds in single-tier systems. In order to translate them into
effective thresholds, two further assumptions need to be made.
One is that party support is distributed evenly across a country
instead of being regionally concentrated. The other concerns the
frequent use of multiple criteria for barring small parties from
participating in the allocation of seats at the higher tier. When
these are alternative criteria (for instance, in recent German elections, winning either 5 per cent of the national vote or three seats
in the lower-tier single-member districts), the criterion that is the
easiest to satisfy becomes the basis for determining the effective
threshold. When they are joint criteria (for instance, in recent
Italian elections, winning both 300,000 votes nationally and at least
one seat at the lower tier), the effective threshold must be based
on the stricter requirement.

On the basis of these assumptions, about half of the two-tier
systems can be assigned effective thresholds fairly easily. For the
four systems without any legal thresholds, the effective thresholds
can be calculated simply from the upper-tier district magnitude
(Italy in 1946, the Italian Euro-election system, Greece in 1989–
90, and Malta in 1987). For the six systems with legal thresholds
expressed in terms of a minimum percentage of the national vote,
this percentage automatically becomes the effective threshold (the
three German systems from 1953 on, Denmark since 1964, Sweden since 1970, and Norway in 1989). For Denmark from 1953 to
1960, the national threshold of 60,000 votes represented an average
of approximately 2.6 per cent of the total valid vote in these three
elections and hence a 2.6 per cent effective threshold. And for the
first German electoral system in 1949, the 5 per cent threshold
applied at the regional (*Land*) level translates, on the assumption
of an even spread of party support, into a national effective
threshold of 5 per cent. (This example shows that the assumption
of even distribution of party support is based on an average
situation. Uneven support can obviously help a small party: with
6 per cent support in one half and 3 per cent support in the other
half of a country, a party would not meet a national 5 per cent
threshold but would meet the regional 5 per cent barrier in half of

the country. But it could also hurt: if the percentages were 7 per cent and 4 per cent respectively, the full national minimum would be met, but the regional minimum would be met in only half of the country.)

The remaining eight systems have legal thresholds formulated in more complex special rules (marked 'SR' in Tables 2.4 and 2.5). Four patterns can be distinguished:

1. The legal threshold for receiving seats in the national higher-level district is that a party has already won at least one seat at the lower level. In the two Italian systems since 1948, a small party has been able to do so by receiving at least the respective Imperiali quota of the votes in the largest lower-level district, namely Rome; this required an average of 2.6 per cent of the vote in 1948 and 1953, but only an average of 2.0 percent later when the quota was changed from the reinforced Imperiali to the slightly higher normal Imperiali quota, but the magnitude of the Rome district was increased considerably. In the two Icelandic systems, the requirement of winning at least one lower-level seat could be achieved most easily by winning a seat in the Reykjavik district with respectively 8 and an average of 12.22 seats. The effective thresholds for these magnitudes are 8.7 and 5.8 per cent.

2. The legal threshold for receiving seats in the national district is to have won a certain minimum number of votes in one or more specified areas. The one example here is Denmark from 1945 to 1953: parties needed to win a Hare quota of the total national vote in one of the country's three regions. This could be achieved most easily in Jutland, where about 42 per cent of all votes were cast, and where about 1.6 per cent of the regional vote equalled the national Hare quota.

3. The legal threshold for receiving seats in higher-level regional districts—not a national district, in contrast with the first pattern —is winning at least one seat in one of the region's lower-level districts. The two Austrian electoral systems, with initially four and later two upper-tier districts, belong to this type. In order to convert this rule into a national effective threshold, another average assumption has to be made: between the situation where a party barely fails to win any lower-tier seats and is hence completely excluded from representation, and the situation where the party just manages to win such seats in all of the higher-tier districts and therefore fully participates in the proportional allocation of seats.

The midway point is meeting this requirement in half of the upper-tier districts (i.e. from which about half of the total assembly seats are filled) that have the largest-magnitude lower districts. In the first Austrian system, this required enough strength to win a Droop quota in a ten-member and later in an eleven-member district—yielding an effective threshold of 8.5 per cent; this threshold decreased sharply to about 2.6 per cent in the second Austrian system when a Hare quota in a much larger district varying from 36 to 42 seats in six elections was sufficient.

4. Finally, the Belgian system resembles the Austrian except for the lower minimum required at the lower tier—0.66 of a Hare quota instead of a full Hare or Droop quota—and the larger number of both lower-tier and upper-tier districts. For the rest, the logic for converting the Belgian rules into an effective threshold is the same as in the Austrian case. Meeting this requirement in a thirteen-member or, more usually, a fourteen-member district permits a party to share in the allocation of about half of the available upper-tier seats.[39]

The earlier Tables 2.2 and 2.3 were organized in terms of increasing district magnitude. This corresponds with decreasing effective thresholds except where these are overridden by higher legal thresholds. Because the various legal thresholds are so common in two-tier systems and because they clearly and strongly override the effects of the high-magnitude upper-tier districts, the electoral systems in Tables 2.4 and 2.5 are listed in decreasing order of effective threshold—which is the most important feature that distinguishes these systems from each other.

INTERMEDIATE SYSTEMS: SEMI-PR, REINFORCED PR, AND MIXED PR-MAJORITY

The remaining six electoral systems do not fit either the majoritarian or the PR categories: semi-PR in the two Japanese systems, reinforced PR in three Greek systems from 1974 to 1985, and a mixture of PR and majority in the French system in 1951 and 1956. However, I shall argue that five of the six can be regarded as sufficiently similar to PR that they can be included in the comparative analyses of all PR systems.

The Japanese limited vote (LV) and single non-transferable vote (SNTV) systems are usually referred to as semi-PR systems, and SNTV is usually regarded as a special case of LV. Voters cast their votes for individual candidates and, as in plurality systems, the candidates with the most votes win. However, unlike in plurality systems, the voters do not have as many votes as there are seats in the district (and districts have to have at least two seats): this is the reason why the formula is called the 'limited' vote. The more limited the number of votes each voter has, and the larger the number of seats at stake, the more LV tends to deviate from plurality and the more it resembles PR. In the 1946 LV election in Japan, each voter had only two votes in districts with 4 to 10 seats, and only three in districts with 11 to 14 seats. SNTV is the special case of LV where the number of votes cast by each voter is reduced to one. In Japan from 1947 on, SNTV has been applied in districts with an average of almost four seats. Table 2.6 presents the vital statistics of the two Japanese electoral systems.

LV and SNTV offer good opportunities for minority representation. The SNTV threshold of exclusion (the upper threshold, above which a candidate is guaranteed a seat) is the Droop quota: 20.2 per cent in the average Japanese electoral district in all elections from 1947 on. The LV upper threshold in the 1946 election was a similar 20.5 per cent.[40] LV and SNTV have the unusual property of having an extremely low threshold of representation (the threshold above which it becomes possible to win a seat): the most extreme example in, say, a three-member district would be one candidate receiving all but two of the votes, and hence obviously being elected, and two other candidates receiving one vote each—and also winning seats! For this reason, Japan has imposed a legal threshold equalling one-fourth of a Hare quota at the district level. These are still relatively low thresholds—and much lower than the effective thresholds calculated on the basis of the average district magnitudes.

In many respects, including the average district magnitude, Japanese SNTV resembles Irish STV. The principal difference, of course, is that SNTV appears to be less proportional because no votes can be transferred. However, this disproportionality does not stem from the usual cause of discrimination against the smaller parties. In fact, the non-transfer of votes among candidates tends to present a considerable problem for the larger parties: a large

TABLE 2.6. The Japanese limited vote and single non-transferable vote systems, 1946–90

Electoral system[a]	Number and years of elections	Electoral formula	District magnitude[b]	Number of districts	Assembly size	Legal threshold N/R/D[c] (%)	Effective threshold (%)
JPN1	1: 1946	Limited vote	8.75	53	464	2.9(D)	8.0
JPN2	17: 1947–90	SNTV	3.95	122.94	486.06	6.3(D)	16.4

Notes:
[a] See description of electoral systems on pp. 13–14, 16.
[b] See description of integers used on p. 16.
[c] See description of level at which the threshold is applied on p. 11.

party has to make sure not to nominate too many candidates (which may cause these candidates to lose in spite of a high total vote for the party's candidates) and to have its voters cast their votes as evenly as possible for its candidates. In contrast, a small party only needs to nominate one candidate in order to maximize its chances of winning a seat. And, in LV systems, a small party only needs to nominate as many candidates as the number of votes that each voter has. Therefore, as far as their political effects are concerned, SNTV and LV can be regarded more legitimately as unusual forms of PR and not highly proportional forms of PR—but more as a result of their relatively small magnitudes and high effective thresholds than because of their electoral formulas—than as non-PR systems. Unless specifically stated otherwise, I shall include them in all future comparisons of PR systems, and I shall group them together with the Irish and Maltese STV systems.[41]

As noted in Chapter 1, PR systems are all too readily characterized as highly complex. But this description does fit Greek reinforced PR from 1974 to 1985.[42] These three systems are also quite idiosyncratic, but they can still be made comparable to the mainstream PR systems. Let me use the first Greek system, used in the 1974 election, as the basic example. For clarity's sake, I shall focus on the principal rules and omit the many minor details and special provisions.

Superficially, the system looks like a four-tier remainder-transfer system: seats not allocated at lower tiers by the Hare quota are transferred to higher tiers (with the exception of the fourth tier, consisting of the 12 so-called 'State seats', which are awarded separately on the basis of the parties' national vote totals). The big difference with remainder-transfer systems is that the remaining *seats* are transferred, but not the remaining *votes*. At the middle and high tiers, the remaining seats are allocated on the basis of the parties' vote totals instead of their remaining votes. This means that, in a typical lower-tier district with five seats and four sizeable parties (a reasonable assumption for the Greek situation), the average remainder would be half a Hare quota, and the total remaining votes would add up to two Hare quotas: only three seats would be allocated, and all of the remaining votes would be lost. The crucial point to understand here is that this system effectively operates like d'Hondt (which, as explained earlier in this chapter and in Appendix A, also disregards all remaining votes) in a district that is considerably smaller than its formal district magnitude.

At the middle tier, this process is repeated: the seats transferred to this level are allocated on the basis of the parties' votes and Hare quotas in nine districts. And, at the third tier, the transferred seats are again allocated on the same basis, but now all still remaining seats are given to the largest party—a formula much closer to d'Hondt than LR-Hare. At these two levels, an additional disadvantage for small parties is the 17 per cent national threshold.[43] At each tier (including, as indicated above, the highest tier of State seats), the results are calculated on the basis of the parties' vote totals. This means—the second crucial point that must be emphasized—that the parliamentary election takes the form of four separate and parallel elections of four mini-assemblies.

The 1974 Greek system is presented in these terms in Table 2.7. The lower districts have a formal average magnitude of 5.14 seats (the total assembly size of 300 seats less the 12 State seats, divided by the 56 districts), but 2 seats are assumed to go to the second level—which means that the estimated true district magnitude is only 3.14 and that, while the quota that is applied is the Hare quota, the true formula is not LR-Hare but d'Hondt. At the next level, there are now assumed to be 112 seats in 9 districts—an average formal magnitude of 12.44 but an estimated true magnitude of only 10.44. And, at the third level, the still remaining estimated number of 18 seats are allocated.[44] The effective threshold at each level is based on the district magnitude or the legal threshold of 17 per cent, whichever is higher. The overall characteristics of the system are the dominant formula (d'Hondt) and the weighted averages (weighted according to the number of seats allocated at each level) of the effective thresholds and the 'assembly sizes' of the four parallel mini-assemblies.

The description of the second and fourth Greek systems in Table 2.7 follows the same logic. The only important change in the second system was the substitution of the Droop for the Hare quota at the lower tier. Assuming the same typical lower-tier district with five seats and four sizeable parties, the average remainder is now half a Droop quota and the total remaining votes, adding up to two Droop quotas, are still lost, but, because of the lower quota, four instead of three seats can be allocated. This was a major change because it made the system considerably less disproportional—by

TABLE 2.7. The Greek four-tier districting systems, rearranged according to effective formula, district magnitude, and assembly size, 1974–85

Electoral system[a]	Number and years of elections	Tier	Electoral formula	District magnitude[b]	Number of districts	Assembly size[d]	Legal threshold N/R/D[c] (%)	Effective threshold (%)
GRE1	1: 1974	L	d'Hondt	3.14	56	176	—	20.0
		M	d'Hondt	10.44	9	94	17(N)	17
		H	d'Hondt[d]	18.00	1	18	17(N)	17
		State	LR-Hare	12	1	12	17(N)	17
Weighted Mean			d'Hondt	6.67		134.27		*18.8*
GRE2	2: 1977–81	L	d'Hondt	4.14	56	232	—	15.8
		M	d'Hondt	4.22	9	38	17(N)	17
		H	d'Hondt[d]	18.00	1	18	17(N)	17
		State	LR-Hare	12	1	12	17(N)	17
Weighted mean			d'Hondt	5.30		184.77		*16.1*
GRE4	1: 1985	L	d'Hondt	4.14	56	232	—	15.8
		M	d'Hondt	4.22	9	38	—	15.5
		H	d'Hondt[d]	18.00	1	18	—	4.0
		State	d'Hondt	12	1	12	—	5.9
Weighted mean			d'Hondt	5.30		184.77		*14.7*

Notes:
[a] See description of electoral systems on pp. 13–14, 16.
[b] See description of integers used on p. 16.
[c] See description of level at which the threshold is applied on p. 11.
[d] Approximation.

increasing the lower-tier magnitude by an estimated one seat (and hence decreasing the effective threshold at this tier as well as the weighted mean for the whole system) and by increasing the weighted assembly size by more than a third. The main change in the fourth Greek system was the abolition of the 17 per cent legal threshold—again a substantial shift away from disproportionality because it lowered the effective thresholds at the three higher levels and, as a result, also the weighted average.[45] Recast in terms of these measurements, the three Greek systems can be compared with the other PR systems. In spite of the deceptive label of 're-inforced' PR, these systems are not highly proportional—as a result of the use of d'Hondt, low district magnitudes, and high effective thresholds—but still, like the Japanese systems, per-mitting an appreciable degree of proportionality and minority representation.

Finally, the French electoral system used in the 1951 and 1956 elections may also be called a reinforced PR system—reinforced not to help the largest parties, as in Greece, but the medium-sized parties in the political centre. Unlike the Greek systems, unfortun-ately, it cannot be made amenable to comparative analysis together with the other PR systems.

It was engineered by the centre parties in order to maximize their own representation and to discriminate against the big parties on the left and right, the Communists and Gaullists. One of the devices they used for this purpose was *apparentement*: the possi-bility of linking two or more party lists, and of thereby gaining the advantage that majoritarian and most PR systems give to large parties, but without having to present joint lists. And while *apparentements* could in principle be negotiated between any two or more parties, they constituted a much more feasible option for the centre parties than for the extreme right and left. The second device was the majority principle: if one party would win an ab-solute vote majority in a multi-member district, that party would win all seats; failing a one-party victory (an unlikely outcome in a multi-party system), all seats would be given to the *apparentement* with a majority of the votes. If neither type of majority materialized, the system would revert to PR with the d'Hondt formula, but their *apparentements* would still give the centre parties the same advan-tage that d'Hondt gives to the larger parties. This was the system everywhere except in the eight electoral districts in the Paris region, where the centre parties were too weak to be able to profit from the majority rule. Hence the very opposite system was engineered: no *apparentements*, no majority rule, and LR-Hare in relatively large districts.

Table 2.8 provides the basic facts for the 1951–6 French system. For Paris, the system was a straightforward LR-Hare system. For the rest of the country, the results are broken down according to whether PR-d'Hondt or the majority rule operated in the districts. The figures are averages for the two elections. The majority rule came into force in 40 districts, with 173 seats, in 1951, but in only 11 districts, with 59 seats, in 1956.[46] The average district magnitude of the majority-rule districts (4.84 seats) as well as the range of magnitudes of these districts (from 2 to 10 seats) appear to contradict my earlier statement concerning the rarity of the use of majoritarian formulas in larger than single-member districts. However, in only one case was there a majority party that won all the seats—in a two-member district in 1951; all other majority winners were majority *apparentements* of two or more parties which then divided up the seats won among themselves according to the respective strengths of their separate party lists. (For this reason, I have computed the effective threshold for the majority districts as if they were PR districts, instead of assigning them the arbitrary 35 per cent attributed to the other majoritarian systems.)

Although more than three-fourths of the seats were allocated by PR, the majority-rule component in these elections was still so strong and its application so interwoven with PR in the areas outside of Paris, that it is impossible to disentangle them. Moreover, the two PR formulas belong to opposite extremes. For these reasons, the mixed French system used in the 1951 and 1956 elections will have to be left out of most of the analyses in Chapters 4 and 5, for instance, when the effects of PR and majoritarian systems are compared and when PR systems are compared with each other.

GENERAL PATTERNS

By presenting the seventy electoral systems in terms of groups of systems with similar key characteristics (majoritarian versus

TABLE 2.8. The French mixed PR-majority system, 1951–6

Electoral system[a]	Number and years of elections	Area	Electoral formula	District magnitude[b]	Number of districts	Assembly size[c]	Legal threshold N/R/D[d] (%)	Effective threshold (%)
FRA2	2: 1951–6	Paris	LR-Hare	9.38	8	75	—	7.5
		Other	d'Hondt	5.13	69.50	353.00	—	13.0
		Other	Majority	4.84	25.50	116.00	—	35[c]
		France	Mixed	5.28	103	544	—	12.7

Notes:
[a] See description of electoral systems on pp. 13–14, 16.
[b] See description of integers used on p. 16.
[c] Approximation.
[d] See description of level at which the threshold is applied on p. 11.

PR systems, d'Hondt versus other PR formulas, one-tier versus two-tier systems) and, within each group, according to other important features (district magnitude and effective threshold), I have already implicitly pointed at some of the general patterns in the electoral systems used by the twenty-seven stable democracies in the 1945–90 period (for their national first-chamber or only-chamber elections). In this section, I shall treat these general patterns in an explicit and systematic manner.

The most striking general aspect of the electoral formulas is their widely different frequency of application. Of the three major categories, PR has been used in about three-fourths of the systems: of the seventy systems, fifty-two are unambiguously PR, and this number rises to fifty-five if the three reinforced PR systems of Greece are added. Majoritarian formulas have been used in twelve systems, and semi-PR only twice, in Japan. Within the broad majoritarian and PR categories, some formulas have never been used —even such well-known possibilities as the majority run-off,[47] the pure Sainte-Laguë, the STV with a quota other than the Droop quota, and the cumulative vote[48]—while, among those that have been in use, two account for more than half of the cases: plurality has been far more prevalent than the other two majoritarian formulas together (in seven out of twelve systems and, even more strikingly, in five out of seven countries), and d'Hondt has been used more often than all of the other divisor, quota, and STV systems combined (in twenty-seven out of fifty-two PR systems and, if reinforced PR is added, in thirty out of fifty-five PR systems).

The same general pattern of uneven usage also occurs with regard to district magnitudes. Majoritarian formulas can in principle be applied in districts ranging from single-member to at-large. In practice, single-member districts have been the rule; two-member districts have been rare, larger multi-member districts even more exceptional, and at-large elections have never been used. The theoretical range for PR systems is from two-member districts to at-large, and most of this range has actually been used, but the lowest magnitudes of between 2 and 5 seats have been rare. Of the fifty-two unambiguous PR systems, only two have used average magnitudes (the higher-tier magnitudes in the case of two-tier districts) of less than 5 seats, and only fifteen have used average magnitudes of less than 10 seats. This means that both majoritarian and PR systems have avoided district magnitudes that seriously

limit proportionality and raise disproportionality. Two general conclusions emphasized by Rae are that all electoral systems tend to
be disproportional, but that some (especially majoritarian ones)
tend to be more disproportional than others (especially PR).[49] A
third, partly contradictory, conclusion could be added: as a result
of their choice of district magnitudes, all electoral systems are reasonably proportional—or at least far less disproportional than they
could potentially be made to be.

We do find many relatively small lower-tier districts in two-tier
PR systems, but their effects are overridden at the higher level.
As stated earlier, the most important reason for instituting
two-tier districting is to combine the advantage of closer voter-
representative contact in smaller districts with the greater proportionality of larger districts. Comparing single-tier and two-tier
systems, we would therefore generally expect lower-tier magnitudes to be lower and upper-tier magnitudes to be higher than the
magnitudes of one-tier systems. This is indeed the case. The means
for the twenty two-tier systems are 8.28 and 207.83 seats, compared
with a mean of 35.70 seats in the thirty-two one-tier systems. The
medians can express these differences more sensitively; they are
6.37 and 91.50 in the two-tier systems, and 12.20 in the single-tier
systems.

Legal thresholds can take away the proportionalizing effect of
large district magnitude again and, not surprisingly, thresholds are
most common in two-tier systems and in high-magnitude single-
tier systems. These legal thresholds tend not to be excessively
high, however; the 17 per cent thresholds in the Greek reinforced
PR systems are exceptional. The highest legal threshold among
the fifty-two unambiguous PR systems is only 8.7 per cent. It is
instructive to compare the effective thresholds of these systems:
the average effective threshold of the twenty-eight PR systems
that do not have legal thresholds (that is, where the effective
threshold is entirely based on the district magnitude) is 7.5 per
cent; in the twenty-four systems with legal thresholds it is 3.8 per
cent. The medians are 8.4 and 4.0 per cent respectively. This means
that while legal thresholds do raise the effective thresholds, they
do not raise them to the level, or even close to the level, of the
systems without legal thresholds.

The fourth and final major dimension of the electoral system
on which this study focuses—assembly size—varies a great deal.

The parliaments (lower or only houses) range in total membership from 40 in Malta until the mid-1950s to an average of 632.85
in the United Kingdom during the entire 1945–90 period (650 in
the 1987 election). The sizes of the national delegations to the
European Parliament range from 6 to 81. These numbers are closely
related to population sizes: large countries tend to have larger
parliaments than smaller countries, and the larger members of the
European Community have larger Euro-delegations than the
smaller members—although the smaller countries are still considerably overrepresented. Taagepera has suggested and proved
an even more specific and quite remarkable relationship: the cube
root law of assembly sizes. This law holds that assembly size tends
to be roughly the cube root of the population size.[50] The delegations to the European Parliament are all considerably smaller than
the national Parliaments, of course—closer to a fourth root than
a cube root relationship.[51]

EMPIRICAL LINKS AMONG THE DIMENSIONS

In Chapters 4 and 5, I shall analyse the influence of the electoral
system dimensions on proportionality and multipartism. I shall do
so by means of multivariate comparisons in order to control for
any empirical relationships among the independent variables
themselves. At this point, however, let us take a direct look at the
mutual relations of these independent variables: the electoral
formula, the effective threshold (as a composite variable based on
legal thresholds and district magnitudes), and assembly size. As in
later chapters, I shall include Japanese semi-PR and Greek reinforced PR among the PR systems (reinforced PR as a d'Hondt
and semi-PR as a non-d'Hondt formula), but I shall also report
the results for the fifty-two unambiguous PR systems without semi-
PR and reinforced PR (by means of endnotes); the latter option
never materially affects the results. The mixed system used by
France in the 1951–6 period will be omitted.

The strongest relationship is between the two major categories
of electoral formula (majoritarian versus PR systems) on the one
hand and the effective threshold on the other. The twelve majoritarian systems all have an effective threshold of 35 per cent

compared with an average effective threshold of only 6.6 per cent for the fifty-seven PR systems; the respective medians are 35 and 5 per cent.[52] As explained earlier, the 35 per cent threshold for the majoritarian systems is an arbitrarily assigned estimate, and a reasonable argument could be made that the estimate should be lower, perhaps as low as 30 per cent. However, even this lower percentage clearly does not change the stark contrast between the majoritarian and PR systems in this respect.

One might plausibly surmise that, within the broad category of PR systems, there would be a similar difference between the less proportional (d'Hondt and LR-Imperiali) and the more proportional formulas (all other formulas, including the combination of LR-Droop and LR-Imperiali used in Italy in 1946). This turns out not to be the case. The average effective threshold of 6.5 per cent in the d'Hondt and LR-Imperiali systems is actually lower than the 6.7 per cent threshold in the other PR systems, but the difference is slight and not statistically significant. The medians are an identical 5.0 per cent.[53]

The majoritarian–PR dichotomy is also related, but much less strongly, to assembly size. Table 2.1, which lists the majoritarian systems, suggests such a relationship because it includes some of the largest countries with, consequently, the largest assemblies: India, the United States, the United Kingdom, and France. The average assembly size of the majoritarian systems is indeed well above that of the PR systems: about 323 compared with about 202 members. The respective medians are even farther apart: about 352 versus 152 members.[54] However, the correlation coefficient between the majoritarian–PR contrast as a dummy variable and assembly size is only 0.25 (statistically significant at the 5 per cent level in a two-tailed test, but only barely). Because of the wide range of assembly sizes with a concentration of cases at the lower end of the range, it is more appropriate to use the logged than the raw assembly sizes. This reduces the correlation coefficient slightly to 0.23 (which is no longer statistically significant). Nevertheless, the important substantive conclusion is that the tendency to disproportionality of systems with majoritarian formulas is to a small extent compensated by their larger assembly sizes.

Again, there is no corresponding difference between the more and less proportional PR formulas. The mean assembly size of the d'Hondt and LR-Imperiali systems is about 211, and of the other

PR systems about 191 members. The medians are an almost identical 150 and 152 respectively.[55]

To turn to the third leg of the triad, we would expect a positive relationship between the effective threshold and assembly size on the basis of our earlier findings of positive relationships between the majoritarian–PR difference and both effective threshold and assembly size. For all 69 cases, the correlation coefficient is indeed a positive 0.22, and the correlation between logged assembly size and effective threshold is a similarly positive 0.19, but neither correlation is statistically significant. Among the fifty-seven PR systems, the two dimensions are almost completely unrelated.

The only strong relationship that we have discovered among our three electoral system dimensions, therefore, is the link between electoral formula and effective threshold, and this relationship is strong only if the formula is defined in terms of the majoritarian–PR dichotomy. One the other hand, the relationship is so strong (the correlation coefficient is a highly significant 0.92) that this finding has major consequences for the multivariate analysis in Chapter 5: in order to avoid the problem of multicollinearity, the two variables cannot be entered together as independent variables in any multivariate regression equations.

TRENDS

One of the best-known generalizations about electoral systems is that they tend to be very stable and to resist change. In particular, as Dieter Nohlen has emphasized, 'fundamental changes are rare and arise only in extraordinary historical situations'.[56] The most fundamental change that Nohlen has in mind is the shift from plurality to PR or vice versa. Indeed, in our universe of twenty-seven countries from 1945 to 1990, this kind of change has not just been rare but completely absent. And only one country—France— has experienced changes back and forth between a majoritarian system and PR.

As far as less fundamental changes are concerned, our twenty-seven countries do show considerable variability by producing seventy different electoral systems—an average of more than two and a half electoral systems per country. And, while these may not be what Nohlen calls 'fundamental' changes, they are not minor changes either: they entail clear changes in electoral formula and/ or changes of at least 20 per cent on the other dimensions. But the countries differ considerably with regard to their predilection for change: the number of electoral systems per country ranges from one to six.

Three broad categories, based on the presentation of the electoral system characteristics in Tables 2.1 to 2.8, can be distinguished. The first consists of countries that had only one electoral system during the entire 1945–90 period: three plurality countries (Canada, New Zealand, and the United States) and two PR countries (Finland and Switzerland). To these should be added the six countries in which the only change was the adoption of a new system for the European Parliament elections: Belgium, Ireland, Luxembourg, Portugal, Spain, and the United Kingdom. Because the sizes of the Euro-delegations was set at a level far below the sizes of the national parliaments, this change necessarily produced a new electoral system according to my criteria. It should be noted, however, that only Ireland and the United Kingdom adopted Euro-election systems that are true miniatures of their parliamentary election systems; the other four also adjusted their effective thresholds.

The second broad group consists of countries that changed but did not completely overhaul their electoral systems: two with majoritarian systems (Australia and India), one with semi-PR (Japan), and five PR countries (Austria, Costa Rica, Iceland, Italy, and the Netherlands). Each of these countries could be easily accommodated within the same table earlier in this chapter. Two countries fit this description except for their Euro-elections: Denmark and Germany. They can therefore also be placed in this middle category (although Germany had no less than six different electoral systems).

Six countries that experienced the most radical changes, and whose parliamentary election systems had to be included in more than one table, make up the final group. France and Greece are the clear leaders with major shifts from PR to majority-plurality systems and vice versa (France) and from reinforced PR to a highly proportional form of PR (Greece); moreover, Greece used five different systems from 1974 to 1990—which is, in relative terms, a much larger number than the six used by France (and by Germany) in a time-span of more than forty years. The others are

Israel, Malta, Norway, and Sweden. The Norwegian and Swedish cases are especially important because their reforms represent broader trends: the establishment of two-tier districting systems (also adopted by Malta on a contingency basis), the abandonment of the d'Hondt in favour of a more proportional formula (as in Germany and Greece), and the adoption of a 4 per cent national threshold. As far as the last reform is concerned, Germany was the only country in the 1950s that had a 5 per cent national threshold for its parliamentary elections; since then, national thresholds of 4 or 5 per cent have been adopted not only by Norway and Sweden but also, for their Euro-elections, by France, Germany, and the Netherlands.

The above changes point to a trend of greater proportionality in electoral systems. Let us examine these trends systematically in terms of the three basic dimensions. The clearest patterns appear with regard to assembly size. The only significant (that is, 20 per cent or greater) changes in the total memberships of the national parliaments are increases: in Australia (twice), Germany, Malta, the Netherlands, and Sweden.[57] On the other hand, all of the new systems adopted for the Euro-elections entailed substantial decreases.

The patterns of changes in electoral formula and significant (20 per cent or greater) changes in effective threshold are more complex. They are shown in Table 2.9, subdivided according to (1) changes in parliamentary election systems versus changes to or in Euro-election systems and (2) changes to more versus less proportional features. Several instances of change appear twice; for instance, the shift from the first to the second Austrian electoral system entailed the adoption of both a more proportional formula and a lower threshold. For the sake of simplicity, however, the major system shifts in France are listed only as changes in formula. Overall, the trend has been to greater proportionality: adoptions of more proportional formulas and thresholds for parliamentary elections have been twice as numerous as the adoption of less proportional rules, and almost the same statement can be made for the adoption of Euro-election rules. No plurality countries are included in Table 2.9, but it is worth recalling that plurality systems have also tended to greater proportionality—or, more accurately, less disproportionality—as a result of the universal abolition of multi-member districts.

TABLE 2.9. Changes in electoral formula and effective thresholds in 21 countries, 1945–90

Dimension of change	Parliamentary elections		European elections	
	Less proportional	More proportional	Less proportional	More proportional
Electoral formula	FRA1-2 FRA2-3 FRA5-6 ISR2-3 ITA1-2	AUT1-2 FRA3-5 GER3-5 GRE4-5 ISR1-2 ITA2-3 MAL2-3 NOR1-2 SWE1-2	DEN3-4E	FRA3-4E GER4E-6E GRE2-3E ITA3-4E
Effective threshold	DEN1-2 ISR1-2 ITA1-2 JPN1-2	AUT1-2 CR1-2 DEN2-3 GRE4-5 ICE1-2 ITA2-3 MAL2-3 NET1-2 NOR2-3 SWE2-3	BEL1-2E DEN3-4E LUX1-2E NET2-3E	GRE2-3E ITA3-4E POR1-2E SPA1-2E

Another way of summarizing the major trends in systems for parliamentary elections is to compare the system used for the first with that for the last election in each country in the 1945–90 period. Of the sixteen countries that underwent changes, only five ended up with a less proportional system than they started out with: France, Denmark, Israel, Italy, and Japan. Moreover, with the exception of France and Japan, the shifts away from proportionality were relatively small, mainly involving minor increases in effective thresholds. Eleven countries ended up with more proportional systems: Australia, Austria, Costa Rica, Germany, Greece, Iceland, India, Malta, the Netherlands, Norway, and Sweden.

It is by no means certain, of course, that these trends will persist. For the 1992 elections, Israel increased its national threshold from 1 to 1.5 per cent, and Malta did not have to use its contingent upper tier. Following its highly proportional 1990 election, Greece has already changed its electoral law back to reinforced PR. And in 1992 Austria adopted a new electoral law with a national threshold of 4 per cent—higher than its previous effective threshold of 2.6 per cent (see Table 2.4). However, regardless of the strength of the trend towards greater proportionality, it is clear that many countries are making, if not fundamental reforms, at least major adjustments in their electoral laws. It is important to describe these not just in terms of their basic tendencies towards proportionality or disproportionality—as I have done throughout this chapter —but to measure the influence of the three electoral system dimensions on the proportionality of election outcomes and on multipartism as precisely as possible. This will be the task of Chapters 4 and 5, after the various indices of proportionality and multipartism are presented in Chapter 3.

3

Disproportionality, Multipartism, and Majority Victories

THE two main political consequences of electoral systems on which this study focuses are (1) their effects on the proportionality or disproportionality of the electoral outcomes and (2) their effects on the party system, particularly the degree of multipartism and the tendency to generate majority victories. Four measures will be proposed and applied for each of these effects.

Disproportionality means the deviation of parties' seat shares from their vote shares, and it appears prima facie to be a simple and straightforward concept, while multipartism and other party system characteristics appear to be considerably more complex and multifaceted. Rather surprisingly, however, the question of how best to measure disproportionality has been much more difficult and controversial than the question of how to measure the key party system characteristics. As a consequence, the four indices of disproportionality that I shall present in this chapter are alternative ways of trying to measure the same phenomenon. I shall argue that one of them—the least-squares measure—is preferable to the others, and I shall rely on it as my principal measure of disproportionality in Chapters 4 and 5. But I shall also occasionally report the results for the other indices, and the values of all four are listed in Appendix B—allowing readers who prefer one of the alternatives to do their own reanalysis of the data with their favourite index. In contrast, the four measures of party system characteristics are measures of different, albeit not unrelated, aspects of the party systems: the effective number of elective parties, the effective number of parliamentary parties, the tendency of the electoral system to manufacture a parliamentary majority for parties that have not received majority support from the voters, and the tendency to generate a parliamentary majority party regardless of whether the party's majority of the seats was manufactured or earned.

MEASURES OF DISPROPORTIONALITY

The measures of the deviation of seat shares from vote shares may be alternatively referred to as measures of proportionality or *dis*proportionality—two sides of exactly the same coin. I shall generally use the latter term because the values of all indices increase with increasing disproportionality. All of the measures have the same point of departure: they begin by noting the differences between the percentages of the seats and the percentages of the votes received by the different parties; these (absolute) differences are listed for each party in the three hypothetical election results presented in Table 3.1. But the measures disagree on how these seat and vote share deviations should be aggregated. The oldest measure (I), proposed by Douglas W. Rae,[1] simply uses the average of the deviations; that is, it sums the absolute differences between the vote percentages (v_i) and seat percentages (s_i), and then divides by the number of parties (n):

$$I = \frac{1}{n} \sum \left| v_i - s_i \right|$$

A big problem with the Rae index is that it is overly sensitive to the presence of very small parties. Examples A and B in Table 3.1 both have two large parties that are equally overrepresented or underrepresented, but in B ten small parties have also participated although quite unsuccessfully—receiving only 1 per cent of the vote each and no seats. As a result, the average deviation goes down considerably—and quite deceptively—from 5 per cent to 1.67 per cent. In general, the Rae index has the tendency to understate the disproportionality of systems with many small parties, and, as a result, tends to understate the disproportionality of PR systems which generally have more small parties than non-PR systems. As Richard S. Katz has pointed out, 'at the extreme, if the infinite number of (hypothetical) parties that receive no votes and obtain no seats is included, every electoral system would appear perfectly proportional'.[2] Rae tries to avoid this problem by disregarding parties with less than 0.5 per cent of the vote, but this arbitrary cut-off point is still quite low; it does not change the calculation of his index in hypothetical situation B at all. Rae is also forced to exclude any small parties that are lumped together

TABLE 3.1. Three hypothetical election results and five measures of disproportionality

Example	Number of parties	Votes (%)	Seats (%)	Difference (%)	
A	1	55	60	5	I (Rae index) = 5.00
	1	45	40	5	D (Loosemore–Hanby index) = 5.00
					LSq (least-squares index) = 5.00
					LD (largest-deviation index) = 5.00
					b (regression coefficient) = 2.00
B	1	50	55	5	I (Rae index) = 1.67
	1	40	45	5	D (Loosemore–Hanby index) = 10.00
	10	1	0	1	LSq (least-squares index) = 5.48
					LD (largest-deviation index) = 5.00
					b (regression coefficient) = 1.13
C	5	15	16	1	I (Rae index) = 1.00
	5	5	4	1	D (Loosemore–Hanby index) = 5.00
					LSq (least-squares index) = 2.24
					LD (largest-deviation index) = 1.00
					b (regression coefficient) = 1.20

as 'other' parties in election statistics, because it is impossible to calculate the individual differences between vote and seat shares of these parties, and it would be incorrect and lead to misleading results to treat these 'other' parties like a single party.

An index that avoids Rae's problem and that has become the most widely used measure of disproportionality was proposed by John Loosemore and Victor J. Hanby.[3] Their index (D) is the total percentage by which the overrepresented parties are overrepresented—which is, of course, the same as the total percentage of underrepresentation. In contrast with the Rae index, which registers the average deviation from proportionality per party, the Loosemore–Hanby index registers the total deviation. In order to calculate the Loosemore–Hanby index, the absolute values of all vote–seat share differences are added, as for the Rae index, but then divided by 2, instead of Rae's division by the number of parties:

$$D = \frac{1}{2} \sum \left| v_i - s_i \right|$$

Hence, except in the hypothetical case of a pure two-party system, such as example A in Table 3.1, the Loosemore–Hanby index will always yield higher values than the Rae index.

The Loosemore–Hanby index represents the difference between examples A and B much more satisfactorily than the Rae index, since the value of the index goes up instead of down. On the other hand, it tends to err in the opposite direction of exaggerating the disproportionality of systems with many parties—and hence of overstating the disproportionality of PR systems; for instance, it yields exactly the same value of 5 per cent for the highly disproportional situation A and the highly proportional situation C in Table 3.1. One minor but attractive advantage of the Loosemore–Hanby index is that it does not have to disregard the 'other' small parties, since these can all be safely assumed to be underrepresented instead of overrepresented parties.

An excellent solution was proposed recently by Michael Gallagher. His least-squares index (LSq) steers a middle course between the Rae and Loosemore–Hanby indices. Its key feature is that it registers a few large deviations much more strongly than a lot of small ones. Its computation is as follows: the vote–seat share differences for each party are squared and then added; this total is divided by 2; and finally the square root of this value is taken:[4]

$$LSq = \sqrt{\left(\frac{1}{2} \sum (v_i - s_i)^2\right)}$$

Another way of thinking about what the least-squares index does is that it weights the deviations by their own values, making the larger deviations account for a great deal more in the summary index than small deviations. When there are only two parties, the least-squares index yields exactly the same values as the Rae and Loosemore–Hanby indices, as example *A* in Table 3.1 illustrates. For the somewhat more disproportional situation in example *B*, the least-squares index gives a suitably higher value. And, for the much more proportional situation in example *C*, it gives a much lower value that also intuitively appears to be a correct representation of the degree of disproportionality.

In the computational example that Gallagher supplies for his index, he includes the votes and seats of the 'other' parties as if they were the seats and votes of one additional party. For the reason indicated above in connection with the discussion of the Rae index, I believe that this is an incorrect procedure; especially because of the squaring of the deviations in the calculation of his index, treating the deviations of two or more parties like one deviation of one party can lead to a considerable overstatement of the extent of disproportionality. Therefore, in all of my calculations of the least-squares index, the 'other' parties are disregarded.

These three indices obviously do not exhaust the possibilities; several others have been proposed and still more could, and probably will, be designed. Typically, these have also represented efforts to find a middle course between the Rae and Loosemore–Hanby indices. For instance, Bernard Grofman has suggested that the total percentage of vote–seat share deviation be divided not by the number of parties, as Rae does, nor by 2, as prescribed by Loosemore–Hanby, but by the effective number of parties; this number, which will be explained in the next section, weights the parties by their relative sizes, and is almost always a number between 2 and the raw number of parties. Another similar measure is the two-major-parties index which I have proposed and used myself. Its rationale is that the discrepancy between the Rae and

Loosemore–Hanby indices can be alleviated by averaging the vote–seat share differences of the larger parties only (e.g. those winning more than, say, 5 or 10 per cent of the vote) and solved completely by averaging the deviations of exactly the same number of parties in different elections in different countries; in order to be able to apply this measure to both two-party and multi-party systems, this 'same number' should be set at two. How the two largest parties fare is assumed to be a good reflection of the overall disproportionality of the election results.[5]

To take this line of reasoning one step further—the ultimate step—is simply to use the largest deviation in an election result (which will generally be the percentage of overrepresentation of one of the largest parties) as the overall index of disproportionality. The beauty of this index is that it not only makes good sense but that it is also the simplest possible way of measuring disproportionality. For this reason, I shall use it as my fourth index of disproportionality in this study. But I shall rely mainly on the least-squares index which I regard as the most sensitive and faithful reflection of the disproportionality of election results, easily counterbalancing the disadvantage of its greater computational complexity—although it would be quite wrong to think of the least-squares measure as an unduly complicated measure.

ABSOLUTE VERSUS RELATIVE VOTE–SEAT SHARE DEVIATIONS

Three general objections can be raised to the entire family of disproportionality measures discussed above. One is based on the important and prima facie highly pertinent observation by Gallagher, and further developed by Gary W. Cox and Matthew S. Shugart, that instead of one generally accepted notion of proportionality there are many divergent notions, and that the various PR formulas described in the previous chapter embody these different notions: what each PR formula does is to define proportionality in a particular way, and it then allocates seats to parties so as to maximize proportionality on the basis of its particular definition.[6] There is an especially wide gap between the notions of proportionality underlying the LR-Hare and d'Hondt formulas. It is also correct to observe that my four measures of disproportionality are all based on absolute differences between vote and seat percentages—and hence not only reflect the same notion of proportionality that inspires LR-Hare but, as a logical consequence, also display a systematic bias in favour of LR-Hare systems. However, this is a serious flaw only if one focuses on the different outcomes exclusively at the district level. As Cox and Shugart concede, 'whether *national* seat totals will be proportional to *national* vote totals depends on many factors—such as additional seats, thresholds, malapportionment, and the geographical distribution of party support—in addition to the formula used to allocate seats within districts'.[7]

The second objection is not just that my measures of disproportionality are biased in favour of a particular PR formula, but that they reflect the general normative perspective that what matters are absolute instead of relative differences between vote and seat shares. For instance, a 1 per cent overrepresentation for a party winning 40 per cent of the votes and 41 per cent of the seats is counted on a par with a 1 per cent overrepresentation of a party with 10 per cent of the vote and 11 per cent of the seats. The opposite perspective, which underlies the d'Hondt method, would argue that the degrees of deviation are very different in the two cases: relatively speaking, the deviation from proportionality is only one-fourth as pronounced for the larger party because it is four times as large as the smaller party. I believe that most people would agree that, in these illustrative cases of $v_1 = 40\%/s_1 = 41\%$ and $v_2 = 10\%/s_2 = 11\%$, the larger party's deviation from proportionality is indeed not as serious as the smaller party's, because it is a smaller relative deviation. But I would also suggest that this criterion becomes operative only in a *ceteris paribus* situation, that is, only when the absolute deviations are the same. When, for instance, the two situations of $v_1 = 40\%/s_1 = 42\%$ and $v_2 = 10\%/s_2 = 11\%$ are compared, I submit that the most commonly accepted notion of proportionality would judge that it is the larger rather than the smaller party that has a worse deviation. And I think that few people would agree that a 4 per cent deviation in the case of $v_1 = 40\%/s_1 = 44\%$ is normatively on par with $v_2 = 10\%/s_2 = 11\%$, $v_3 = 5\%/s_3 = 5.5\%$, or $v_4 = 1\%/s_4 = 1.1\%$, as the d'Hondt notion of proportionality would maintain.

To take this argument one step further, let us look at the

hypothetical example of two parties with 41,000 and 10,000 votes in a four-member district. The d'Hondt formula would award all 4 seats to the larger party because of its concern with minimizing relative disproportionality, whereas LR-Hare would reason that the larger party had won 3.2 quotas and the smaller party 0.8 quotas, and that the seat distribution should therefore be 3 to 1. Here again, I would submit that the most widely held view of proportionality would consider the second result to be the more just and equitable. The principles on which the different PR formulas are based are not normatively neutral, and the formulas themselves cannot be considered equally proportional on the basis of merely diverging notions of proportionality. The d'Hondt method is still basically a PR formula, but with a built-in advantage for larger parties—not a formula that can be argued to be just as proportional as LR-Hare.

This does not mean that d'Hondt is inferior to LR-Hare, of course, and it may well be considered to have some clear advantages over LR-Hare. In fact, its very bias in favour of large parties may be regarded as an advantage since this reduces party system fragmentation. And because it favours the larger parties, it is also free from two drawbacks of LR-Hare: d'Hondt will never reward a party for splitting or for tactically presenting two separate lists, and it will never deny a majority of the seats to a party with a vote majority (in a district with an odd number of seats). But these are advantages that are conceptually distinct from the idea of proportionality. D'Hondt is simply not as proportional a formula as LR-Hare. This reinforces my response to the first objection: to the extent that the least-squares index and the other measures of proportionality are biased in favour of LR-Hare, this is not an arbitrary prejudice but a proper reflection of the inherently greater proportionality of the LR-Hare formula.[8]

The third objection is that disproportionality, however measured, should not be the focus of attention, and that the focus should be on the type or, in Cox and Shugart's words, the 'political character' of disproportionality: 'the extent to which different methods of PR favour large parties over small'.[9] My response here is that all of my measures of disproportionality already do exactly that. Disproportionality is not a random phenomenon but a pattern in which larger parties are systematically overrepresented and smaller parties are systematically underrepresented. As shown above, big-party bias is logically inherent in the d'Hondt formula, and it is just as logical a consequence of decreasing district magnitudes or increasing electoral thresholds. And it is amply confirmed by empirical analysis of election results. For instance, in the next section I shall show that the effective number of parties in the legislature is almost invariably smaller than their effective number in the electoral arena as a result of the systematic advantages enjoyed by the larger parties and the systematic disadvantages suffered by the smaller ones.

Moreover, it turns out to be very hard to develop a satisfactory measure of big-party bias that can compete successfully with the measures of disproportionality. Cox and Shugart offer one intriguing proposal. They regress the parties' seat percentages on the vote percentages, and argue that the unstandardized slope (regression coefficient) of the regression line provides a simple index of big-party bias. A slope (b) of 1.00 indicates an absence of bias; higher values indicate a systematic advantage for larger parties, and lower values would mean a small-party bias.

In addition to the four indices of disproportionality, Table 3.1 presents the values of big-party bias b for the three hypothetical election outcomes. For example A, the value of b is a suitable 2.00, but for examples B and C the values of 1.13 and 1.20 run counter to common sense: the highly disproportional situation in B with a big-party bias similar to A is registered not only as much less biased than A, but also less biased than the highly proportional situation in C, in which the big parties do not appear to be extremely favoured. The obvious problem is that, like the Rae index of disproportionality, Cox and Shugart's b is overly sensitive to the presence of small parties: they force the regression line to go through, or close to, the origin and, as a result, greatly reduce its slope. Since this measure of big-party bias is less accurate than the indices of disproportionality (with the possible exception of the Rae index) and since it does not add any crucial feature—in particular, the tendency to overrepresent large parties—that is not already implicit in the indices of disproportionality, there is no reason to switch from these four indices to a more 'refined' measure of big-party bias.

Table 3.2 presents two sets of correlation coefficients among the four indices of disproportionality: for all seventy electoral systems, including the mixed French system in 1951 and 1956, and for the

TABLE 3.2. Correlation matrices for four indices of disproportionality in 70 electoral systems and 57 PR systems

Systems	Rae index	Loosemore–Hanby index	Least-squares index	Largest-deviation index
70 electoral systems				
Rae index	1.00			
Loosemore–Hanby index	0.77	1.00		
Least-squares index	0.85	0.97	1.00	
Largest-deviation index	0.80	0.95	0.99	1.00
57 PR systems				
Rae index	1.00			
Loosemore–Hanby index	0.84	1.00		
Least-squares index	0.94	0.96	1.00	
Largest-deviation index	0.93	0.92	0.99	1.00

Note: All of the correlation coefficients are statistically significant at the 1 per cent level (one-tailed test).

fifty-seven PR systems; removing France from the first set does not change any of the coefficients. Four aspects of these matrices stand out. First and most obviously, all four indices are all highly and significantly correlated. Second, the nature of the least-squares index as a compromise between the Rae and Loosemore–Hanby indices is confirmed: its correlations with both indices is strong, while the correlations between Rae and Loosemore–Hanby are the weakest in both sets. Third, among all the impressively high correlations, those of the Rae index with the other indices are the least strong. Fourth, the strongest correlations (0.99 in both sets) are between the least-squares and the largest-deviation indices— confirming the latter as a useful and attractively simple measure of disproportionality.

THE EFFECTIVE NUMBER OF PARTIES

The most important difference among democratic party systems is that between two-party and multi-party systems. In parliamentary types of government, two-party systems make one-party majority cabinets possible, whereas such cabinets are not impossible but much less likely in multi-party systems. In presidential forms of government, two-party systems may have two quite different but equally significant results: either the president will enjoy majority support from the legislature or he or she will be faced by a hostile legislative majority. In addition to the distinction between two-party and multi-party systems, a further distinction must be made between moderate and extreme multi-party systems—with commensurate consequences for cabinet formation in parliamentary systems and legislative support for presidents in presidential systems. The variable that underlies both of the distinctions is the number of parties.

The practical problem in measuring the number of parties is how to count parties of unequal size and, in particular, how to count very small parties. The assumption in the comparative politics literature has long been that some kind of weighting is necessary. For instance, the British party system has long been described as a two-party system even though, throughout the twentieth century, there have always been more, and usually quite a few more, than two parties in the House of Commons—which means that third parties have simply been discounted.

In modern comparative politics, a high degree of consensus has been reached on how exactly the number of parties should be measured. Here, too, Rae has played a pioneering role. He proposed an index of party system fractionalization based both on the numbers of parties and on their relative sizes. If v_i is the vote proportion of the i-th party, the party system fractionalization based on the parties' vote shares (F_v) is:

$$F_v = 1 - \sum v_i^2.$$

The theoretical rationale for F_v is that it represents 'the frequency with which pairs of voters would disagree [in their choice of parties] if an entire electorate interacted randomly'.[10] In a pure one-party system, all voters would agree on their choice of this one party, and fractionalization would be zero; in the most extreme case of fractionalization, each voter would have his or her own party, and fractionalization would reach the maximum value of 1. A similar index can be constructed on the basis of the parties' seat shares, that is, the party system fractionalization in parliament instead of among the voters (F_s):

$$F_s = 1 - \sum s_i^2,$$

in which s_i is the seat proportion of the i-th party.

Markku Laakso and Rein Taagepera improved these indices by transforming them into the 'effective number of parties', which again can be calculated either on the basis of vote shares or seat shares.[11] The two equations are:

$$N_v = \frac{1}{\sum v_i^2}$$

and

$$N_s = \frac{1}{\sum s_i^2}.$$

The effective number of parties carries the same information as the Rae index of party system fractionalization. In fact, N can easily be calculated from F as follows:

$$N = \frac{1}{1 - F}.$$

The big advantage of N is that it can be visualized more easily as the number of parties than the Rae abstract index. In a two-party system with two equally strong parties, the effective number of parties is exactly 2.00 ($F = 0.50$). If one party is considerably stronger than the other, with, for instance, respective vote or seat shares of 70 and 30 per cent, the effective number of parties is 1.72—in accordance with our intuitive judgement that we are moving away from a pure two-party system in the direction of a one-party system ($F = 0.42$). Similarly, with three exactly equal parties, the effective number formula yields a value of 3.00 ($F = 0.67$). If one of these parties is weaker than the other two, the effective number of parties will be somewhere between 2.00 and 3.00, depending on the relative strength of the third party (F would be between 0.50 and 0.67).

There are two major alternatives to the effective number of parties—measures proposed by John K. Wildgen and by Juan Molinar—but neither is very different from the effective number of parties.[12] Wildgen's index of 'hyperfractionalization' accords special weight, as its name indicates, to small parties. Molinar's index does the opposite: it gives special weight to the largest party. In cases where all parties have equal strength, the three measures yield exactly the same values: 2.00 for a two-party system, 3.00 for a three-party system, and so on. For party systems with unequal parties, Wildgen's index generally has the highest values, the effective number of parties lower values, and Molinar's index the lowest values. For instance, when there are two large parties and one considerably smaller party—with respective strengths of 45, 45, and 10 per cent—the Wildgen index is 2.58 parties; the effective number of parties is 2.41; and the Molinar index is 2.23.

The above hypothetical example, which looks more like a two-and-a-quarter than a two-and-a-half party system, shows one advantage of the Molinar index: it often appears to be closer to what one intuitively thinks of as the number of parties than the other two indices. On the other hand, the Molinar index can also produce values that appear to be too low. For instance, when in a pure two-party system one party splits down the middle, so that the distribution of votes or seats changes from 50–50 to 50–25–25, most people would say that the number of parties has increased from 2 to a higher number, but, measured by the Molinar method, it goes down to 1.89.[13] The reason is that Molinar measures not just the number of parties but also the saliency of the largest party. Because the effective number of parties is the purest measure of the number of parties, because it has become the most widely used measure, because the alternative measures are quite similar to it in most respects, and, last but not least, because it is computationally much simpler than the alternatives, it will be my number-of-parties measure in this study.

As indicated above, the effective number of parties can be based either on the parties' vote shares or on their seat shares, yielding the two distinct measures of the effective number of elective parties and the effective number of parliamentary parties. Because electoral systems tend to favour the larger and to discriminate against the smaller parties, the effective number of parliamentary parties should be expected to be lower than the effective number of elective parties. At the same time, we would expect the two measures to be strongly correlated, especially in PR systems. Both expectations are correct for our electoral systems. The correlation coefficient for all seventy systems is 0.91 and for the fifty-seven PR systems 0.94 (see Table 3.3). And, in sixty-eight of the seventy systems, the effective number of parliamentary parties is lower than the number of elective parties; the two exceptions are the French 1951–6 system which was deliberately engineered against the largest parties and in favour of the medium-sized parties, and the highly proportional Italian system for Euro-elections (LR-Hare, large district magnitude, and no legal threshold) which has happened to work out slightly less favourably for the two largest parties than for the other parties. In these two exceptional cases, however, the effective number of parliamentary parties is only slightly higher than the number of elective parties: 5.83 compared with 5.75 parties in the French case, and 4.42 compared with 4.31 parties in the Italian Euro-elections.

The distinction between the two measures is also theoretically very important, because they are affected differently by what Maurice Duverger has called the 'mechanical' and 'psychological' and Rae the 'proximal' and 'distal' effects of electoral systems.[14] The mechanical or proximal effects are simply the immediate effects of the translation of votes into seats in a particular election.

TABLE 3.3. Correlation matrices for four party system characteristics in 70 electoral systems and 57 PR systems

Systems	Effective number of elective parties	Effective number of parliamentary parties	Frequency of parliamentary majorities	Frequency of manufactured majorities
70 electoral systems				
Effective number of elective parties	1.00			
Effective number of parliamentary parties	0.91**	1.00		
Parliamentary majorities	−0.56**	−0.71**	1.00	
Manufactured majorities	−0.34**	−0.54**	0.82**	1.00
57 PR systems				
Effective number of elective parties	1.00			
Effective number of parliamentary parties	0.94**	1.00		
Parliamentary majorities	−0.53**	−0.63**	1.00	
Manufactured majorities	−0.28*	−0.41**	0.75**	1.00

Notes:
* Statistically significant at the 5 per cent level (one-tailed test).
** Statistically significant at the 1 per cent level (one-tailed test).

To the extent that this translation discriminates against the smaller parties, voters as well as politicians, political activists, and financial backers—not wanting to waste their votes, energies, and money—will tend to favour the larger parties. Such strategic behaviour underlies the psychological or distal effects of electoral systems. The effective number of elective parties is affected solely by the psychological effects of electoral systems—*expectations* about how votes will be translated into seats—whereas the effective number of parliamentary parties is influenced both by these expectations (psychological effects) and the actual (mechanical) process of translating votes into seats. Put another way, the effective number of elective parties is likely to be reduced by psychological effects, but any further reduction from the effective number of elective to the effective number of parliamentary parties is exclusively the work of the mechanical factors.

GENERATING MAJORITY VICTORIES

The second pair of indicators of party system characteristics are the generation of majority parties in the legislature and the artificial generation of such majority parties out of parties that have not won vote majorities. Like the effective number of parties, these measures may be thought of as improvements of the classic, but very rough and simple, distinction between two-party and multiparty systems. The rationale is that the importance of two-party systems is that they make one-party majority cabinets in parliamentary systems (or one-party majorities supporting or opposing presidents in presidential systems) possible; if this is the crucial concern, why not measure it directly instead of merely as a probable consequence of two-party systems? The most straightforward measure, therefore, is simply whether or not electoral systems generate majority parties in the legislature; for a series of elections, the measure is the percentage of elections that produce such majorities, to which I shall henceforth refer as the percentage of parliamentary majorities.

The second measure is the percentage of 'manufactured majorities'. This is one of the terms coined by Rae to describe the four possible outcomes of elections: (1) an 'earned majority' of seats won by a party that has also won a majority of the votes; (2) a 'manufactured majority' in the legislature won by a party that has won less than a vote majority; (3) a 'natural minority' where no party wins either a vote or a seat majority; and (4) an 'artificial minority' where one of the parties does win a vote majority but not a majority of the seats.[15] The categories of this typology are exhaustive but not quite mutually exclusive: an election may result in both a manufactured majority for one party and the reduction of the winner of the popular vote to an artificial minority.

Given the tendencies of most electoral systems to favour the larger parties, artificial minorities are not very likely. Rae even suggests that 'no such electoral system exists', because 'it would be intolerable if an electoral law robbed leading parties of their majorities'.[16] Actually, two elections included in this study do exemplify the phenomenon: in the 1954 Australian election, the Labour Party won a narrow vote majority but fell short of a majority in the legislature, and in the 1981 election in Malta, the Labour Party won a manufactured majority while the Nationalists were reduced to an artificial minority. The fact that there are only two examples does prove the rarity of artificial minorities, and the latter example also shows that artificial minorities are hard to tolerate: the institution of the contingent upper tier in the Maltese election law after 1981 was designed to prevent a repetition of the 1981 anomaly.

Mechanical and psychological factors also affect the generation of parliamentary majorities and manufactured majorities differently. In the artificial manufacturing of a majority, the psychological factors may play a certain role by increasing the votes for the largest parties, but the mechanical factors obviously play the crucial role. Since parliamentary majorities can be either earned or manufactured majorities, both psychological and mechanical factors may contribute to them and their effects are much harder to disentangle.

Because both types of majorities are likely to be associated with electoral systems that favour large parties, and because they are partly related by definition (that is, a manufactured majority is also automatically a parliamentary majority), we would expect the two measures to be closely correlated. As Table 3.3 shows, this is indeed the case: the correlation coefficient is 0.82 for all electoral systems (excluding the French 1951–6 system does not change this

figure) and 0.75 for the PR systems. The reason why these coefficients are not even higher is that, while both types of majorities
are concentrated among the plurality systems and both types are
much rarer among PR systems, the measures may assume extreme
values (for instance, in an electoral system used for one election,
the values will be either 100 per cent or 0 per cent), and plurality
systems may show quite different patterns of majority generation;
for instance, US Congressional elections have resulted in 100 per
cent majorities but only 8.7 per cent manufactured majorities,
whereas British parliamentary elections have produced 92.3 per
cent majorities, all of which have been manufactured majorities.

POLITICAL PARTIES, PARTY ALLIANCES, AND FACTIONS

A short comment is required about the definition of political
parties. All eight of the basic measures of disproportionality and
party system characteristics introduced in this chapter crucially
depend on which entities are counted as parties: the vote and seat
shares of these parties, their effective number (also calculated
on the basis of their vote and seat shares), and whether or not one
of them attains majority status. In practice, there is usually not
much disagreement on the identification of the parties, but problems arise in two situations. The first is the problem of highly factionalized parties like the Italian Christian Democrats and the
Japanese Liberal Democrats: should these two parties be counted
as parties, or are their factions the real parties? The second problem is that of close alliances between parties like the Australian
Liberal and National parties, the German Christian Democratic
Union and Christian Social Union, and the Belgian Christian
People's and Christian Social parties as well as the other Belgian
linguistic parties that are similarly allied with their ideological
partners across the linguistic divide: are these alliances or the
alliance members the true parties?

The definitions one chooses are by no means inconsequential.
For instance, in the Australian electoral system used from 1949 to
1983, the percentages of parliamentary and manufactured majorities would go up dramatically if the Liberal and National parties
would be counted as one party. My criterion will be to follow the

parties' own definitions. This means that, in the above examples of factionalized parties, the parties as they define themselves rather than their factions will be considered the real parties. Similarly, parties that give themselves different names will be regarded as separate parties—including the Christian Democrats and the Christian Social Union in Germany which are more often counted as a single party.[17] This is also the practice that Thomas T. Mackie and Richard Rose follow in their *International Almanac*.[18] The few doubtful cases of alliances among small parties that remain, none of which are of great consequence, are explained in Appendix C.

INTERACTIONS BETWEEN DISPROPORTIONALITY AND THE PARTY SYSTEM

Disproportionality is a centrally important phenomenon in this study for two reasons. First, as I have emphasized before, while all electoral systems tend to be at least somewhat disproportional, they also tend to avoid extreme disproportionality. In other words, proportionality is one of the aims, albeit not necessarily the most important aim, of most electoral systems. The analysis of the degrees of disproportionality is important in order to determine to what extent this aim is realized. Moreover, it is important to determine how the different dimensions of electoral systems contribute to the proportionality or disproportionality of election outcomes. In this analysis, disproportionality is of intrinsic interest as the dependent variable—the focus of what we try to explain in terms of the electoral system dimensions as the independent or explanatory variables.

The other dependent variables on which this study focuses are the different aspects of party systems. In this analysis, disproportionality serves as the hypothesized link between the electoral system variables and the party system variables: the hypothesis is that it is the disproportionality of electoral systems that, by mechanical and psychological means, reduces the number of parties and increases the chances of having majority party victories. Table 3.4 shows that this hypothesis is borne out—with the exception of the link between disproportionality, as measured by the least-squares index, and the effective number of elective parties which

TABLE 3.4. Correlations between the least-squares index of dispropor-tionality and four party system characteristics in 70 electoral systems and 57 PR Systems

Party system characteristics	Least-squares index	
	70 Electoral systems	57 PR systems
Effective number of elective parties	−0.11	−0.02
Effective number of parliamentary parties	−0.45**	−0.29*
Frequency of parliamentary majorities	0.58**	0.42**
Frequency of manufactured majorities	0.63**	0.41**

Notes:
   * Statistically significant at the 5 per cent level (one-tailed test).
  ** Statistically significant at the 1 per cent level (one-tailed test).

is weak, and statistically not significant—both for all seventy elec-toral systems and for the fifty-seven PR systems. (Excluding 1951–6 France from the set of seventy systems makes virtually no difference, and roughly similar patterns appear when the other three indices of disproportionality are used.)[19]

The other correlations are statistically significant, but they dif-fer considerably in strength. The strongest correlations appear in the set of all seventy electoral systems—reflecting the wide differ-ences between majoritarian and PR systems with regard to both disproportionality and party systems. But even the strongest rela-tionship, between disproportionality and manufactured majorities, is not overwhelmingly strong: the coefficient of 0.63 means that the degree of disproportionality explains less than 39 per cent of the variance in manufactured majorities (in terms of the adjusted R^2). And it explains only about 19 per cent of the variance in the effective number of parliamentary parties. In the PR systems, it explains less than 16 per cent of the variance of any of the party system variables.

One explanation may be that the link between disproportionality and the party system is a two-way relationship. Disproportionality affects the degree of multipartism, but multipartism can in turn affect the degree of disproportionality. The reason for this is es-pecially clear in plurality systems, where a substantial part of the disproportionality of the election outcome is caused by small parties that fail to win representation or that are severely underrepresented. For instance, in US Congressional elections, in which for various reasons—including direct primary elections that weed out minor contenders and state laws that discriminate against third parties[20]—virtually no small parties compete, the degree of disproportionality is considerably lower (5.41 per cent) than in British parliamentary elections in which a significant number of more substantial small parties tend to participate (10.55 per cent). Among PR systems, the most highly proportional ones may tempt politicians to form small parties and voters to vote for these parties—creating a large number of parties but also, if many of these parties fail to win seats, a relatively high degree of disproportionality.

This two-way relationship is especially difficult to sort out because disproportionality and multipartism affect each other in opposite directions: disproportionality *decreases* multipartism but, to at least some extent, multipartism *increases* disproportionality. Chapter 5 will show that the direct influence of one of the electoral system dimensions, the effective threshold, on multipartism is actually stronger than the effect of disproportionality.

The link between the party system as the independent variable and disproportionality as the dependent variable also has an important implication for two of the four additional dimensions of electoral systems—presidentialism and ballot structure—mentioned in Chapter 2. Both presidential government and categorical ballots are hypothesized to decrease multipartism. There is no plausible direct link between these two variables and disproportionality, but indirectly, via the party system, there could be a causal connection. Hence we can infer the further hypotheses that presidentialism and categorical ballots decrease disproportionality.

These hypotheses will be tested in Chapter 6. First, however, the next two chapters will focus on the effects of the basic triad of electoral system dimensions: the effective threshold, the electoral formula, and assembly size.

4

Changes in Election Rules between Systems in the Same Country

BEFORE turning to the more conventional cross-sectional analysis of the effects of electoral systems on disproportionality and party systems in the next chapter, I shall devote this brief chapter to a series of analyses by means of the comparative method. This method, which may also be called the method of controlled comparison, focuses on comparable cases: cases that differ with regard to the variables one wants to investigate, but similar with regard to all other important variables that may affect the dependent variables; these other important variables can then be treated as control variables. In Neil J. Smelser's words, comparable cases offer the following great advantage: 'The more similar two or more [cases] are with respect to crucial variables . . . the better able is the investigator to isolate and analyze the influence of other variables that might account for the differences he wishes to explain.'[1] It is usually not easy, however, to find appropriate comparable cases.

In this study, several of the cases under investigation—that is, the electoral systems—are perfect candidates for analysis as comparable cases: successive electoral systems in the same country. Many potentially important explanatory variables can be controlled in the sense that they can be assumed not to differ or to differ only marginally: the same country, the same political parties, the same voters, and so on. Moreover, if one or two of the electoral system dimensions has not changed, they are similarly controlled. The ideal situation is one in which, in the same country, two successive electoral systems differ with regard to only one dimension, because this allows us to gauge the influence of this one dimension with the knowledge that neither the other dimensions nor other background variables could have had a substantial effect on the outcome. It is on these ideal comparable cases that I shall focus in this chapter, but I shall also analyse within-country changes of electoral system that involve two dimensions, as well as small changes that have occurred within the same electoral system.

ONE-DIMENSIONAL CHANGES IN ELECTORAL FORMULA

Tables 4.1 to 4.3 present the effects of changes in one dimension of the electoral system—the electoral formula, the effective threshold, and the assembly size respectively—on disproportionality and the effective numbers of parties.[2] The evidence is derived from the electoral systems of twelve countries. The next section, where two-dimensional changes will be examined, will present evidence from seven additional countries. These nineteen countries are mainly PR countries. The reason is not only that there are more PR than non-PR countries in our universe in the first place, but also that PR countries have tended to change their electoral systems more frequently than the others. Of the five plurality countries, for instance, three (Canada, New Zealand, and the United States) did not change their electoral systems at all during the 1945–90 period; hence they are logically excluded from the analysis. And the other two (India and the United Kingdom) changed only once. The party system characteristics reported in the tables are the effective numbers of elective and parliamentary parties; the frequencies of majority victories are not included because such majorities, whether manufactured or earned, were relatively rare in these PR systems.

A quick glance at the tables reveals that some PR countries are much more strongly represented among the comparable cases than others. An especially interesting example is provided by the last four German electoral systems which, juxtaposed in two different ways, yield four pairs of comparable cases (see Tables 4.1 and 4.3): two one-dimensional changes in electoral formula, from d'Hondt to LR-Hare, in the last two parliamentary election systems and in the two Euro-election systems, and two drastic reductions in assembly size, but no other changes, when the two parliamentary and the two Euro-election systems are compared. In three other countries (Denmark, Israel, and Norway), two successive changes provide two pairs of comparable cases in each country. The inclusion of the shift from the first (1949) to the second Israeli system (1951–69) requires a special explanation,

TABLE 4.1. Controlled changes in electoral formula, and changes in disproportionality and effective numbers of parties

Electoral system[a]	Electoral formula	Disproportionality (%)	Effective number of elective parties	Effective number of parliamentary parties
FRA1	d'Hondt	3.65	4.59	4.23
FRA2	Mixed	5.48	5.75	5.83
CHANGE		+1.83	+1.16[b]	+1.60[b]
GER3	d'Hondt	2.18	3.17	2.95
GER5	LR-Hare	0.67	3.56	3.47
CHANGE		-1.51	+0.39	+0.52
GER4E	d'Hondt	4.24	3.18	2.76
GER6E	LR-Hare	1.91	4.02	3.74
CHANGE		-2.33	+0.84	+0.98
ISR1	d'Hondt	2.47	5.39	4.73
ISR2	LR-Hare	0.86	5.10	4.92
CHANGE		-1.61	-0.29	+0.19
ISR2	LR-Hare	0.86	5.10	4.92
ISR3	d'Hondt	2.61	4.36	3.82
CHANGE		+1.75	-0.74	-1.10
NOR1	d'Hondt	8.53	3.87	2.92
NOR2	Modified Sainte-Laguë	4.38	3.77	3.26
CHANGE		-4.15	-0.10	+0.34
SWE1	d'Hondt	3.51	3.43	3.06
SWE2	Modified Sainte-Laguë	2.36	3.30	3.11
CHANGE		-1.15	-0.13	+0.05

Notes:
[a] See description of electoral systems on pp. 13–14, 16.
[b] The changes that run counter to the hypothesized influence of the electoral formula are in italics.

because technically two dimensions were changed: LR-Hare replaced d'Hondt and a 1 per cent national threshold was introduced. However, because this threshold is extremely low and because no party would have been barred from representation if the threshold had already been in place in 1949, I decided to ignore the threshold change in this case—in the interest of making maximum use of the available evidence.[3]

Let us take a closer look at the controlled changes in electoral formula in Table 4.1. Increases are indicated by plus and decreases by minus signs, and the increases and decreases that run counter to the hypothesized direction of the change are highlighted by being italicized. All of the changes entail shifts from or to the d'Hondt formula, and they all result in the increase or decrease in disproportionality (measured by the least-squares index) expected on the basis of the proportional or disproportional tendencies of the formulas. In absolute terms, the change from d'Hondt to one of the non-d'Hondt formulas results in a roughly 2 per cent change in disproportionality; the mean change is 2.05 per cent and the median 1.75 per cent. In relative terms, the change from d'Hondt increases or decreases disproportionality by roughly one-third to two-thirds.

The main hypothesis with regard to the effective numbers of parties is that they should be increased by a more proportional and reduced by a less proportional formula. As the italicized changes in Table 4.1 show, there are several disconfirming instances. The first change, that of the French electoral system change from the first post-war to the second post-war system (at the top of the table), is not really an invalidating case, however. As emphasized earlier, the 1951–6 system was the unusual mixed system with both majoritarian and PR elements and, as far as the PR side was concerned, with both d'Hondt and LR-Hare formulas. Because the majority rule could be applied, and actually was applied, in more districts and for the allocation of more seats than LR-Hare (see Table 2.8), I am treating the shift from d'Hondt to the mixed formula as a change in an inherently disproportional direction. In accordance with this assumption, the least-squares index of disproportionality increases substantially, but the effective numbers of both elective and parliamentary parties rise substantially, too. The reason, as also already indicated earlier, is that the French 1951–6 system was deliberately engineered to be disproportional in favour of the medium-sized parties and against the largest parties—contrary to the normal pattern of increasing discrimination as party sizes decrease—and hence it should be expected to increase the number of parties. It is the kind of exception that proves the rule—or, more accurately, that reminds us forcefully of what the normal hypothesis is.

Nevertheless, there are several other exceptions, and these form a theoretically significant pattern. All three deviations occur among the changes in the effective number of *elective* parties; excluding the French system, three of the changes are in accordance with the hypothesis that increasing proportionality will increase the number of parties and vice versa, and three run counter to this hypothesis. The sizes of the unexpected changes in multipartism are relatively small, and they are all smaller than the sizes of the expected changes, but the conclusion can only be that the effect of the different PR formulas on elective multipartism is, at best, quite weak. On the other hand, the effective numbers of parties in parliament all change in the hypothesized direction.

Giovanni Sartori has made the useful distinction between 'strong' (plurality) and 'feeble' (PR) electoral systems as far as their effects on party systems are concerned. His 'strong' plurality systems are strong in their capacity to reduce the number of parties—a proposition that will be confirmed by the evidence to be presented in the next chapter. Within the family of PR systems, Sartori makes a further distinction between highly proportional, hence completely 'feeble', systems and less proportional 'strong-feeble' systems.[4] To the extent that all electoral systems, including PR systems, tend to decrease the effective number of parties in the process of converting the elective into parliamentary parties, there are no truly and totally 'feeble'—or what might also be called neutral—systems. Nevertheless, the evidence of Table 4.1 does support the proposition that d'Hondt is a 'strong-feeble' formula in its capacity to produce a lower degree of multipartism in parliament than the other more proportional formulas. The second significant aspect of the evidence of Table 4.1 is that this decrease in multipartism is only marginally due to Maurice Duverger's 'psychological' factors, since elective multipartism is minimally affected by the changes in electoral formula.[5] Hence the reduction that does take place is almost entirely the effect of the mechanical factors of the electoral systems' translation of votes into seats.

Only two of the changes in Table 4.1 involved the generation of majority parties. In Norway, manufactured majorities occurred in both elections of the 1945–9 d'Hondt system but in only two of the nine elections under the 1953–85 system that used the modified Sainte-Laguë formula—in accordance with our theoretical expectations. In Sweden, one majority was generated, an earned majority, but—contrary to expectations—in the modified Sainte-Laguë rather than the d'Hondt system.

ONE-DIMENSIONAL CHANGES IN EFFECTIVE THRESHOLD AND ASSEMBLY SIZE

Table 4.2 shows the changes in effective threshold when the other electoral system dimensions—formula and assembly size—do not change. Unfortunately, there are only four changes of this kind, but the resulting changes in disproportionality and effective numbers of parties are all in the expected direction. In Denmark, the two changes in effective threshold were relatively small, and the corresponding changes in disproportionality were equally small. In Iceland, a bigger reduction in effective threshold resulted in an impressive drop in disproportionality, but an even larger reduction in Norway resulted in only a relatively small drop in disproportionality. The changes in multipartism, while all in the expected direction, do not correspond closely in size with the amounts of change in the effective thresholds.

A fifth instance of change could be added: the change from the first (1952–7) to the second (1962–84) Indian electoral system. India changed from an average magnitude of 1.21 seats to exactly 1 seat per district. In terms of the effective threshold of 35 per cent that I assigned to all majoritarian systems regardless of the type of majority or plurality formula and regardless of district magnitude, formally no change took place on this dimension—nor on the other two dimensions. But for the present analysis, it would be correct to interpret a reduction in district magnitude (in a majoritarian system) as the equivalent of a reduction in effective threshold. On the basis of this interpretation, the changes in disproportionality and multipartism are all in the expected direction. Disproportionality, while high in both systems, decreased from

TABLE 4.2. Controlled changes in effective threshold, and changes in disproportionality and effective numbers of parties

Electoral system[a]	Effective threshold (%)	Disproportionality (%)	Effective number of elective parties	Effective number of parliamentary parties
DEN1	1.6	1.81	4.08	3.96
DEN2	2.6	2.01	3.84	3.66
CHANGE	+1.0	+0.20	−0.24	−0.30
DEN2	2.6	2.01	3.84	3.66
DEN3	2.0	1.74	5.22	4.92
CHANGE	−0.6	−0.27	+1.38	+1.26
ICE1	8.7	7.49	3.66	3.44
ICE2	5.8	2.86	4.06	3.84
CHANGE	−2.9	−4.63	+0.40	+0.40
NOR2	8.9	4.38	3.77	3.26
NOR3	4.0	3.65	4.84	4.23
CHANGE	−4.9	−0.73	+1.07	+0.97

Note:
[a] See description of electoral systems on pp. 13–14, 16.

20.77 to 16.76 per cent; the effective number of elective parties increased, though only slightly, from 4.21 to 4.31; and the number of parliamentary parties rose more impressively from 1.79 to 2.27 parties. There was no change in the generation of majority parties: both systems had a 100 per cent incidence of such majorities, all of them manufactured. The only other change that involved majority parties in this group of countries was the change from the 22 per cent incidence of manufactured majorities in the Norwegian 1953–85 system, already mentioned, to no majority party in the one election, in 1989, in the third Norwegian electoral system.

There is a more abundant supply of changes in assembly size, as Table 4.3 shows. And the supply of deviant findings increases even more. In all but one of the nine changes, the index of disproportionality still goes up or down as expected, but the effective numbers of parties change more often in the unexpected than in the expected direction. The first finding is not very surprising because it occurs in a change in the Australian alternative vote systems; majoritarian systems tend to yield not only more disproportional results than PR systems, but also results that fluctuate more in their degree of disproportionality from election to election. The pattern of changes in multipartism—basically showing no clear impact of assembly size—are extremely surprising, especially because the changes in the least-squares indices show that changes in assembly size do have the hypothesized effect on disproportionality.

Changes in parliamentary and manufactured majorities in the five countries where they occurred show a similar divided pattern. Smaller assembly size was associated with a higher incidence of majorities of both kinds in the first change in Australia and, although only marginally so, in Ireland, but it was associated with a lower incidence of such majorities in the other change in Australia and in Malta. In the United Kingdom, there were more manufactured majorities but fewer earned majorities in the parliamentary election system than in the Euro-election system.

The tentative conclusions that emerge from the total of twenty instances of one-dimensional electoral system change (excluding the change in the French system for the reasons discussed above, but including, for the sake of maximizing the number of cases, the change in the Indian system) are the following: first, changes to more proportional electoral system characteristics almost invariably

TABLE 4.3. Controlled changes in assembly size, and changes in disproportionality and effective numbers of parties

Electoral system[a]	Assembly size	Disproportionality (%)	Effective number of elective parties	Effective number of parliamentary parties
AUL1	74	9.61	2.74	2.40
AUL2	122	8.55	2.76	2.53
CHANGE	+48	-1.06	+0.02	+0.13
AUL2	122	8.55	2.76	2.53
AUL3	148	10.24	3.02	2.35
CHANGE	+26	+1.69[b]	+0.26	-0.18
GER1	402	3.80	5.71	4.65
GER2	487	3.67	4.21	3.63
CHANGE	+85	-0.13	-1.50	-1.02
GER3	497	2.18	3.17	2.95
GER4E	78	4.24	3.18	2.76
CHANGE	-419	+2.06	+0.01	-0.19
GER5	497	0.67	3.56	3.47
GER6E	78	1.91	4.02	3.74
CHANGE	-419	+1.24	+0.46	+0.27

GRE1[c]	134	15.79	2.74	1.72
GRE2	185	10.99	3.21	2.22
CHANGE	+51	-4.80	+0.47	+0.50
IRE1	152	3.49	3.10	2.79
IRE2E	15	10.83	4.45	3.43
CHANGE	-137	+7.34	+1.35	+0.64
MAL1	40	3.79	2.97	2.79
MAL2	57	3.73	2.33	2.14
CHANGE	+17	-0.06	-0.64	-0.65
UK1	633	10.55	2.65	2.10
UK2E	78	19.45	2.94	1.85
CHANGE	-555	+8.90	+0.29	-0.25

Notes:

[a] See description of electoral systems on pp. 13–14, 16.

[b] The changes that run counter to the hypothesized influence of the assembly size are italicized.

[c] In the Greek case, the change was not in the formal assembly size (which remained steady at 300 members) but in what may be called the effective assembly size, as explained in Ch. 2 and Table 2.7.

resulted in lower disproportionality as measured by the least-squares index. Second, the effective number of parliamentary parties changed as hypothesized in three-fourths (15 out of 20) of the changes. Third, the effective number of elective parties changed as hypothesized in only about half (11 out of 20) of the recorded instances. Fourth, the effective threshold appears to have the greatest and the assembly size the least influence on the effective numbers of parties.

A MORE REFINED TEST

The above conclusions about the electoral system's influence on the number of parties are less than totally convincing for two reasons. In the first place, while it is easy to understand that electoral system differences within the PR family have much less impact than the differences between PR and plurality, it is difficult to understand and accept that the former appear not to have at least some, however weak, influence. Second, while it is easy to understand that the effective number of parliamentary parties is more responsive to electoral system changes than the effective number of elective parties, it is difficult to understand that it is not even more responsive; after all, even if, on the average, the latter is not affected at all by the electoral system changes, we would still expect the effective number of parliamentary parties to change by the sheer mechanical force of the electoral system changes.

A possible explanation of the first of these anomalies is that changes in the effective number of elective parties are based on psychological factors—expectations about the effects of electoral system changes—and that it may take more time for these expectations to change than for the electoral systems to change themselves. The politicians who have engineered the change in the electoral system presumably know and understand its likely impact right away, but the voters and some of the activists and financial supporters may need some actual experience with the new system in order to understand it. This explanation may be tested by comparing the effects of the old system not with those of the entire new system, but with the new system beginning with the second or the third election after the change.

The second possible explanation is of a methodological nature. I have used electoral systems within the same country as comparable cases, on the grounds that while these electoral systems were undergoing changes, the political parties and electorates could be assumed to remain basically unchanged. However, the period under observation is so long—close to half a century for most of the countries—that this assumption may well be questioned. Moreover, some of the electoral systems themselves extend over such long periods of time and so many elections that significant changes in parties and electorates may have occurred even within these systems. This explanation suggests an alternative method of measuring changes in the effective numbers of parties when the electoral system is changed: instead of comparing two entire systems—that is, all of the elections in the two systems—we should focus on elections that are as close together as possible in order to maximize comparability. Matthew S. Shugart has successfully used this kind of strategy in his study of electoral reform in some PR countries: he compares the results of the last two elections under the old rules with those of the first two elections under the reformed system.[6] There is an obvious drawback to this strategy as well: using just one or two elections, instead of all of the elections available for an electoral system, deprives one of the advantage of the greater accuracy and reliability that repeated observations of the operation of the same system provide.

The above two considerations suggest the following alternative tests of the influence of changes in the electoral system on multipartism: in order to give the explanation of lagged response a fair chance and in order to maximize comparability (and in spite of a reduction in the reliability of the evidence), compare the results of the last election of the old electoral system with the second and with the third election under the new system. When the change is a change from a parliamentary election system to a Euro-election system, the last election in the former is defined as the election just prior to the first Euro-election; in Ireland, for instance, this last parliamentary election took place in 1977, because it was the last election before the first Euro-election in 1979, and it is compared with the second and third Euro-elections in 1984 and 1989. Parenthetically, another small but not insignificant drawback of these alternative tests must be noted here: since not all of the electoral systems have second and third elections, focusing on these elections reduces the instances of change available for analysis—from 20 to 15 and from 20 to 13 respectively.

The results of one of the alternative tests are presented in Table 4.4 in abbreviated form; in order to save space, the indices of disproportionality and the effective numbers of parties of the two comparable elections are omitted, and merely the increases and decreases are included in the table. The table gives the results for the changes to the second election in the new system rather than the third; the results of the two comparisons are quite similar, but the latter is based on fewer cases of change.

Table 4.4 shows again that actual changes in the disproportionality of elections, as measured by the least-squares index, follow changes in electoral system properties very closely. As far as the effects on the effective number of parties are concerned, the table solves one anomaly and confirms the other. The more refined test demonstrates clearly that the degree of multipartism in parliament does respond quite faithfully to changes in the proportional or disproportional tendencies of electoral systems: in the fifteen instances of change, there is only one exception to this proposition. On the other hand, the lack of responsiveness of the effective number of elective parties is confirmed: the ratio of positive (expected) to negative reactions is 6 to 9. When the three majoritarian systems are removed, the ratio for the PR systems becomes an even more damning 4 to 8.

The conclusion is now inescapable that differences in disproportionality in PR systems do not appreciably affect the effective number of elective parties. These differences are clearly not large enough to produce commensurate differences in the strategic calculations by élites and voters and hence insufficient psychological forces systematically to affect the party system. The systematic influence by the electoral system on the party system that does occur is the impact on the effective number of parliamentary parties, and it is due almost entirely to the mechanics of the translation of votes into seats.

TWO-DIMENSIONAL CHANGES

We can seek further confirmation from the instances of change in electoral systems that entailed changes on two dimensions, as long

TABLE 4.4. One-dimensional changes in the electoral system and changes in disproportionality and effective numbers of parties, from the last election in the old to the second election in the new electoral system.

Electoral system change[a]	Disproportionality (%)	Effective number of elective parties	Effective number of parliamentary parties
ISR1–2	−1.25	+0.92	+1.23
ISR2–3	+1.94	+1.40[b]	+0.81
NOR1–2	−5.60	−0.28	+0.32
SWE1–2	−1.08	−0.05	+0.12
IND1–2	−9.95	+1.25	+1.40
DEN1–2	+1.00	−0.01	−0.08
DEN2–3	−0.27	+0.42	+0.37
ICE1–2	−4.75	−0.03	+0.13
AUL1–2	−4.25	−0.25	+0.18
AUL2–3	0.00	+0.23	+0.05
GER3–4E	+4.55	+0.46	−0.01
GRE1–2	−7.40	−0.05	+0.37
IRE1–2E	+8.80	+0.97	−0.11
MAL1–2	+4.55	+0.33	+0.01
UK1–2E	+6.95	+0.09	−0.16

Notes:
[a] See description of electoral systems on pp. 13–14, 16.
[b] The changes that run counter to the hypothesized influence of the electoral system dimensions are italicized.

as both changes were in the same direction of proportionality or disproportionality. There are eleven changes of this kind among our electoral systems. They all involve a change in the effective threshold combined with either a change in formula or a change in assembly size. Table 4.5 presents the increases and decreases in the least-squares indices of disproportionality and in the effective numbers of parties from the last election of the old system to the second election of the new system. As in the earlier tables in this chapter, the figures that run counter to the hypothesis are italicized.

The evidence should be stronger and clearer than in Table 4.4, because the changes are the results of two shifts in the same direction instead of just one shift of the electoral system. However, the impact on the effective number of parliamentary parties is now slightly weaker. On the other hand, the changes in the index of disproportionality are again almost entirely as hypothesized, and the changes in the effective number of elective parties are again about evenly divided—showing essentially no impact of the electoral system on elective multipartism.

WITHIN-SYSTEM CHANGES

I made a final attempt to use the comparative method by focusing on small changes that occurred entirely within a particular electoral system. These are changes that are not large enough to signify the start of a new system, that is, they are neither a clear change of electoral formula nor a change of 20 per cent or more in the effective threshold or the assembly size. Most of them were slight upward or downward adjustments of the effective threshold: modifications in the average district magnitude, as in Finland, Ireland, Malta, and Portugal, or in the legal threshold, as in Denmark and Italy. I examined seventeen changes of this kind, again attempting to achieve as much comparability as possible by comparing the last election before the change with the second election after. My rationale was that, however small, these changes might be discovered to affect disproportionality and multipartism to some degree, since the effective threshold had proved to be the strongest of the electoral system dimensions, and since these small changes

TABLE 4.5. Two-dimensional changes in the electoral system and changes in disproportionality and effective numbers of parties, from the last election in the old to the second election in the new electoral system

Changes in electoral system[a]	Disproportionality (%)	Effective number of elective parties	Effective number of parliamentary parties
Effective threshold and electoral formula			
AUT1–2	−1.95	*−0.03*[b]	+0.09
FRA2–3	+11.72	−1.16	−2.30
ITA1–2	+2.08	−0.51	−0.85
ITA2–3	−1.07	−0.02	+0.20
JPN1–2	+4.39	−3.72	−2.99
Effective threshold and assembly size			
BEL1–2E	+3.70	*+0.40*	*+0.83*
CR1–2	−0.45	−1.24	−1.07
LUX1–2E	+7.65	−0.41	−0.89
NET1–2	*+0.14*	−0.53	*−0.50*
NET2–3E	+2.45	*+0.09*	−0.13
SWE2–3	−1.51	+0.33	+0.48

Notes:

[a] See description of electoral systems on pp. 13–14, 16.

[b] The changes that run counter to the hypothesized influence of the electoral system dimensions are italicized.

occurred in optimally controlled circumstances within the same electoral system.

The results, however, turned out to be entirely negative. The changes in disproportionality and in the effective numbers of elective and parliamentary parties were all about evenly divided between changes that confirmed and that disconfirmed the basic hypothesis. The small shifts in effective threshold were evidently too small to have a measurable impact.

There is also a positive aspect to this finding, however. It shows that the electoral systems, even when they include a long series of elections, have a high degree of internal uniformity. This increases the confidence we can have in the electoral systems as our basic cases for analysis—and the proper cases to be examined by means of a cross-sectional research design in the next chapter.

5

Bivariate and Multivariate Analyses

AFTER the comparable-cases analyses of the previous chapter, this chapter turns to the systematic analysis of all cases, that is, all seventy electoral systems—with the exception of the highly unusual case of the mixed PR–majority system used in the 1951 and 1956 elections in France, which cannot be made to fit our general categories. Most of the time, the remaining sixty-nine cases will be the focus of attention, but I shall also single out the fifty-seven PR cases for special examination on many occasions.

I shall start with the bivariate relationships between the three electoral system dimensions on the one hand and disproportionality and party system characteristics on the other. My next topic will be the multivariate relationships among these variables, which I shall examine by means of both cross-tabulations and regression analysis. Finally, I shall test whether the empirical relationships discovered in this chapter hold up when a more conservative criterion—generally, a 50 per cent instead of a 20 per cent cut-off point—is used to distinguish between cases. This leads to several instances of consolidation of two or more cases in the same country into a single case—and the reduction from sixty-nine to fifty-two electoral systems (excluding 1951–6 France).

BIVARIATE PATTERNS

Table 5.1 presents the bivariate relationships between the electoral formula on the one hand and disproportionality and the four party system variables on the other. The formulas are broken down into five categories: (1) plurality, (2) other majoritarian formulas, (3) d'Hondt and LR-Imperiali, the least proportional of the PR formulas, (4) the more proportional LR-Droop, STV, and modified

TABLE 5.1. The effects of electoral formulas on disproportionality and party systems in 69 electoral systems

Electoral formula	Disproportionality (%)	Effective number of elective parties	Effective number of parliamentary parties	Frequency of parliamentary majorities	Frequency of manufactured majorities
Plurality (7)	13.56	3.09	2.04	0.93	0.71
Other majoritarian (5)	10.88	3.58	2.77	0.52	0.52
D'Hondt, etc. (32)	5.22	4.35	3.70	0.18	0.14
LR-Droop, etc. (13)	4.15	3.80	3.29	0.24	0.14
LR-Hare (12)	1.88	3.62	3.46	0.23	0.04
All (69)	5.69	3.94	3.34	0.30	0.21

Note: The numbers of cases on which the average numbers and percentages are based are in parentheses.

Sainte-Laguë formulas, and (5) the most proportional LR-Hare formula. As explained in Chapter 2, the Japanese limited vote and single non-transferable (SNTV) systems are grouped in the middle PR category, and the Greek reinforced PR systems, after being reconfigured, belong to the d'Hondt formulas.

The percentage of disproportionality decreases as hypothesized from the plurality formula to LR-Hare. This decrease is both monotonic and dramatic: from almost 14 per cent to less than 2 per cent. The principal difference is between the majoritarian systems and the PR systems. The percentages in this column confirm the three general rules emphasized earlier. One, all electoral systems, including PR, are disproportional to some extent. Second, they are all also reasonably proportional, in the sense that even the highest disproportionality is not outrageously disproportional; the disproportionality of the plurality systems, for instance, is less than three times that of the d'Hondt PR system. But, third, there are obviously big and important differences among the various systems, and the systems of proportional representation are indeed much more proportional than the non-proportional systems.

An important caveat needs to be attached to the second of these rules. Electoral systems that provide incentives for strategic behaviour, especially plurality systems, significantly understate the degree of disproportionality: assuming that many voters cast their votes for larger parties because they do not want to waste their votes on small parties with poor chances of being elected, the parties' seat shares deviate much more from the pattern of the voters' true preferences than from the actual vote shares—and it is the latter on which the index of disproportionality is based.

An excellent indication of the strength of strategic behaviour can be found in the difference in effective numbers of elective parties between plurality and other majoritarian formulas.[1] The two formulas are alike in most respects—including the fact that they are normally applied in single-member districts—but differ in that strategic voting is, by and large, not necessary in the non-plurality systems. In France, voters can vote for their favourite small party in the first round without wasting their votes, because the second round, if no candidate wins in the first round, offers them another chance to vote for a candidate of one of the major parties.[2] In Australia, giving one's first preference to a candidate of a small party is not a wasted vote because, if the contest is not decided on the basis of first preferences, second preferences will be counted and may help to elect one of the major candidates. The difference between the effective numbers of elective parties in plurality and other majoritarian systems—3.09 compared with 3.58 parties—must be attributed mainly to the strong presence versus the virtual absence of strategic voting. It is worth noting that the effective number of elective parties in the French and Australian systems is lower than in the PR systems, but not a great deal lower—and almost the same as that in the LR-Hare systems.

That disproportionality does not automatically lead to fewer elective parties is again demonstrated by the PR systems: the least proportional d'Hondt formula has the most parties, and the most proportional LR-Hare has the fewest parties. However, in line with the findings in the previous chapter, this order is partly reversed and the differences are narrower as far as the effective numbers of parliamentary parties are concerned. The less proportional formulas do cause a sharper reduction in the effective number of parties from elective to parliamentary parties. The greatest reduction, both in absolute and in relative terms, takes place in plurality systems.

In fact, by far the most striking difference in Table 5.1 is that between plurality and the other formulas: only plurality succeeds in creating a two-party system, by reducing the average effective number of about three elective parties to one with two parliamentary parties.[3] The one qualification that needs to be emphasized here is that the Indian party system has usually been one of a dominant party and several smaller parties, which adds up to an effective number of roughly two parties, instead of a system with two more or less balanced parties. Both the two-party and the dominant-party patterns are associated with a very high incidence of parliamentary majorities: an average of more than 90 per cent, of which more than two-thirds are manufactured majorities. In the other majoritarian systems, all of the parliamentary majorities are manufactured, and they occur in only slightly more than half of the elections. Parliamentary and manufactured majorities are not uncommon in PR systems either but they occur at a much lower frequency. The three PR formulas do not differ greatly among themselves except that, under the most proportional LR-Hare system, manufactured majorities are extremely rare.

For the PR systems of election, Table 5.2 demonstrates that the

TABLE 5.2. The effects of effective thresholds on disproportionality and party systems in 69 electoral systems

Effective threshold (%)	Disproportionality (%)	Effective number of elective parties	Effective number of parliamentary parties	Frequency of parliamentary majorities	Frequency of manufactured majorities
35 (12)	12.44	3.30	2.34	0.76	0.63
12.9 to 18.8 (9)	7.24	3.28	2.71	0.61	0.38
8.0 to 11.7 (13)	5.74	3.99	3.31	0.25	0.18
4.0 to 5.9 (17)	3.68	4.56	3.99	0.05	0.04
0.1 to 3.3 (18)	2.29	4.07	3.74	0.11	0.03
All (69)	5.69	3.94	3.34	0.30	0.21

Note: The numbers of cases on which the average numbers and percentages are based are in parentheses.

differences in effective thresholds are considerably more conse-
quential than the differences in formula. The effective threshold
is a continuous variable, but naturally occurring discontinuities
make it easy to divide the values into five categories. The largest
break occurs between the 35 per cent arbitrarily assigned to all
majoritarian systems and the highest threshold—18.8 per cent under
reinforced PR in Greece—in any PR system. But the effective
thresholds of PR systems also clearly cluster in four groups, as
shown in the first column of the table.

Because plurality and majority formulas have the highest
effective thresholds, the top row of the table merely repeats the
information that was already contained in the two top rows of
Table 5.1. Table 5.2 is therefore mainly important for what it tells
us about PR systems. Disproportionality decreases, as hypothesized, as the effective threshold decreases—both monotonically
and with sizable differences between each of the four categories.
The effective numbers of parties increase as the threshold decreases, but what looks like a clear pattern is upset by the PR
systems with the lowest thresholds. However, the occurrence of
parliamentary and manufactured majorities is highly sensitive to
the threshold level. Among the least proportional systems—those
with the highest thresholds—the average percentage of parliamentary majorities, 61 per cent, is even higher than that for the
non-plurality majoritarian systems. In the next category with
threshold levels between 8.0 and 11.7 per cent, such majorities are
rarer but still occur in one-fourth of the elections. At lower
threshold levels, both parliamentary and manufactured majorities
become quite rare.

Table 5.3 shows the effects of the third electoral system dimension: assembly size. This is also a continuous variable, and I
again converted it into discrete categories by taking advantage of
naturally occurring discontinuities, as shown in the first column.
The table is limited to the fifty-seven PR systems. The reason is
that, as shown in Chapter 2, assembly size and formula are correlated: plurality and majority systems are used most often for the
election of the largest assemblies. As a result, the bivariate relationship between assembly size and disproportionality for all sixty-
nine electoral systems appears to be curvilinear: as assembly size
increases, disproportionality decreases from 5.96 to 4.62 per cent,
but then goes up to 4.92 and, for the largest assemblies, to 7.03 per

TABLE 5.3. The effects of assembly size on disproportionality and party systems in 57 PR systems

Assembly size	Disproportionality (%)	Effective number of elective parties	Effective number of parliamentary parties	Frequency of parliamentary majorities	Frequency of manufactured majorities
6 to 81 (20)	4.86	3.96	3.42	0.21	0.08
100 to 200 (19)	4.12	4.10	3.65	0.28	0.19
211 to 350 (7)	4.00	3.66	3.19	0.15	0.11
402 to 626 (11)	3.63	4.50	3.87	0.10	0.09
All (57)	4.27	4.07	3.55	0.20	0.12

Note: The numbers of cases on which the average numbers and percentages are based are in parentheses.

cent. There is no plausible theoretical reason for this, and the most likely explanation is that it is merely an artefact of the relationship between assembly size and plurality-majority systems. In order to control for this disturbing influence, therefore, only the PR systems are included in the table.

As hypothesized, the percentage of disproportionality now decreases monotonically as assembly size increases. The biggest difference is between the smallest assemblies, with up to 81 members, and the next category of assemblies with 100 to 200 members. This makes good theoretical sense, because, while the technical possibility of achieving perfect or near-perfect proportionality keeps improving as assembly size goes up, only the smallest assembly sizes entail serious restrictions on proportionality. In line with this finding, we would expect lower effective numbers of parties and higher frequencies of parliamentary and manufactured majorities in these small assemblies. Table 5.3 shows that this is not the case; in fact, the values for the smallest assemblies are very close to the average values for all assemblies. For the larger assemblies, there is no discernible pattern either. Of the three sets of bivariate relationships, those of the effects of assembly size are plainly the weakest.

MULTIVARIATE PATTERNS

The multivariate relationships are shown in a series of five tables (Tables 5.4 to 5.8). In order to have sufficient cases in each category, the two classes of PR systems with the highest thresholds were merged and, similarly, the two most proportional PR formula groups were consolidated. The juxtaposition of three types of formula and four categories of effective thresholds yields 12 cells, but 5 of these are logically empty. The first table, which presents the multivariate results for disproportionality, makes a further dichotomous contrast according to assembly size, using the difference between the smallest assemblies (with up to 81 members) and the larger ones (with 100 or more members) that we just discovered to be the most important dividing line.

Table 5.4 is the kind of table that is a researcher's pure delight because of the beautifully regular pattern it displays. Part A shows a completely perfect relationship between formula and threshold

TABLE 5.4. Average percentages of disproportionality, classified by electoral formula, effective threshold, and assembly size, in 69 electoral systems

Assembly size	Effective threshold (%)	Plurality and other majoritarian formulas	D'Hondt and LR-Imperiali	Other PR
A. All 69 systems				
	35	12.44 (12)	—	—
	8.0–18.8	—	8.07 (11)	4.64 (11)
	4.0–5.9	—	4.21 (13)	1.98 (4)
	0.1–3.3	—	2.96 (8)	1.76 (10)
B. 22 systems with small assemblies				
	35	14.53 (2)	—	—
	8.0–18.8	—	10.32 (2)	5.26 (5)
	4.0–5.9	—	4.95 (7)	1.91 (1)
	0.1–3.3	—	4.80 (2)	1.38 (3)
C. 47 systems with large assemblies				
	35	12.03 (10)	—	—
	8.0–18.8	—	7.57 (9)	4.12 (6)
	4.0–5.9	—	3.33 (6)	2.00 (3)
	0.1–3.3	—	2.34 (6)	1.92 (7)

Note: The numbers of cases on which the average percentages are based are in parentheses.

on the one hand and disproportionality on the other: the indices of disproportionality gradually decrease from the top left-hand cell to the bottom right-hand cell. The plurality and majority systems have the highest disproportionality. After that, the indices of disproportionality of the d'Hondt and LR-Imperiali systems are higher than those of the other PR systems in each of the threshold categories; and within the two PR formula categories, the indices decrease as the effective threshold decreases. When assembly size is controlled, by separating the small from the large assemblies in parts B and C of the table, the same perfect pattern is repeated twice.

TABLE 5.5. Average effective numbers of elective parties, classified by electoral formula and effective threshold, in 69 electoral systems

Effective threshold (%)	Plurality and other majoritarian formulas	D'Hondt and LR-Imperiali	Other PR
35	3.30 (12)	—	—
8.0–18.8	—	3.83 (11)	3.57 (11)
4.0–5.9	—	4.73 (13)	4.00 (4)
0.1–3.3	—	4.46 (8)	3.76 (10)

Note: The numbers of cases on which the average effective numbers of parties are based are in parentheses.

By comparing the corresponding cells in parts B and C, we can also gauge the effect of assembly size when formula and threshold are controlled. Disproportionality is generally lower in the larger assemblies, but here two slight imperfections appear: in the two lowest threshold groups of the other PR systems. The difference in disproportionality in the 4.0 to 5.9 per cent threshold category is very small, and should probably not be taken too seriously because of the few cases in these cells, but the entries in the two bottom right-hand cells clearly deviate from the expected pattern. A plausible explanation is at hand, however: it makes sense that in this most proportional category, with an overall disproportionality well below 2 per cent, small assembly size does not contribute any further to lower disproportionality.

The classification by assembly size is not repeated in Tables 5.5 to 5.8 because the effect of assembly size now largely disappears. There are still slightly more differences in the expected direction than in the contrary direction, but the pattern is too erratic to warrant the conclusion that even a slight influence of assembly size remains. Table 5.5 does not show a very clear pattern for the influence of electoral formula and effective threshold on the number of elective parties either. There are more parties in the PR systems than in the plurality and majority systems, but among the six PR categories the differences are more often than not against expectations: there are more instead of fewer parties in d'Hondt and LR-Imperiali than in the other PR systems, and the systems with the lowest thresholds have fewer instead of more parties than

TABLE 5.6. Average effective numbers of parliamentary parties, classified by electoral formula and effective threshold, in 69 electoral systems

Effective threshold (%)	Plurality and other majoritarian formulas	D'Hondt and LR-Imperiali	Other PR
35	2.34 (12)	—	—
8.0–18.8	—	3.09 (11)	3.04 (11)
4.0–5.9	—	4.08 (13)	3.71 (4)
0.1–3.3	—	3.91 (8)	3.61 (10)

Note: The numbers of cases on which the average effective numbers of parties are based are in parentheses.

those with medium thresholds. This finding confirms the lack of influence of different PR systems on the effective number of elective parties that already emerged from the comparative analysis in the previous chapter.

However, the previous chapter did show a substantial influence of different forms of PR on the effective number of parliamentary parties. At least at first sight, Table 5.6 does not appear to confirm this finding. In fact, all of the differences in this table are exactly in the same direction as those in the previous table—but they are all much smaller. The one clear pattern that Table 5.6 does show is the major difference between PR systems with thresholds of 8.0 per cent and higher and those with thresholds of 5.9 per cent and lower. Within the latter category, the differences are very small. Thresholds therefore clearly matter in the sense that thresholds of 8.0 per cent and higher substantially reduce the effective numbers of parliamentary parties: these numbers are roughly half-way between those of the plurality-majority and the other PR systems. But there is no gainsaying of the contradiction between the evidence of Table 5.6 and the comparative evidence in the previous chapter with regard to PR formulas. Since the positive finding in the previous chapter was based on the more tightly controlled comparable-cases analysis, it can obviously not be abandoned, but it is weakened at least slightly.

The pattern of a major division between systems with thresholds above 8.0 per cent compared with lower-threshold systems found in Table 5.6 also shows up very clearly in Tables 5.7 and 5.8. Both

TABLE 5.7. Average frequencies of parliamentary majorities, classified by electoral formula and effective threshold, in 69 electoral systems

Effective threshold (%)	Plurality and other majoritarian formulas	D'Hondt and LR-Imperiali	Other PR
35	0.76 (12)	—	—
8.0–18.8	—	0.40 (11)	0.40 (11)
4.0–5.9	—	0.06 (13)	0.00 (4)
0.1–3.3	—	0.06 (8)	0.15 (10)

Note: The numbers of cases on which the frequencies are based are in parentheses.

TABLE 5.8. Average frequencies of manufactured majorities, classified by electoral formula and effective threshold, in 69 electoral systems

Effective threshold (%)	Plurality and other majoritarian formulas	D'Hondt and LR-Imperiali	Other PR
35	0.63 (12)	—	—
8.0–18.8	—	0.31 (11)	0.22 (11)
4.0–5.9	—	0.05 (13)	0.00 (4)
0.1–3.3	—	0.06 (8)	0.00 (10)

Note: The numbers of cases on which the frequencies are based are in parentheses.

parliamentary majorities and manufactured majorities occur with considerably greater frequency at the higher threshold levels. As in Table 5.6, these figures are roughly in the middle between the frequencies of plurality-majority and other PR systems. What Tables 5.7 and 5.8 partly obscure, but what was already shown in the earlier Table 5.2, is that the majority-generating capacity is especially strong among the PR systems with the highest thresholds of 12.9 per cent and above. This small group contains some of the more unusual PR systems: Irish and Maltese STV, Japanese SNTV (literally a semi-PR rather than a PR system), and Greek reinforced PR. A slightly greater tendency of d'Hondt and LR-Imperiali systems compared with other PR systems to yield manufactured majorities also appears in Table 5.8, but there is no clear pattern differentiating the two PR formula groups as far as the generation of parliamentary majorities is concerned.

REGRESSION ANALYSES

Most of our variables are cardinal in nature and hence capable of being subjected to regression analysis. And the one variable that is discrete—the electoral formula—can be dichotomized and thus also included in this kind of analysis. Tables 5.9 and 5.10 show the regression analyses for all sixty-nine electoral systems (again with the exception of 1951–6 France); in Table 5.10, a PR dummy variable is used—essentially dichotomizing the electoral formulas into plurality and majority versus PR systems. Table 5.11 shows the regression analyses for the fifty-seven PR systems only; here a d'Hondt and LR-Imperiali dummy represents the dichotomy between these least proportional PR formulas and all other PR formulas.

The tables show the regression of each of the dependent variables on the three independent variables (the three electoral system dimensions). For each regression, the tables present the estimated (unstandardized) regression coefficients, the standardized regression coefficients (betas), and the t-values for each independent variable, as well as the intercept, the square of the correlation coefficient (R^2), and the adjusted R^2. The betas can be interpreted as rough indicators of the strength of each independent variable in explaining the dependent variables. Because of the relatively large number of cases and the small number of independent variables, the adjusted R^2 is generally only slightly lower than the unadjusted R^2, but my measure of the proportion of variance explained will be the former, more conservative R^2. The tables also indicate whether or not the regression coefficients are statistically significant at the 5 per cent or 1 per cent level.

Because the majoritarian–PR contrast and the effective threshold are so highly correlated, they cannot be entered into the same regression equation. Therefore, as Tables 5.9 and 5.10 show, they were entered into separate regression equations together with assembly size. Uniformly, the results—both the percentage of variance explained and the betas—are stronger when the effective

TABLE 5.9. Regression analyses of the influence of the effective threshold and assembly size on disproportionality and party system variables in 69 electoral systems

Independent variables	Disproportionality	Effective number of elective parties	Effective number of parliamentary parties	Frequency of parliamentary majorities	Frequency of manufactured majorities
Effective threshold[a]	0.32**	−0.03**	−0.05**	0.02**	0.02**
	0.82	−0.34	−0.55	0.66	0.65
	(10.93)	(2.82)	(5.26)	(7.04)	(6.85)
Assembly size (log)	−1.52*	0.12	0.12	−0.03	0.02
	−0.15	0.05	0.05	−0.04	0.03
	(2.04)	(0.39)	(0.50)	(0.42)	(0.29)
Intercept	5.31	4.07	3.66	0.12	−0.05
R^2	0.64	0.11	0.30	0.43	0.43
Adjusted R^2	0.63	0.08	0.28	0.42	0.41

Notes:
[a] The estimated regression coefficients are listed first, followed by the standardized coefficients; absolute t-values are in parentheses.

* Statistically significant at the 5 per cent level (one-tailed test).

** Statistically significant at the 1 per cent level (one-tailed test).

TABLE 5.10. Regression analyses of the effect of the electoral formula and assembly size on disproportionality and party system variables in 69 electoral systems

Independent variables	Disproportionality	Effective number of elective parties	Effective number of parliamentary parties	Frequency of parliamentary majorities	Frequency of manufactured majorities
PR dummy	-8.61**	0.81*	1.24**	-0.57**	-0.50**
	-0.72	0.26	0.45	-0.55	-0.57
	(7.96)	(2.13)	(3.92)	(5.20)	(5.50)
Assembly size	-1.60*	0.11	0.11	-0.03	0.02
(log)	-0.16	0.04	0.05	-0.04	0.02
	(1.78)	(0.34)	(0.43)	(0.36)	(0.21)
Intercept	16.26	3.04	2.07	0.84	0.59
R^2	0.49	0.06	0.19	0.30	0.33
Adjusted R^2	0.47	0.04	0.17	0.27	0.31

Notes:

[a] The estimated regression coefficients are listed first, followed by the standardized coefficients; absolute t-values are in parentheses.

* Statistically significant at the 5 per cent level (one-tailed test).

** Statistically significant at the 1 per cent level (one-tailed test).

threshold rather than the PR dummy is used as one of the independent variables. The reason, of course, is that the effective threshold is capable of capturing the less proportional and more majority-generating tendencies of the high-threshold PR systems, whereas the PR dummy assumes no differences within the broad group of PR systems. Because of the differences within the majoritarian group between plurality and non-plurality systems (see Table 5.1), I also tried using a plurality dummy (contrasting plurality on the one hand with the other majoritarian systems plus the PR systems on the other), but this always yielded weaker results than those produced by the PR dummy.

It comes as no great surprise after all the evidence that has already been presented, that disproportionality is the variable that is best explained by the electoral system dimensions. The proportion of variance explained by the effective threshold and assembly size is almost two-thirds (63 per cent). The effective threshold by itself—that is, in a bivariate regression equation—already explains 61 per cent of the variance. Assembly size adds a bit more than one percentage point, but this contribution is still statistically significant at the 5 per cent level. The unequal impact is also reflected by the widely different betas. When we look at the unstandardized regression coefficients, each percentage increase in the effective threshold produces almost a third (0.32) of a percentage increase in disproportionality, and each unit increase in the logged assembly size (which means a tenfold jump in assembly size from, say, 10 to 100 or from 50 to 500) yields a decrease of about a percentage point and a half (1.52 per cent) in disproportionality.

Since I introduced three alternative measures of disproportionality in Chapter 3 (the Rae, Loosemore-Hanby, and largest-deviation indices), it is worth enquiring at this point whether the impressive total percentage of variance explained can be raised further when these are used instead of the least-squares index. The answer is yes for the Rae index for which the variance explained is 74 per cent—probably due to this measure's tendency to overstate the proportionality of PR systems (see Chapter 3)—but no for the Loosemore–Hanby and largest-deviation indices for which the variance explained is 52 and 57 per cent respectively. Using the Taagepera–Shugart threshold instead of my preferred effective threshold lowers the variance explained only slightly: from 63 to 61 per cent.

The variance explained of the other variables is considerably lower—especially low for the effective number of elective parties (again, not much of a surprise), but a respectable 28 to 42 per cent for the other three. It should be noted that assembly size is no longer a significant explanatory variable, and that the total amount of explained variance is explained almost entirely by a single variable: the effective threshold. Each percentage increase in the effective threshold reduces the effective number of elective parties by 0.03 and the effective number of parliamentary parties by 0.06, and it increases the frequency of parliamentary and manufactured majorities by about 4 and 2 per cent respectively. All of the coefficients of the regressions of the dependent variables on the effective threshold as well as on the PR dummy are statistically significant, usually at the 1 per cent level; in fact, as the high t-values show, most of the coefficients that are significant at the 1 per cent level are also significant at the 0.1 per cent level.

In the regression analyses of the fifty-seven PR systems, all three independent variables could be entered simultaneously (see Table 5.11), but the results are similar in many respects to those of the regression analyses of all sixty-nine systems. Disproportionality is again the variable of which the largest amount of variance can be explained, and the proportion explained is again almost two-thirds (63 per cent). The effective threshold is also again the strongest force, but, as the betas indicate, the electoral formula (the d'Hondt and LR-Imperiali dummy) and assembly size also make important contributions; all of the regression coefficients are statistically significant at the 1 per cent level. In a stepwise regression, the effective threshold by itself explains almost 45 per cent of the variance in disproportionality; the electoral formula raises this percentage by 12 points to 57 per cent; and assembly size adds the final 6 per cent. The unstandardized regression coefficients show that each percentage increase in effective threshold increases disproportionality by 0.42 per cent, that moving from one of the more to one of the less proportional PR formulas raises the index of disproportionality by 2.19 per cent, and that each unit increase in logged assembly size decreases disproportionality by 1.68 per cent.

The Rae index of disproportionality again gives a somewhat better result (71 per cent of variance explained), and the Loosemore–Hanby and largest-deviation measures again perform not as well as the least-squares index (55 and 58 per cent respectively).

TABLE 5.11. Regression analyses of the effect of three electoral system dimensions on disproportionality and party system variables in 57 PR systems

Independent variables	Disproportionality	Effective number of elective parties	Effective number of parliamentary parties	Frequency of parliamentary majorities	Frequency of manufactured majorities
Effective threshold[a]	0.42**	-0.06*	-0.09**	0.04**	0.02**
	0.66	-0.27	-0.42	0.54	0.48
	(8.13)	(2.09)	(3.39)	(4.70)	(4.06)
d'Hondt and LR-Imperiali dummy	2.19**	0.63	0.31	-0.05	0.05
	0.36	0.26	0.15	-0.08	0.10
	(4.35)	(2.06)	(1.23)	(0.68)	(0.86)
Assembly size (log)	-1.68**	-0.07	0.04	0.02	0.07
	-0.25	-0.03	0.02	0.02	0.12
	(3.09)	(0.21)	(0.13)	(0.22)	(1.02)
Intercept	3.86	4.29	3.88	-0.04	-0.21
R^2	0.65	0.14	0.20	0.30	0.25
Adjusted R^2	0.63	0.09	0.15	0.26	0.21

Notes:

[a] The estimated regression coefficients are listed first, followed by the standardized coefficients; absolute t-values are in parentheses.

* Statistically significant at the 5 per cent level (one-tailed test).

** Statistically significant at the 1 per cent level (one-tailed test).

However, the Taagepera–Shugart threshold now yields a slightly stronger result than my effective threshold: in conjunction with the electoral formula and assembly size, it explains almost 65 per cent of the variance in disproportionality.

The amounts of variance in the other dependent variables that the electoral system dimensions manage to explain is again much lower than the explained variance in disproportionality—and also lower than the corresponding percentages of variance explained in the regression analyses of all sixty-nine systems. The electoral formula dummy appears to be a significant variable (with a beta of 0.26 and a t-value of 2.06) in the explanation of the effective number of elective parties—but note that its sign is wrong: the use of d'Hondt or LR-Imperiali is associated with a larger instead of a smaller number of parties, contrary to the hypothesized effect of these relatively disproportional PR formulas. In the regressions of the other party system variables, the electoral formula is not statistically significant either and adds only slightly to the total variance explained; assembly size makes no contribution at all. The general pattern is that the effective threshold is the most important, and almost the only important, explanatory variable. In several respects, it emerges as a stronger factor among the fifty-seven PR systems than among all sixty-nine electoral systems: each percentage increase produces a greater increase in disproportionality and about twice as much of an increase in the effective numbers of parties and in the frequency of parliamentary majorities.

The strength of the effective threshold as an explanatory variable is also highlighted when we compare Tables 5.9 to 5.11 with Table 3.4 in Chapter 3. This table shows strong correlations between disproportionality and the party system characteristics with the exception of the effective number of elective parties. A reasonable expectation would have been that disproportionality, as the putative causal link between the electoral system and the party system, would be a stronger explanatory variable than any of the electoral system dimensions by themselves or even stronger than all of the electoral system dimensions combined. This is not the case, however: for all four of the party system variables and for both the set of sixty-nine electoral systems and the set of fifty-seven PR systems, just one of the electoral system dimensions, the effective threshold, explains a substantially larger proportion of the variance than disproportionality.

A REPLICATION OF THE REGRESSION ANALYSES WITH
CONSOLIDATED CASES

As promised in Chapter 1, I also replicated the regression analyses on a smaller number of more leniently defined electoral systems.[4] Having more than one electoral system in the same country offers a special advantage because it means that the comparable-cases method can be applied. However, using them as cases in cross-sectional research is at least somewhat problematic because the cases in this type of analysis should ideally be completely independent of each other and, in practice, should be as independent as possible. In order to comply with this requirement, I redefined the electoral systems in such a way as to have fewer systems in the same country: a total of fifty-three cases in the twenty-seven countries—only about two electoral systems per country.

Instead of my earlier 20 per cent criterion, I used the criterion that at least 50 per cent change in the effective threshold or in the assembly size was necessary for a set of elections to be defined as a new electoral system. With regard to the electoral formula, I did not count changes within the family of majoritarian systems or within each of the three major groups of PR systems as changes that triggered the definition of a new electoral system; for instance, the switch from the reinforced to the normal LR-Imperiali in Italy in the 1950s was considered to be a within-system instead of a between-system change. In addition, it seemed reasonable to be even more lenient in the following three cases: (1) the adoption of the very low threshold of 1 per cent in Israel after the 1949 election; (2) the increase in the low effective threshold of 1.6 to a still rather low 2.6 per cent in Denmark in 1953; and (3) the increase in assembly size from 74 to 121 in the late 1940s in Australia. I also dropped the criterion that electoral systems had to consist of successive elections. This meant that the Israeli elections held in 1949 and from 1973 on, held under similar election rules (ignoring the lack of a legal threshold in 1949), could be regarded as elections belonging to the same electoral system. Similarly, the 1945–6 and 1986 elections in France, forty years apart but conducted with strikingly similar election rules, could be treated as a single electoral system. One consequence of all these consolidations was to increase

TABLE 5.12. Regression analyses of the influence of the effective threshold and assembly size on disproportionality and party system variables in 52 electoral systems (consolidated cases)

Independent variables	Disproportionality	Effective number of elective parties	Effective number of parliamentary parties	Frequency of parliamentary majorities	Frequency of manufactured majorities
Effective threshold[a]	0.32**	−0.03*	−0.05**	0.02**	0.02**
	0.83	−0.31	−0.51	0.67	0.69
	(9.88)	(2.22)	(4.02)	(6.18)	(6.57)
Assembly size (log)	−2.36**	−0.11	0.04	0.01	0.02
	−0.26	−0.04	0.02	0.02	0.04
	(3.12)	(0.30)	(0.16)	(0.14)	(0.40)
Intercept	7.00	4.56	3.82	0.02	−0.06
R^2	0.67	0.10	0.25	0.45	0.49
Adjusted R^2	0.66	0.07	0.22	0.43	0.47

Notes:
[a] The estimated regression coefficients are listed first, followed by the standardized coefficients; absolute t-values are in parentheses.

* Statistically significant at the 5 per cent level (one-tailed test).
** Statistically significant at the 1 per cent level (one-tailed test).

TABLE 5.13. Regression analyses of the effect of three electoral system dimensions on disproportionality and party system variables in 44 PR systems (consolidated cases)

Independent variables	Disproportionality	Effective number of elective parties	Effective number of parliamentary parties	Frequency of parliamentary majorities	Frequency of manufactured majorities
Effective threshold[a]	0.38**	−0.04	−0.07*	0.03**	0.03**
	0.62	−0.14	−0.29	0.44	0.57
	(6.50)	(0.95)	(1.96)	(3.09)	(4.46)
d'Hondt and LR-Imperiali dummy	1.90**	0.63	0.33	−0.06	0.05
	0.34	0.26	0.16	−0.11	0.11
	(3.51)	(1.70)	(1.07)	(0.77)	(0.85)
Assembly size (log)	−2.02**	−0.12	0.03	0.02	0.05
	−0.34	−0.05	0.02	0.03	0.12
	(3.56)	(0.31)	(0.10)	(0.23)	(0.90)
Intercept	4.96	4.28	3.76	0.00	−0.19
R^2	0.64	0.10	0.12	0.21	0.34
Adjusted R^2	0.61	0.03	0.05	0.15	0.29

Notes:

[a] The estimated regression coefficients are listed first, followed by the standardized coefficients; absolute t-values are in parentheses.

* Statistically significant at the 5 per cent level (one-tailed test).

** Statistically significant at the 1 per cent level (one-tailed test).

the relative weight of the Euro-elections, which could never be merged with the parliamentary elections.[5]

The results of the replication of the regression analyses in the smaller sets of fifty-two electoral systems and forty-four PR systems (the 1951–6 French system was again excluded) are shown in Tables 5.12 and 5.13. Slight changes in the results of the analysis were to be expected, and they did, in fact, occur. In general, the relationships in the set of all electoral systems turned out somewhat stronger, and considerably stronger as far as the influence of assembly size on disproportionality is concerned: one unit increase in the logged assembly size now decreases disproportionality by as much as 2.36 per cent instead of 1.52 per cent—an 'improvement' of close to a full percentage point. On the other hand, the relationships in the consolidated set of PR cases were somewhat weaker; for instance, the coefficient of the regression of the effective number of elective parties on the effective threshold is no longer statistically significant. But it is worth noting that here, too, the influence of assembly size on disproportionality has become more sizable.

The overall pattern did not change. Of the five dependent variables, disproportionality remained the one best explained by the electoral system dimensions. The assembly size and, among the PR systems, the electoral formula did not significantly affect the party system variables. And, above all, the effective threshold remained the strongest explanatory variable.

6

Four Other Potential Explanations

As I indicated in Chapter 2, in addition to the three basic electoral system dimensions—effective threshold, electoral formula, and assembly size—four more electoral system variables may be hypothesized to affect disproportionality and the various party system characteristics: ballot structure, malapportionment, presidentialism, and *apparentement*. Their influence will be examined by the same methods that I used in Chapters 4 and 5: comparable cases, cross-tabulation, and regression analyses.

ORDINAL VERSUS CATEGORICAL BALLOT STRUCTURE

What Douglas W. Rae calls 'ballot structure' entails the question of whether the voter can only vote for candidates of one party (a categorical ballot) or divide his or her vote among more than one party (an ordinal ballot). Rae hypothesizes that ordinal ballots 'allow each voter's mandate to be dispersed among several parties, thereby producing a sort of micro-fractionalization', and that elections held with such ballots and hence with aggregated and repeated micro-fractionalizations 'produce more fractionalized elective party systems than would be found under other elections'.[1]

Although categorical ballots are the rule and ordinal ballots the exception among electoral systems, ordinal ballots are not all that rare: they have been used in eighteen of our seventy electoral systems. Several electoral formulas logically imply an ordinal ballot. The Australian alternative vote as well as STV in Ireland and Malta are ordinal in the strict sense of the term since they entail the rank-ordering of candidates by the voters. This allows (or, in the Australian case, requires) the voters to vote for candidates of more than one party, and it may well be a voter's lower, instead of his or her first, preference that will contribute to the election of a candidate of a particular party. The French two-ballot formula allows the voters to vote for different parties on the first and second ballots and usually—when candidates are eliminated or withdraw after the first ballot—requires at least some of the voters to do so. Similarly, the Japanese limited vote formula, by giving each voter two or three votes to be cast for two or three candidates of either the same or different parties, by definition allowed these votes to be split among different parties. The same is true in plurality two-member or three-member districts as in the 1952 and 1957 Indian elections.

When an ordinal ballot is not logically implied by the electoral formula and the district magnitude, it may be added as a special feature of the electoral system. The cases in point are Germany, Luxembourg, and Switzerland. Since 1953, the German two-tier system for parliamentary elections has provided for two separate votes to be cast by each voter: a first vote for a candidate at the lower tier (the single-member districts), and a second vote for a party list at the higher tier. Having two separate votes allows voters to vote for two different parties, although it should be emphasized that, since the second votes are the decisive votes for the distribution of the seats among the parties, any split votes are split very unequally. Luxembourg (both for its parliamentary and Euro-elections) and Switzerland use list PR systems with the special feature of *panachage*: they give each voter as many votes as there are seats in the district and allow him or her to distribute these votes over two or more parties, equally or preferentially.

Rae's test of his own proposition led him to the conclusion: 'my theory is absolutely wrong.'[2] This negative result was partly due to two errors of classification. He misclassified the French two-ballot and the post-1953 German systems as categorical; as shown above, they are clearly ordinal. More seriously, he failed to control for his other two independent variables—formula and district magnitude. It is easy to see that controlling for magnitude would have led to a different conclusion. In combination with single-member districts, ordinal ballots do produce a larger number of parties than categorical ballots. This finding is partly tautological because, with the minor exception of the 1952–7 Indian plurality system which was partly categorical and partly ordinal, the categorical-ballot systems coincide exactly with the plurality systems (Canada, New

Zealand, the United Kingdom, the United States, and India from 1962 on) and the ordinal-ballot systems are the 'other' majoritarian systems (the Australian alternative-vote and the French two-ballot system). But one could well argue that the theoretical explanation of the difference between the two types of majoritarian systems hinges on the distinction with regard to ballot structure: categorical ballots provide a strong incentive to vote strategically in order not to waste one's vote, whereas ordinal ballots remove most of the risk of wasting one's vote and hence encourage both sincere voting and multipartism.

In addition, there is at least some anecdotal evidence that ballot structure may stimulate multipartism in PR systems, too. In Germany, for instance, the small but crucially important Free Democratic Party has benefited substantially from its appeal to the voters to give it their second votes (which are the more important of the two votes at the voters' disposal); the Free Democrats have in fact, somewhat sarcastically, been called the 'party of second choice'.[3] It is virtually certain that, without the ordinal ballot, the party would not have fared so well and that multipartism in Germany would have been reduced.

Because Rae's proposition concerning ballot structure does have a good deal of plausibility and because his own test of it was deficient, it deserves to be submitted to a new and more rigorous test. Rae specifically links ballot structure with the number of elective parties but it may be logically extended to links with the other party system variables: if ordinal ballot structure increases the effective number of elective parties, it is likely to increase the number of parliamentary parties as well and to reduce the frequency of parliamentary and manufactured majorities. There is no plausible direct relationship between ballot structure and disproportionality, but, according to the logic that multipartism may result in greater disproportionality (see Chapter 3), the ordinal ballots may be hypothesized to raise indirectly the level of disproportionality.

As a first step, let us examine the available comparable cases; these are, as in Chapter 4, successive electoral systems in the same country that differ on only one dimension as well as the even more closely comparable cases of the last election under the old and the second election under the new system. Changes in ballot structure have taken place in four countries: France, Japan, India, and Germany. Unfortunately, the first two do not provide comparable cases. In France, the shifts back and forth between ordinal and categorical systems simultaneously entailed shifts from majoritarian to PR and from single-member (high effective threshold) to multi-member (medium effective threshold) districts. The change from the first (1946) to the second (1947–90) Japanese system entailed a change from ordinal to categorical ballots but also both a change in electoral formula from the limited vote to the single non-transferable vote and a drastic increase in effective threshold.

The two Indian systems do appear to offer comparable cases: a change from a mixed categorical–ordinal ballot structure to a completely categorical ballot structure, but no change in effective threshold (35 per cent), no change in electoral formula (plurality), and a less than 9 per cent increase in assembly size. As hypothesized, disproportionality decreased but, contrary to the hypothesis, the effective numbers of parties increased, and the frequency of parliamentary and manufactured majorities remained the same (100 per cent for all Indian elections). A comparison of the 1957 election (the last in the 1952–7 system) with the 1967 election (the second in the 1962–84 system) yields the same conclusions. However, since the expectation of decreased disproportionality hinges on decreased effective numbers of parties, and since these numbers of parties were found to increase rather than decrease, the positive finding concerning disproportionality must be taken with a grain of salt.

Moreover, it must be noted that the same change was already used in Chapter 4 as a shift between two comparable cases; there the argument was that, while there was no change in the arbitrarily assigned effective threshold of 35 per cent, the change from partly multi-member to strictly single-member districts did entail a reduction in district magnitude which, in a majoritarian system, can be expected to result in reduced disproportionality and an increase in effective numbers of parties. All three of these changes were found to occur, both from the first to the second electoral system and from the 1957 to the 1967 election (see Table 4.4). It is therefore more plausible to attribute the decrease in disproportionality to the direct effect of the lowering of the district magnitude than to the indirect effect of giving up ordinal ballots. In short, the Indian evidence concerning the hypothesized effects of ballot structure must be regarded as mainly negative.

The changes in ballot structure in Germany were shifts from categorical ballots in the first (1949) to ordinal ballots in the second (1953) electoral system and shifts in the other direction from the two subsequent electoral systems for parliamentary elections to the two Euro-election systems. The latter changes also entailed major reductions in assembly size and therefore do not offer good comparable cases. The change from 1949 to 1953, however, involved only a minor increase in assembly size—just above the 20 per cent criterion—and since assembly size has proved to have only modest explanatory power, the 1949 and 1953 electoral systems can be treated legitimately as comparable cases. The results are again negative: the effective numbers of elective and parliamentary parties and the degree of disproportionality went down instead of up—contrary to the hypothesis—and there was no change in parliamentary and manufactured majorities (zero in both elections).

In spite of these discouraging results, let us proceed to the cross-tabulation analysis. Table 6.1 shows the effects of ballot structure with the influence of the effective threshold—the strongest explanatory variable that we have found—controlled for. In order to have a sufficient number of cases on which to base the average numbers, percentages, and frequencies, the original five threshold levels used in Table 5.2 were reduced to three levels. The 1952–7 Indian system was omitted because it is mainly categorical but also partly ordinal.

For the high-threshold systems—which are also the systems with majoritarian formulas—the hypothesized differences between ordinal and categorical ballot structures emerge very clearly in all instances. As I have emphasized above, these differences coincide with the contrast between plurality and other majoritarian formulas. In fact, if I had included the mainly categorical 1952–7 Indian system among the categorical ballot structures, the differences between the two types of ballot structure would have become identical to the differences between the plurality and other majoritarian formulas shown in Table 5.1. The same pattern appears among the higher-threshold PR systems, but the pattern is reversed among the lower-threshold PR systems for three of the five dependent variables. The finding that the degree of disproportionality consistently behaves in accordance with the hypothesis is again suspect because the effective numbers of parties, which supposedly drive the degree of disproportionality, are not in accordance with

TABLE 6.1. The effects of ballot structure on disproportionality and party system variables at three levels of effective threshold in 68 electoral systems

Variable	Effective threshold					
	35%		8.0–18.8%		0.1–5.9%	
	Ordinal (5)	Categorical (6)	Ordinal (7)	Categorical (15)	Ordinal (5)	Categorical (30)
Disproportionality (%)	10.88	12.36	6.06	6.49	1.99	3.13
Effective number of elective parties	3.58	2.91	4.30	3.42	3.32	4.48
Effective number of parliamentary parties	2.77	2.08	3.51	2.86	3.07	4.00
Frequency of parliamentary majorities	0.52	0.92	0.26	0.46	0.20	0.06
Frequency of manufactured majorities	0.52	0.66	0.13	0.32	0.00	0.04

Note: The numbers of cases on which the average numbers and percentages are based are in parentheses.

the hypothesis. The only other positive result—in addition to the differences found among the majoritarian systems—is that categorical ballot structures manufacture majorities with consistently higher frequencies than ordinal ballot structures.

This last conclusion also emerges from the multiple regression analyses shown in Tables 6.2 and 6.3. I treated ballot structure as a dummy variable in which the seventeen ordinal-ballot systems were assigned a value of 1 and all others a value of 0; the problematic Indian system used in 1952 and 1957 was assigned a score of 0.35 on the ground that about 35 per cent of the members of parliament were elected in multi-member, and hence ordinal-ballot, districts. All of the other electoral system variables—the basic three dimensions that have been the focus of this study so far plus the three additional variables to be discussed at greater length in this chapter—were also entered as potential control variables.[4] However, in order to avoid overly complex tables with many statistically insignificant regression coefficients, I used the stepwise regression method so that only the significant variables ended up in the regression equations.

There is no significant bivariate link between ballot structure and disproportionality or any of the party system variables, but, with the influence of the effective threshold controlled for, ballot structure does turn out to be a significant explanatory variable for one of these variables: the frequency of manufactured majorities. And this influence appears both in the full set of sixty-nine electoral systems and in the set of fifty-seven PR systems. The coefficients are not highly significant in statistical terms (only at the 5 per cent level), but a change from categorical to ordinal ballots produces sizeable 14 and 15 per cent reductions in manufactured majorities in the two sets of systems. This is still not an extremely impressive result, but at least our search for an additional explanation has not come up completely empty-handed.

MALAPPORTIONMENT

Michael Gallagher has suggested that malapportionment may be an additional component of the electoral system that may influence electoral disproportionality: 'disproportionality can arise if some areas of a country are allocated more seats in relation to

TABLE 6.2. Stepwise regression analyses of the effect of five electoral system variables on disproportionality and party system variables in 69 electoral systems

Independent variables	Disproportionality	Effective number of elective parties	Effective number of parliamentary parties	Frequency of parliamentary majorities	Frequency of manufactured majorities
Effective threshold[a]	0.35** 0.90 (12.62)	-0.03** -0.30 (2.63)	-0.05** -0.54 (5.29)	0.02** 0.64 (7.00)	0.02** 0.70 (7.43)
Assembly size (log)	-2.32** -0.23 (3.26)	—	—	—	—
Apparentement	-2.34** -0.22 (3.08)	—	—	—	—
Presidentialism	-4.66** -0.21 (3.04)	-1.25* -0.22 (1.90)	—	0.32* 0.17 (1.87)	—
Ordinal ballots	—	—	—	—	-0.14* -0.17 (1.82)
Intercept	7.49	4.34	3.91	0.04	0.01
R^2	0.71	0.15	0.30	0.46	0.46
Adjusted R^2	0.70	0.13	0.28	0.44	0.44

Notes:
[a] The estimated regression coefficients are listed first, followed by the standardized coefficients; absolute t-values are in parentheses.
* Statistically significant at the 5 per cent level (one-tailed test).
** Statistically significant at the 1 per cent level (one-tailed test).

TABLE 6.3. Stepwise regression analyses of the effect of six electoral system variables on disproportionality and party system variables in 57 PR systems

Independent variables	Disproportionality	Effective number of elective parties	Effective number of parliamentary parties	Frequency of parliamentary majorities	Frequency of manufactured majorities
Effective threshold[a]	0.42** 0.68 (8.67)	−0.06* −0.27 (2.07)	−0.09** −0.42 (3.43)	0.03** 0.52 (4.63)	0.03** 0.54 (4.49)
d'Hondt and LR-Imperiali dummy	2.14** 0.35 (4.45)	—	—	—	—
Assembly size (log)	−2.08** −0.31 (3.83)	—	—	—	—
Apparentement	−1.53** −0.20 (2.48)	—	—	—	—

Presidentialism	—	—	—	0.33* 0.19 (1.68)	—
Ordinal ballots	—	—	—	—	−0.15* −0.24 (1.96)
Intercept	5.03	4.50	4.13	−0.03	−0.03
R^2	0.68	0.07	0.18	0.33	0.28
Adjusted R^2	0.66	0.06	0.16	0.30	0.25

Notes:

[a] The estimated regression coefficients are listed first, followed by the standardized coefficients; absolute t-values are in parentheses.

* Statistically significant at the 5 per cent level (one-tailed test).

** Statistically significant at the 1 per cent level (one-tailed test).

population than are others.'[5] Malapportionment is especially hard to avoid in majoritarian systems with single-member districts, because equal apportionment requires that relatively many small districts be drawn with exactly equal electorates or populations. It is hardly a problem in PR systems that use relatively large districts of varying magnitudes, because seats can be proportionally allocated to pre-existing geographical units like provinces or cantons. And malapportionment is entirely eliminated as a problem when elections are conducted at-large, as in The Netherlands, Israel, and many of the Euro-elections, or with a nation-wide upper tier, as in Germany and Denmark (as long as enough adjustment seats are available at the upper level).

Substantial disproportionality, measurable by the least-squares and other indices, should be expected only if malapportionment systematically favours particular areas of a country and/or particular parties. Gallagher states that, where it has been a significant factor, it has 'usually [involved] the deliberate over-representation of rural areas'.[6] Rural overrepresentation may also be the result of increasing urbanization combined with infrequent re-districting. Among our seventy electoral systems, there are nine cases of substantial rural overrepresentation: the United States (until the reapportionment revolution in the 1960s), the first and second Australian systems, the French two-ballot single-member district system (from 1958 to 1981), the Japanese SNTV system, the two Norwegian systems before 1989, Iceland from 1946 to 1959, and Spain (the system for parliamentary elections—not the Euro-elections, which are conducted at-large). In addition, there are three cases of deliberate regional overrepresentation: the overrepresentation of Scotland and Wales in British parliamentary and Euro-elections and the overrepresentation of French speakers in the Belgian Euro-elections.

Gallagher's hypothesis can be extended to the party system variables. The logic is that disproportionality generally favours the larger instead of the smaller parties, and that malapportionment as an additional source of disproportionality is therefore also more likely to help the larger parties—and hence reduce the effective numbers of parties and increase the chances of parliamentary and manufactured majorities. A clear example is Japan, where the Liberal Democratic Party has profited greatly from malapportionment in favour of the rural areas. On the other hand, the principal beneficiary of rural overrepresentation in Australia has been the National Party (formerly the Country Party), which is a relatively small party—but the faithful ally of the large Liberal Party.

Changes from malapportionment to more equally apportioned districts or vice versa took place in eight countries, but usually other important changes in the electoral system occurred at the same time. Nevertheless, there are three pairs of comparable cases. In the United States electoral system, we can compare the elections before the reapportionment revolution, from 1946 to 1962 (the year of the Supreme Court's *Baker* v. *Carr* decision), with the elections from 1972 to 1990; there were no changes in the plurality single-member district system, and the total membership of the House of Representatives also remained virtually unchanged. Contrary to the hypothesis, disproportionality did not decrease; instead, it increased rather substantially from 4.25 to 6.22 per cent. And the four party system variables hardly changed at all. The second pair of comparable cases are the 1949–83 and 1984–90 Australian electoral systems: malapportionment was reduced, while the alternative vote formula and single-member districting remained the same, and the assembly size increased by only 21 per cent. Here again, the evidence disconfirms the hypothesis; disproportionality increased from 8.55 to 10.24 per cent, and three of the four party system variables also changed in the 'wrong' direction.

The French parliamentary election systems used in 1958–81 and 1988 present very closely matched cases: malapportionment was reduced, but the majority-plurality formula and single-member districting did not change, and the assembly size increased by less than 20 per cent. The only reason why these two electoral systems have been treated as separate systems is that the 1986 PR system intervened between them. Disproportionality decreased as hypothesized from 14.15 to 11.84 per cent, but only two of the four party system variables changed in the expected direction. (Comparing closely matched elections, in addition to similar electoral systems, is not very fruitful for these three countries because our main interest is in changes in disproportionality, and disproportionality tends to vary a great deal from election to election in all single-member district systems.)

The evidence provided by the comparable cases is therefore mainly negative. The same applies to the exercise of cross-tabulating malapportionment with disproportionality and the party system variables while controlling for the impact of the effective threshold—similar to the cross-tabulations in Table 6.1. In fact, the results of this exercise are not worth reproducing because there is simply no interpretable pattern at all.

For the regression analysis, I operationalized malapportionment mainly as a dummy variable with the malapportioned systems being assigned a value of 1 and the others a value of 0. I made two adjustments, however: I gave the United States a score of 0.5 in order to reflect the elimination of malapportionment after 1970, and I assigned the same score to the British Euro-election system because its degree of overrepresentation of Scotland and Wales is only about half of that of the parliamentary election system.

The results are entirely negative. There are statistically significant bivariate correlations between malapportionment on the one hand and disproportionality, parliamentary majorities, and manufactured majorities on the other, but the influence of malapportionment disappears completely in the multiple regression equations. This is why malapportionment does not even feature in Tables 6.2 and 6.3. The main explanation is that malapportionment is correlated with the effective threshold: among the sixty-nine electoral systems, malapportionment occurs especially in the single-member district systems, and, among the fifty-seven PR systems, it has occurred especially in relatively low-magnitude—and hence high-threshold—systems such as Japan, Spain, and Norway. Consequently, when the influence of effective threshold is controlled for, malapportionment turns out not to be a factor of any significance for disproportionality or the party system variables. Additional explanations are that the effect of malapportionment may be neutralized by other factors (as the Labour Party's advantage in Scotland and Wales in counteracted by its disadvantage of having high concentrations of support in urban areas of England), and that malapportionment may benefit a small instead of a large party (as in the example of the Australian National Party mentioned above).

PRESIDENTIAL GOVERNMENT

In presidential systems of government, the presidency is the biggest political prize to be won, and only the largest parties have a realistic chance to win it. This advantage for the large parties is likely to carry over to legislative elections. It is therefore logical to expect that presidential systems, all other factors being equal, will have smaller effective numbers of parties than non-presidential systems of government. One generally accepted explanation of the American two-party system—which is a much more exclusive two-party system, with virtually no third parties at all, than the British, Canadian, and New Zealand two-party systems—is the impact of presidential elections. In Latin America, the same mechanism appears to operate even when legislative elections are conducted under PR. As Matthew S. Shugart and John M. Carey have pointed out, this is especially the case when the presidential election is decided by plurality rather than by majority (which may require a run-off election) and, more importantly, when the legislative election is held at the same time as the presidential election, as in Costa Rica.[7] Indirectly, by limiting the number of parties, presidentialism can also be hypothesized to reduce the degree of electoral disproportionality.

There are no comparable cases to take advantage of because the United States and Costa Rica were presidential systems without change or interruption in the 1945–90 period. However, a very clear picture emerges from Table 6.4. It compares the United States with the other single-member district systems, and it compares the 1953–8 and 1962–90 Costa Rican systems, which have effective thresholds of 10.6 and 8.5 per cent respectively, with the other PR systems that have effective thresholds in the 8.0 to 11.7 per cent range. Among systems with similar threshold levels, the presidential systems are indeed characterized by lower electoral disproportionality, lower effective numbers of parties, and, with one small exception, higher frequencies of parliamentary and manufactured majorities. The one exception is the very low level of manufactured majorities in the United States; the explanation is that the United States approaches the pure two-party model (with no third parties at all) in which, except in the unlikely event of a tie, parliamentary majorities are not only guaranteed but also extremely likely to be earned instead of manufactured majorities.

Because the non-presidential single-member district systems in Table 6.4 include the French and Australian ordinal-ballot systems, their differences with the United States with regard to the party system variables are exaggerated. Excluding France and Australia

TABLE 6.4. The effects of presidential government on disproportionality and party system variables at two levels of effective threshold in 25 electoral systems

Variable	Effective Threshold			
	35%		8.00–11.7%	
	United States (1)	Non-presidential (11)	Costa Rica (2)	Non-presidential (11)
Disproportionality (%)	5.41	13.08	3.98	6.06
Effective number of elective parties	2.03	3.41	2.80	4.21
Effective number of parliamentary parties	1.92	2.38	2.49	3.46
Frequency of parliamentary majorities	1.00	0.74	0.62	0.19
Frequency of manufactured majorities	0.09	0.68	0.25	0.17

Note: The numbers of cases on which the average numbers and percentages are based are in parentheses.

—that is, comparing the United States with the plurality systems only—yields somewhat smaller but still sizeable differences. In particular, the effective number of elective parties in the United States is 2.03 and in the other plurality systems 3.27—a difference of more than one party.

In the full set of sixty-nine electoral systems, there are significant bivariate correlations (at the 5 per cent level) between presidentialism on the one hand and the effective numbers of elective and parliamentary parties and parliamentary majorities on the other. As Table 6.2 shows, the impact of presidentialism on two of these variables remains significant when the influence of the effective threshold is controlled for. Moreover, there is no direct bivariate relationship between presidentialism and disproportionality, but when the effective threshold and two other explanatory variables are controlled for, presidentialism starts playing a highly significant role (at the 1 per cent level) in decreasing disproportionality. It reduces electoral disproportionality by 4.66 per cent and the effective number of elective parties by 1.25; it raises the frequency of parliamentary majorities by 32 per cent. Among the fifty-seven PR systems (where Costa Rica is now the only instance of presidential government), there is only one significant bivariate correlation (at the 5 per cent level): between presidentialism and parliamentary majorities. This relationship also survives, though barely, the imposition of the effective threshold as a control variable. Presidentialism increases the frequency of parliamentary majorities by 33 per cent.

While these positive findings are gratifying, it must be remembered that they are based on only three electoral systems in two countries. In order to strengthen our confidence in these conclusions about presidentialism, I tested whether other systems with directly elected presidents might have the same or similar consequences. My argument was that large parties may enjoy special advantages not only in fully presidential systems of government but also—although perhaps not to the same degree—wherever there are popularly elected presidents, even when these presidents are not as powerful as presidents in presidential systems, when they are not elected simultaneously with the legislature, and when they are not elected by plurality. In France, for instance, under a two-ballot system for both presidential and legislative elections, a multi-party system has been maintained but in a two-bloc or bipolar format and with considerably fewer parties than in the parliamentary Third Republic which used the same electoral system. Maurice Duverger asks 'why the same electoral system coincided with a dozen parties in the Third Republic but ended up with only four in the Fifth Republic'. His main explanation is 'the direct popular election of the president, which has transformed the political regime'.[8] Similarly, it may be hypothesized that pressures to reduce the numbers of parties operate in the other two semi-presidential systems—Portugal (until 1982) and Finland—as well as in the parliamentary systems of government that have directly elected, though not very powerful presidents—Austria, Iceland, Ireland, and Portugal (after 1982).

The above six countries, together with the United States and Costa Rica, account for a total of sixteen electoral systems. I again treated presidentialism—now meaning any system with a popularly elected president—as a dummy variable. Unfortunately, the results were completely negative without even a hint of an occasional weak relationship. Extending the range of the presidentialism hypothesis to systems that are not fully presidential clearly does not work well. The most likely explanation is that, as Shugart and Carey maintain, concurrent presidential-legislative elections and the election of the president by plurality are necessary conditions for presidentialism to have the hypothesized effect; it is probably also necessary that the directly elected president be a powerful political leader instead of merely a ceremonial head of state.

INTER-PARTY ELECTORAL LINKS

Apparentement is the French term for the formal linking of party lists that is allowed in some list PR systems. English translations that have been proposed include 'cartel'[9] and 'association',[10] but *apparentement* is the most commonly used term in English, too. The party lists that are thus linked appear separately on the ballot, and each voter normally votes for one list only (except in the case of *panachage*), but in the initial allocation of seats, all of the votes cast for the linked lists are counted as having been cast for one list. The next step is the proportional distribution of the seats won by the *apparentement* to the individual parties that belong to it.

Because even PR systems tend to favour the larger parties to some extent, the possibility of *apparentement* makes it possible for small parties to counteract to some extent the disadvantages of their small size. Enid Lakeman expresses this argument in the following words: 'The existence of many splinter parties [may result in] a distortion of representation if the votes for a certain opinion-group are split among several parties. This effect can be mitigated by *apparentement*'.[11] The major examples of list PR systems with *apparentement* are Switzerland, Israel, The Netherlands (both the parliamentary elections since 1977 and the Euro-elections), and the Danish Euro-elections, but it was also used in Sweden in 1948 and in Norway in 1945 and 1985.[12] (As discussed in Chapter 2, it was also an integral part of the mixed PR–majority system in France in 1951 and 1956, which is left out of consideration in the current chapter.)

Since *apparentement* helps the smaller parties, and since disproportionality tends to be especially at the expense of small parties, *apparentement* can be expected to reduce disproportionality. It can also be expected to have an effect on the party system: since it reduces the disadvantage of being a small party, it removes an important incentive for small parties to merge, and hence, all other factors being equal, it should increase the effective numbers of parties and decrease the incidence of parliamentary and manu- factured majorities.

It is important to realize that the formation of such inter-party electoral links is allowed not only as a special feature of some list PR systems, but also as a logical consequence of several other electoral systems. By definition, both the alternative vote and STV always permit parties to link up for maximum electoral gain by simply agreeing to ask their respective voters to cast first prefer- ences for their own candidates but the next preferences for the candidates of the linked party. In Australia and Ireland, but not in Malta, parties often take advantage of this opportunity. Simi- larly, the French two-ballot system implies the possibility for parties to link for the purpose of reciprocal withdrawal from the second ballot in different districts—an opportunity that has been used fre- quently by the parties of the left and the parties of the right.

Among the sixty-nine electoral systems, twenty have explicit or implied *apparentement* provisions. In order to examine their influ- ence, let us again first examine the available comparable cases: the elimination of *apparentement* between the 1945 and 1949 elections in Norway in what was in all other respects the same electoral system, its readoption by Norway in 1985, the last election in the 1953–85 system, and its adoption in the middle of the 1956–89 electoral system in the Netherlands (for the last five of the eleven elections in this system).

The shifts to and away from *apparentement* in Norway are not optimal for within-system comparisons, because there were no second elections after the switch was made; the 1949 and 1985 elections were the last elections in each system. However, a comparison of the two elections immediately before and after the shift reveals changes in disproportionality in the expected direction: an increase from 7.83 per cent in 1945 to 9.23 per cent in 1949, and a decrease from 4.93 per cent in 1981 to 4.74 per cent in 1985. In The Netherlands, the second-election test yields a disconfirm- ing result—an increase from 1.19 per cent in 1972 to 1.29 per cent in 1981—but the difference is small and the first percentage was already very low. But the changes in the effective numbers of parties in the two countries show mainly negative results; there were no changes with regard to parliamentary and manufactured majorities in any of the three pairs of comparable cases.

A similar picture emerges from the cross-tabulation analysis in Table 6.5. Within the three categories of effective thresholds, the *apparentement* systems have consistently less disproportionality than the systems without *apparentement*, although the difference is very small in the low-threshold systems. Five of the six differences with regard to the effective numbers of parties are in line with the hypothesis, but two of these differences are rather small. And only three of the six differences in the generation of parliamentary and manufactured majorities turn out as hypothesized. It should also be noted that, in the category of single-member district systems, the difference between systems with and without *apparentement* coincides with the difference between ordinal and categorical ballot structures. In fact, in the set of sixty-nine electoral systems, these two variables are strongly correlated (the correlation coefficient is 0.51), and they should therefore not be allowed to enter into the same regression equation; this is not a problem in Table 6.2, because the stepwise regression procedure never selected both variables at the same time.

For the purpose of the multiple regression analyses, I again treated the independent variable mainly as a dummy variable (with a value of 1 for the *apparentement* systems and 0 for the others), but the three systems already singled out for the comparable-cases analysis required special treatment because they used *apparentement* for some but not all of the elections; accordingly, the 1956–89 Dutch system was assigned a score of 0.45, the 1945–9 Norwegian system a score of 0.50, and the 1953–85 Norwegian system a score of 0.11.[13] Tables 6.2 and 6.3 further confirm the conclusion that *apparentement* is not a significant predictor of party system characteristics, but that it does explain variations in disproportionality very well. These relationships appear only when the other variables are controlled for; there are no significant bivariate correlations between *apparentement* and any of the dependent variables. In both tables, the regression coefficients are highly significant (at the 1 per cent level), and *apparentement* lowers the level of disproportionality by 2.34 and 1.53 per cent respectively.

TABLE 6.5. The effects of *apparentement* on disproportionality and party system variables at three levels of effective threshold in 69 electoral systems

Variable	Effective Threshold							
	35%		8.0–18.8%		0.1–5.9%			
	Apparentement (5)	No *Apparentement* (7)	*Apparentement* (7)	No *Apparentement* (15)	*Apparentement* (7)	No *Apparentement* (28)		
Disproportionality (%)	10.88	13.56	5.18	6.90	2.83	3.00		
Effective number of elective parties	3.58	3.09	3.67	3.71	4.63	4.23		
Effective number of parliamentary parties	2.77	2.04	3.18	3.01	4.08	3.81		
Frequency of parliamentary majorities	0.52	0.93	0.40	0.40	0.14	0.07		
Frequency of manufactured majorities	0.52	0.71	0.28	0.26	0.00	0.04		

Note: The numbers of cases on which the average numbers and percentages are based are in parentheses.

Apparentement therefore joins ballot structure and presidentialism as important influences on disproportionality and/or the party system that have been discovered in this chapter. It is especially gratifying that these three additional elements of the electoral system were found to affect not just disproportionality but also aspects of the party system. Tables 6.2 and 6.3 can serve as grand summaries of my findings, although they are too conservative in one respect: the comparable-cases analysis in Chapter 4 has shown clearly that the electoral formula and assembly size strongly influence the effective number of parliamentary (but not elective) parties. Although the two tables do not reflect this finding, it must be regarded as a firm conclusion. What the tables do point up very accurately is that (1) of all of the dependent variables, disproportionality can be explained best by the various dimensions of the electoral system, and that (2) of all of the explanatory variables, the effective threshold is by far the best explainer. This was already the main conclusion of Chapter 5. The findings of this chapter add several refinements, but they do not change the overall thrust of the earlier conclusion.

7

Electoral Engineering:
Limits and Possibilities

WHAT is the practical significance of the analysis presented in this volume for electoral engineers? In a frequently cited statement, Giovanni Sartori characterizes the electoral system as 'the most specific manipulative instrument of politics'.[1] But while election rules are undoubtedly more manipulable than other components of the political system, two questions remain: how effective can the manipulation of the electoral system be, and to what extent are politicians able and willing to manipulate the electoral system? In this concluding chapter, I shall discuss these questions with regard to the two major consequences of electoral systems —their effects on electoral disproportionality and on the party system—discussed in this book. I shall also discuss several other lessons that electoral systems may be able to learn from each other: five examples of especially successful devices used in some countries that others may well want to imitate.

FINE-TUNING THE DEGREE OF PROPORTIONALITY

One major message of this book is that the degree of electoral disproportionality or proportionality responds very sensitively to the rules of the electoral system. The evidence of the comparable-cases analyses (Tables 4.1 to 4.5), the three-way cross-tabulation (Table 5.4), and the regression analyses (Tables 5.9 to 5.11) consistently demonstrate that the effective threshold is the strongest instrument for influencing proportionality but that the electoral formula and assembly size are also strong and useful instruments. In addition, as shown in the previous chapter, explicit or implied *apparentement* provisions and having a presidential form of government offer further instruments for improving the proportionality of the election outcome (see Tables 6.2 and 6.3)—although it would be absurd, of course, to recommend presidentialism just for the sake of attaining a bit more electoral proportionality.

These five dimensions of the electoral system do not explain the degree of proportionality perfectly; the fact that they succeed in explaining about two-thirds of the variance means that about a third remains unexplained. But given the roughness of the operational definition of the crucial variable of effective threshold—based on a series of drastic simplifying assumptions, as explained in Chapter 2—and given the many political factors outside of the electoral system that affect the degree of proportionality—such as the political cleavages in a society, the relative sizes of the major social groups, and the regional distribution of the vote—it is amazing that as much as two-thirds of the variance in disproportionality is explained by the electoral system alone. It is not an exaggeration to conclude that, if electoral engineers want to increase or decrease that degree of proportionality, the four instruments of the electoral system offer them the opportunity to fine tune the electoral system for the purpose of the particular outcome that they aim for.

This is an important practical conclusion because there is wellnigh universal agreement that electoral proportionality is a major goal of electoral systems and a major criterion by which they should be judged. For many PR supporters, proportionality is a goal in and of itself—virtually synonymous with electoral justice—but it is also regarded as an important means for minority representation. Majoritarian systems can also make provisions for minority representation, of course—such as the special Maori districts in New Zealand, reserved seats for the scheduled castes and tribes in India, and affirmative gerrymandering in the United States—but PR has the great additional advantage of enabling any minority, not just those specifically favoured by the electoral law, to be represented (as long as they attain a stipulated minimum level of electoral support). Compared with majoritarian systems, PR can be said to have the advantage of permitting representation by minorities that define themselves as groups wishing to have representation as minority parties. PR thus avoids any invidious choices in favour of certain minority groups and, as a consequence, against other minorities.[2]

The importance of proportionality as a normative principle is also shown by the trends in the electoral laws discussed at the end of Chapter 2. The overall direction of the changes in election rules was towards more proportional rules. However, since the plurality countries did not change at all and since France is the only country that shifted back and forth between majoritarian and PR systems, this trend towards greater proportionality was a trend among countries that were already committed to PR.

For the supporters of majoritarian election systems, proportionality is obviously not the major goal but at least a secondary goal. It is probably more accurate, however, to say that this secondary aim is not so much a relatively high degree of proportionality as the avoidance of too much disproportionality. The fact that the non-proportional systems have eliminated multi-member districts (see Chapter 2) and have reduced the problem of malapportionment (see Chapter 6) demonstrates this concern. But regardless of the degree to which electoral reformers want to achieve electoral proportionality or the degree to which they are willing to tolerate disproportionality, the basic dimensions of the electoral system give them effective instruments to reach their goals.

SHAPING PARTY SYSTEMS AND MAJORITY VICTORIES

The links between the electoral system and the four characteristics of party systems emphasized in this study are much weaker than those between the electoral system and the degree of disproportionality. This also means that for electoral engineers the electoral system is not as strong an instrument for shaping the party system. The influence of the electoral system on the effective number of elective parties is especially weak. The comparable-cases evidence indicated that there was no systematic relationship between the two at all, and the cross-tabulations and the regression analyses showed no more than a tenuous relationship; in the two regression analyses shown in Tables 5.9 and 5.11, the electoral system dimensions explained only 8 and 9 per cent of the variance in elective multipartism.

At the same time, it would be quite wrong to belittle the

importance of the influence of the electoral system on the party system and its practical utility to electoral engineers. First of all, although it is true that there are no major differences with regard to the effective number of elective parties among most PR systems and the non-plurality majoritarian systems, the effect of strategic behaviour (or the psychological factors) does substantially reduce elective multipartism in plurality systems.

Second, for the operation of the political system the effective number of parties in parliament is much more important than the number of elective parties. And here the link with the electoral system is much stronger. In the set of sixty-nine electoral systems, for instance, the electoral system variables explain as much as 28 per cent of the variance in parliamentary multipartism (Tables 5.9 and 6.2). And in the comparable-cases analysis, changes in all three of the principal electoral system dimensions yielded the expected increases or decreases in the effective number of parliamentary parties with only few exceptions (Chapter 4). The effective threshold turned out to be especially influential—an important fact for electoral engineers to note. However, the comparable-cases analysis also showed the formula and assembly size to be strong factors. This finding was not supported by the cross-tabulation and regression analyses but, in the face of these contradictory pieces of evidence, the comparable-cases evidence should be given greater weight because it is based on a more firmly controlled research design in which more of the *cetera* are held *paria*.

Third, even more important is the frequency of parliamentary and manufactured majorities. And these are the party system features that the electoral system explains best: as much as 44 per cent of their variance is explained in the set of sixty-nine electoral systems (Table 6.2). Here again, considering the roughness of how I had to define and measure the crucially important variable of effective threshold and considering the many socio-political forces mentioned earlier that also affect the emergence of majorities, the fact that the electoral system explains more than two-fifths of the variance must be considered impressive. Moreover, one variable—the effective threshold—does most of the explaining by itself.

Fourth, while the impact of the effective threshold is a matter of degree—generally speaking, as Table 5.2 shows, the higher the threshold the higher the frequency of parliamentary majorities

—Table 5.1 shows that the difference between plurality and all other systems is especially important: the different thresholds in non-plurality systems make parliamentary majorities more or less likely, but the average 93.2 per cent incidence of parliamentary majorities in plurality systems means that these majorities are virtually guaranteed by plurality. As noted above, plurality systems also stand out as the system in which strategic behaviour operates to reduce drastically the effective number of elective parties—to an average of slightly more than three parties (see Table 5.1). This number is further reduced to just above two by the mechanical effect of the plurality formula. And the mechanical effect of plurality is also very important in creating the usual parliamentary majorities, since more than two-thirds of these majorities in parliament are artificially manufactured by plurality.

Clearly, the effective threshold is a strong instrument for electoral engineers, but the plurality formula (with its inherently very high effective threshold) is the strongest instrument. It is rather ironic that the strongest instrument that is potentially available to electoral engineers—switching from PR to plurality or the other way around—is rarely used and, in our set of twenty-seven countries in the 1945–90 period, was never used.

It may be argued that the non-plurality majoritarian systems are quite similar to plurality systems except that they tend to create two blocs (strong coalitions) of parties instead of a two-party system, and parliamentary majorities for one of the blocs rather than for one party. This seems to be especially true for Australia where the pattern of party competition and the alternation in government is between one such bloc (the close alliance of the Liberal and National Parties) and one large party (the Labour Party). In France, competition between the two large blocs of the left and the right has become the normal pattern under the usual majority-plurality system of the Fifth Republic. Another interpretation of the French system is that it can operate like the American system of plurality elections preceded by direct primary elections: the first ballot is seen as the functional equivalent of the primary. On the other hand, as pointed out in the previous chapter, the development of the French two-bloc system was also influenced by the institution of a strong presidency and direct presidential elections; in the Third Republic, under a similar electoral system, no two-bloc competition developed.

This is not the place to discuss the further consequences of different party systems at length. Suffice it to say that the conventional assumption that two-party systems make for more effective and stable democracy than multi-party systems is not valid. As I have shown elsewhere, for instance, majoritarian parliamentary systems do not have a better record with regard to either macroeconomic management (the stimulation of economic growth and the control of inflation and unemployment) or the maintenance of public order and peace than multi-party parliamentary systems.[3]

What two-party systems do excel in, as G. Bingham Powell has demonstrated, is clear government accountability: the voters know that the governing party is responsible for past government performance, and they can decisively return this party to power or replace it with the other major party.[4] But greater accountability does not directly translate into greater responsiveness to citizen interests. There is no evidence that coalition cabinets in multiparty systems are less responsive than one-party majority cabinets; on the contrary, coalition cabinets are usually closer to the centre of the political spectrum—and hence closer in their policy outlook to the average citizen—than one-party cabinets representing either the left or the right.[5] But it is entirely legitimate, of course, to regard government accountability as a value in and of itself—just as proportionality is an ultimate value for many PR supporters.

In the final analysis, therefore, the choice between PR (especially one of the more proportional forms of PR) and multipartism on the one hand and plurality and two-party systems on the other depends on personal normative preferences; does one value minority representation and the principle of proportionality more highly than the two-party principle and government accountability, or the other way around? This is not merely a matter of personal taste but also, and probably more so, of cultural background; plurality is used exclusively in countries with a British political heritage, and it is used in most of these countries—in our set of twenty-seven countries, Ireland and Malta are the only exceptions. (Ireland and Malta are the two principal users of STV, which points to an even broader pattern of the crucial importance of political culture for the choice of electoral systems; STV is used exclusively in countries with British political traditions, in contrast with list PR which is used exclusively in countries without such traditions.)

FIVE EXEMPLARY DEVICES FOR ELECTORAL REFORM

The empirical links between the electoral system dimensions on the one hand and disproportionality and multipartism on the other constitute the most important practical information for electoral engineers. In addition, however, there are a number of specific devices used in some of our electoral systems that appear to work particularly well and that deserve to be recommended as models for electoral engineers elsewhere. I shall make three major and two minor recommendations. The major recommendations are the establishment of two-tier districting for PR systems, two-tier districting of a different type for plurality and majority systems, and national legal thresholds. The two less important bits of advice concern vote transferability and *apparentement*.

1. *Two-tier districting in PR systems*

As discussed in Chapter 2, several PR countries have used two-tier districting during the entire 1945–90 period (Austria, Belgium, Denmark, Germany, Iceland, Italy), but there were quite a few more who adopted it towards the end of the period (Greece, Malta, Norway, Sweden), and none that abolished it.[6] Two-tier districting is a particularly attractive way of combining the advantage of close representative–voter contact in low-magnitude districts with the greater proportionality of high-magnitude districts.

To get the full advantage of two-tier arrangements, the upper-level district should be an at-large national district and the lower-tier districts should be either single-member districts or low-magnitude multi-member districts. Most of the two-tier districting systems have in fact used a single national district at the higher level; the exceptions are Austria, Belgium, and Greece. But the lower-tier districts are often still surprisingly large, especially in the different Italian electoral systems, including the Euro-election system, and in Austria since 1971, where the average magnitudes have ranged from 16.20 to 20.33 seats. Only Germany has consistently used single-member districts at the lower level. Because STV asks the voters to rank order the candidates, high-magnitude districts are impractical—which necessarily puts severe restrictions on the proportionality of the overall election result.

Hence the establishment of a national upper-tier district could be of special benefit to the Irish and Maltese STV systems.[7] Malta has in fact already established such a national district but, as we have seen, only on a contingency basis and only to convert a popular majority into a parliamentary majority.[8]

National at-large districts at the upper level—especially in adjustment-seats rather than remainder-transfer systems and assuming that enough adjustment seats are available—have the added advantage that they entirely eliminate any problems of malapportionment and gerrymandering. Malapportionment has been a special problem in plurality and other single-member district systems, but it can and has occurred in PR systems, too. Malapportionment is logically precluded in electoral systems with a national upper tier of the kind described above—and, of course, also in one-tier systems with only one nation-wide district (such as in Israel, the Netherlands, and most of the Euro-election systems). Gerrymandering is a particularly strong temptation in single-member districts, but it rapidly becomes more difficult with increasing district magnitude; it is safe to say that it is impractical in districts with more than five or six seats. A nation-wide upper-tier district (or again a nation-wide district in a single-tier system) entirely eliminates the temptation and the problem of gerrymandering.

Two-tier districting does have the disadvantage that it makes the electoral system more complex—but two-tier systems need not be extremely complex. The German, Danish, and Swedish examples show that all that is needed is a simple national translation of votes into seats, and the allocation of the adjustment seats to parties in such a way that nation-wide proportionality (except for legal thresholds) is achieved.

2. *Two-tier districting for plurality systems*

Two-tier districting has been used only by PR systems and is usually only discussed as a possible reform for PR systems. However, it is an equally attractive possibility for plurality systems. As emphasized earlier, the plurality rule has a very strong tendency to produce parliamentary majorities—but such majorities are not produced with absolute certainty, and it can also happen that the second largest party wins a majority of the seats (as in Britain in

1951 and in New Zealand in 1978 and 1981). A perfect solution for these problems is to institute a national upper-tier district with sufficient adjustment seats to translate a plurality of the vote into a parliamentary majority of, say, a minimum of 55 per cent of the seats.[9] The remaining seats could then be allocated proportionally to the other parties. If not just a parliamentary majority for one party, but also a strong opposition, is desired, three alternative rules could be introduced: the largest party could be limited to 55 per cent of the seats (even if it has won more than 55 per cent of the votes) and/or the second party could be given a minimum of, say, 35 per cent of the seats with the remaining 10 per cent going to the smaller parties, or the second party could be given all of the remaining 45 per cent of the seats.

In the French and Australian majoritarian systems, similar rules could be introduced to guarantee that either an inter-party alliance or an unallied party, which would get, respectively, the largest number of votes nation-wide or the largest number of first preferences, would receive a minimum of again 55 per cent of the seats in parliament. There are obviously very many other ways to write the specific rules for two-tier districting and adjustment seats in plurality and other majoritarian systems. My main point is not to make a detailed recommendation but to point out to plurality advocates (and proponents of other majoritarian systems) that, if they regard the creation of a parliamentary majority and a clear two-party (or two-bloc) configuration in parliament as the principal objective of their favourite electoral system, two-tier districting can guarantee this result—which is merely probable but not certain without two-tier districting.

Another advantage, similar to that in PR systems but of much greater importance for majoritarian systems, is that two-tier districting with a single nation-wide upper district would eliminate the problems of malapportionment and gerrymandering. Moreover, it would solve another great problem from which political parties in majoritarian systems suffer: their tendency not to make serious efforts to win in areas where they are weak, since spending a great deal of time, energy, and money in districts where they have little chance of winning tends to be regarded as a waste of scarce resources. Counting the votes nation-wide and translating national vote totals into national seat totals—not proportionally but according to majoritarian rules—obviously introduces a strong incentive to try to gain as many votes as possible everywhere, including in districts that are safe for other parties.

3. *National legal thresholds stated in terms of a percentage of the total national vote*

The two basic methods of erecting barriers against the representation of small parties are high district magnitudes and legal thresholds, but there is a great variety of these legal thresholds: at the national, regional, and local levels; stated in terms of a minimum number of votes or a minimum percentage of the vote; predicated (in two-tier systems) on winning at least a seat or a particular quota or part of a quota in a lower-level district; and so on and so forth. For the analysis of this book, I converted all of these magnitudes and thresholds into effective thresholds with functionally equivalent consequences for disproportionality and multipartism.

This does not mean, however, that all these effective thresholds are equally desirable from the point of view of electoral reform. All legal thresholds as well as the thresholds implied by district magnitudes except national legal thresholds stated in terms of a percentage of the total national vote are arbitrary and haphazard because they will bar parties not just on the basis of their lack of a minimum of popular support but also on the basis of how their support and the support of other parties are distributed. Their general bias favours small parties with regionally concentrated support. The only way to avoid this problem is to measure party support nationally and to do so in terms of a particular percentage of the vote, such as 1 per cent in Israel, 2 per cent in Denmark, 4 per cent in Norway, Sweden, and the Dutch Euro-elections, and 5 per cent in the German parliamentary and Euro-elections and in the French Euro-elections.[10] Another advantage of these legal thresholds is their simplicity compared with legal thresholds that are formulated in various other ways. (Legal thresholds based on a particular minimum number rather than a minimum percentage of votes are arbitrary in a different way: they are affected by overall voter turn-out.)

Such minimum national percentages can only be used in one-tier systems that use a single national district, or in two-tier districting systems. Since one-tier national districts tend to be very large, the desirability of using minimum national percentages as thresholds adds another argument in favour of two-tier districting systems.

One disadvantage is that the transition from no representation to full representation may be considered too sudden and sharp. In Germany between 1957 and 1987, for instance, a party with just below 5 per cent of the national votes would not get any seats, whereas a party with exactly 5 per cent or a bit more would be awarded about 25 seats; in principle, one extra vote could spell the winning of 25 seats! In most other types of systems, the threshold is a range from a lower threshold where a party may receive some representation, but is still severely underrepresented, to an upper threshold where full representation is achieved. However, if such a sliding scale is regarded as desirable, the same can be done—much less haphazardly—with national percentages. For instance, a minimum of 1 per cent national support could be considered sufficient for token representation, a minimum of 3 per cent for representation at half-proportionality, and a minimum of 5 per cent for fully proportional representation.

4. *Transferability of votes*

STV achieves as much proportionality as it does (in spite of its relatively small district magnitude) because neither surplus votes of successful candidates nor the votes of unsuccessful candidates are completely wasted. In other words, the proportionality of STV depends on the transferability of votes from both successful and defeated candidates to candidates that are still in the running. It is the non-transferability of votes in SNTV that makes it into a semi-PR instead of a regular PR system. In practice, Japanese SNTV has operated much like STV and in districts with similar magnitudes. But an obvious improvement in the system is to make the votes transferable, that is, to change from SNTV to STV. One objection would be that, as pointed out in Chapter 2, SNTV's lack of proportionality hurts the larger instead of the smaller parties. But if the object is to help the smaller parties, it would make more sense to apply STV in larger districts—or, even better, with a national upper-tier district and adjustment seats—than to retain SNTV.

A similar reform is worth considering in the Finnish list PR system, in which the voters vote for one candidate of one party and where the election of individual candidates depends on how many votes they have individually received; for instance, if a party is entitled to three seats, the three candidates with the highest individual vote totals are elected. This means that *within the party* an SNTV system is used. Here, too, using within-list STV instead of within-list SNTV would yield more accurate and less haphazard results.[11]

5. *Apparentement*

Finally, another minor recommendation concerns an advantage that is sometimes, mistakenly, attributed exclusively to STV in contrast with list PR systems: its encouragement of alliances among parties. For instance, Donald L. Horowitz observes correctly that STV encourages agreements among parties to engage in 'vote pooling' by reciprocally asking their voters to cast their highest preferences for candidates of their own party but their next preferences for the candidates of the other party. Such agreements may well develop into durable alliances. Horowitz is wrong, however, when he argues that 'STV permits a measure of . . . vote pooling that list-system PR completely precludes'.[12] As I pointed out at the end of the previous chapter, the possibility of *apparentement* may be added to any form of list PR, and it gives the linked parties the same advantage of vote pooling and hence the same incentive to form inter-party alliances. Since STV has some distinct disadvantages—such as its small district magnitude (unless alleviated by an upper-tier district) and the negative effects of intra-party competition between candidates on party cohesion—list PR with the possibility of *apparentement* may be a more attractive way of encouraging inter-party alliances than STV.

ELECTORAL ENGINEERING AND ELECTORAL SYSTEM STABILITY

In this chapter, my focus has been on the possibilities of electoral engineering and even the desirability of particular models of electoral reform. However, I have also emphasized various constraints on electoral engineering, such as the crucially important fact that electoral system features explain far from everything about party systems and the cultural obstacles to major changes in election rules. With regard to the latter point, the September 1992 referendum in New Zealand provided an important initial test of the thesis that democracies with a British political heritage are firmly tied to plurality or STV. The New Zealand voters could vote for or against the retention of plurality, and, in the case of a negative decision on plurality, they were presented with further options that included both STV and a German-style list PR. Nearly 85 per cent rejected plurality, and about 70 per cent chose list PR as their favourite alternative. However, this was a decision on broad principles only, and the definitive test will be a second referendum in late 1993 when the voters will be faced with a dichotomous choice between the plurality single-member district system and a specific list PR proposal patterned after the German model.

The Irish voters twice, in 1959 and 1968, rejected proposals to shift from STV to the plurality system—but these were the only two options, and a change to list PR was not considered. Such cultural factors tend to be reinforced by vested partisan interests and sheer institutional conservatism. The fact that most of the new Euro-election systems are so similar to the EC members' parliamentary election systems (apart from the smaller numbers of representatives to be elected) provides evidence of the strong limits to change even within the PR and plurality families.

In addition, there should be—and, quite clearly, there are—moral constraints on electoral change. Healthy partisan competition requires that the electoral system—the basic rules of the democratic election game—be broadly supported and not be changed too frequently. In particular, they should not be changed for narrow partisan purposes. In this respect, France and Greece—the countries that, among our twenty-seven democracies, have been the most frequent and drastic 'reformers'—are not normative models that other democracies ought to emulate. Note that all my specific proposals for electoral reform are minor and modest; they are all suggestions for incremental improvements, not revolutionary upheaval, of existing systems.

The situation is different, however, for democratizing and newly democratic countries. When a first electoral system has to be chosen which will hopefully guide the new democracy's elections for a long time (or, in the case of a redemocratizing country, a new system that will hopefully work better than the old one), it is important to examine all of the options as well as their advantages and disadvantages. This examination should include a careful look at the great variety of electoral rules and experiences of the world's stable and consolidated democracies. Therefore, to the extent that this study of seventy electoral systems in twenty-seven democracies will have some practical utility, it may have more to offer to electoral engineers in the new democracies than in these twenty-seven old democracies.

Appendix A

Proportional Representation Formulas

PR formulas can best be explained by classifying and subclassifying them: the first classification distinguishes between list PR, in which voters cast their votes for party lists of candidates, and the single transferable vote (STV), in which voters vote for individual candidates. List PR can then be classified into highest averages (divisor) and largest remainders (quota) systems.[1] And these can be classified further according to the particular divisor or quota that they employ. I shall use a few simple examples to illustrate their operation.

Table A.1 shows the only two highest averages methods that are in actual use for the allocation of seats to parties: d'Hondt and modified Sainte-Laguë. Seats are awarded sequentially to parties having the highest 'average' numbers of votes per seat until all seats are allocated; each time a party receives a seat, its 'average' goes down. These 'averages' are not averages as normally defined but depend on the given set of divisors that a particular divisor system prescribes. The d'Hondt formula uses the integers 1, 2, 3, 4, and so on. As Table A.1 shows, the first seat (indicated by the number in parenthesis) goes to the largest party, party A, whose votes are then divided by 2. The second seat is given to party B, because its 'average' (29,000 votes, its original vote total) is higher than C's and D's and also higher than A's votes divided by 2. The third seat goes to A because its vote divided by 2 is higher than B's vote divided by 2 and higher than C's and D's votes; and so on.[2] The final seat allocation to parties A, B, C, and D is 3, 2, 1, and 0 seats.

The Sainte-Laguë formula, in the original form proposed by its inventor, uses the odd-integer divisor series 1, 3, 5, 7, and so forth. In practice, it is used only in a modified form which uses 1.4 instead of 1 as the first divisor. Its sequential procedure for allocating seats to parties is identical to that of the d'Hondt method. In the example of Table A.1, the first five seats are awarded to the parties in exactly the same order as in the d'Hondt method, but the sixth seat is won by party D instead of A; the final distribution of seats therefore becomes 2, 2, 1, 1.

The three most common largest remainders (LR) formulas, using the Hare, Droop, and Imperiali quotas, are shown in Table A.2. In all quota

TABLE A.1. Illustrative examples of the operation of two highest averages formulas in a six-member district with four parties

Seats allocated using D'Hondt divisors of 1, 2, 3, 4, etc.

Party	Votes				Total seats
	(v)	v/1	v/2	v/3	
A	41,000	41,000 (1)	20,500 (3)	13,667 (6)	3
B	29,000	29,000 (2)	14,500 (5)	9,667	2
C	17,000	17,000 (4)	8,500		1
D	13,000	13,000			0
TOTAL	100,000				

Seats allocated using modified Sainte-Laguë divisors of 1.4, 3, 5, 7, etc.

Party	Votes				Total seats
	(v)	v/1.4	v/3	v/5	
A	41,000	29,286 (1)	13,667 (3)	8,200	2
B	29,000	20,714 (2)	9,667 (5)	5,800	2
C	17,000	12,143 (4)	5,667		1
D	13,000	9,286 (6)			1
TOTAL	100,000				

Note: The order in which seats are awarded sequentially to parties is indicated by the numbers in parentheses.

systems, the first step is to calculate a quota of votes that entitles parties to a seat; a party gets as many seats as it has quotas of votes; any unallocated seats are then given to those parties having the largest numbers of unused votes (remainders). The Hare quota is the oldest and simplest of the quotas: it is simply the total number of valid votes divided by the number of seats at stake in a district. The Droop quota divides the total number of votes by the number of seats plus 1, and the Imperiali quota by the number of seats plus 2.

The quickest method for calculating the results is to divide each party's votes by the quota, which yields the number of quotas each party has won.[3] Parties then receive one seat for each full quota; any seats that cannot be allocated in this way are given to the parties with the largest fraction of a quota. In the first example of Table A.2, based on the use

TABLE A.2. Illustrative examples of the operation of three largest remainders formulas in an eight-member district with four parties

Hare quota = 100,000 [votes]/8 [seats] = 12,500

Party	Votes	Hare quotas	Full quota seats	Remaining seats	Total seats
A	41,000	3.28	3	0	3
B	29,000	2.32	2	0	2
C	17,000	1.36	1	1	2
D	13,000	1.04	1	0	1
TOTAL	100,000	8.00	7	1	8

Droop quota = 100,000/(8 + 1) = 11,111

Party	Votes	Droop quotas	Full quota seats	Remaining seats	Total seats
A	41,000	3.69	3	1	4
B	29,000	2.61	2	0	2
C	17,000	1.53	1	0	1
D	13,000	1.17	1	0	1
TOTAL	100,000	9.00	7	1	8

Imperiali quota = 100,000/(8 + 2) = 10,000

Party	Votes	Imperiali quotas	Full quota seats	Remaining seats	Total seats
A	41,000	4.10	4	0	4
B	29,000	2.90	2	0	2
C	17,000	1.70	1	0	1
D	13,000	1.30	1	0	1
TOTAL	100,000	10.00	8	0	8

of the Hare quota, parties *A*, *B*, *C*, and *D* have 3, 2, 1, and 1 full Hare quotas respectively and are therefore given 3, 2, 1, and 1 seats—a total of 7 seats—in the initial allocation. Since 8 seats are available, one more seat has to be allocated: it goes to the party with the largest remainder of votes, that is, the largest remaining fraction of a quota. This is party *C* with a remaining 0.36 of a Hare quota; and the final distribution of seats becomes 3, 2, 2, 1. Apart from the use of different (lower) quotas, the procedure for allocating seats to parties with the Droop and Imperiali methods is exactly the same. The LR-Imperiali formula has been used exclusively in Italy, and Italy has also used (in the 1948 and 1953 elections) an even lower quota, also—rather confusingly—referred to as the Imperiali quota: the number of votes divided by the number of seats plus 3. I shall refer to the latter as the reinforced LR-Imperiali quota (and to the corresponding formula as reinforced LR-Imperiali). Both of the Imperiali quotas run the risk of allocating more seats than are actually available; this would happen, for instance, with the reinforced Imperiali quota in the example of Table A.2. The Italian rule for such cases is that the results be recalculated with the use of the next higher quota.

The examples of Tables A.1 and A.2 were selected not just to illustrate the different procedures but also to show that the choice of PR formula can affect the allocation of seats. Such differences do not always appear; in a seven-member district, for instance, the four parties would be awarded exactly the same 3, 2, 1, and 1 seats, respectively, by all five methods. Where differences do appear, however, they are not random but systematically affect the degree of proportionality and the electoral opportunities for small parties. These differences occur within the two groups of quota and divisor systems rather than between them. Among the quota systems, proportionality decreases as the quota decreases; this is illustrated in Table A.2 where the use of the Droop quota instead of the Hare quota causes the small party *C* to lose a seat and the largest party *A* to win an extra seat. This is somewhat counter-intuitive because one would expect smaller parties to benefit from a lower quota. How can this result be explained?

The explanation is that lowering the quota will increase the remainders for the larger parties at a faster pace than for the smaller parties (illustrated in Table A.2 for the shift from the Hare to the Droop quota) and/ or that the number of remaining seats is reduced, which means that fewer of the remaining votes qualify for a seat in the final allocation (illustrated for the shift from the Droop to the Imperiali quota in Table A.2). Disregarding these remaining votes harms small parties because they are a large portion of the small parties' votes—and, of course, the entire vote total of a party that does not win any seats—but only a relatively small portion of the larger parties' votes. As a result, the seat shares of the larger parties will tend to be systematically higher than their vote shares, and the smaller parties will tend to receive seat shares that are systematically below their vote shares. The maximum disadvantage for small parties occurs when there are no remaining seats to be allocated at all.

Although it is a divisor formula, the d'Hondt method can also be interpreted as a particular kind of quota formula—and thus be compared with the other quota formulas. Its purpose can be said to be to find a quota that will allow the allocation of all available seats in the first allocation and to disregard all remainders. This quota equals the last 'average' to which a seat is awarded: 13,667 votes in Table A.1.[4] When the parties' votes are divided by this quota, their quotas are 3.00, 2.12, 1.24, and 0.95 and the seat distribution 3, 2, 1, and 0—without the need to honour any of the remaining votes; note especially party *D*'s large unused fraction of 0.95 of a quota.[5]

The pure Sainte-Laguë formula can be interpreted in a similar way. Its quota is twice the last of the 'averages' to which a seat is awarded. For each quota of votes that a party has won, it is awarded one seat, and all remaining votes of half a quota or more are also honoured. If all remainders were so honoured, a strong bias in favour of the small parties would result—just as the d'Hondt rule of ignoring all remainders entails a bias against the small parties. By setting a boundary of half a quota above which remainders do, and below which they do not, qualify for a seat, Sainte-Laguë treats all parties in an even-handed manner. However, the modified Sainte-Laguë deviates from this high degree of proportionality by raising the first divisor from 1 to 1.4 and thereby making it more difficult for small parties to win their first seats. The formula operates almost like d'Hondt as far as a party winning its first seat is concerned, because the distance from 1.4 to 3 is proportionally nearly the same as the distance from 1 to 2; if the first divisor were 1.5, the first-seat procedure would be exactly like d'Hondt. But for winning seats thereafter, modified Sainte-Laguë works like pure Sainte-Laguë.

STV is more difficult to compare with the other PR formulas because voters cast their votes for individual candidates, in order of the voters' preferences, instead of party lists. Table A.3 presents a hypothetical example that, while it is very simple, illustrates all of STV's basic rules. In a three-member district, there are 100 voters and seven candidates (*P* to *V*). In the top half of the table, the voters' preferences are summarized: there are 15 ballots with candidate *P* as the first preference, *Q* as the second preference, and *R* in third place, with no further preferences indicated; several other ballots also contain three preferences, but the rest indicate only one or two preferences. Like LR systems, STV requires the choice of a quota, which in practice is always the Droop quota. However, it is defined in a slightly different way from the LR Droop quota: the quotient arrived at by dividing the total vote by the number of seats plus 1 is rounded up or, if the quotient is an integer, 1 is added. In the example

TABLE A.3. Illustrative example of the operation of the single transferable vote in a three-member district with seven candidates

Droop quota = $[100/(3 + 1)] + 1 = 26$

15 ballots	P-Q-R	20 ballots	S-T
15 ballots	P-R-Q	9 ballots	T-S
8 ballots	Q-R-P	17 ballots	U
3 ballots	R-P-Q	13 ballots	V

Candidate	First count	Second count	Third count	Fourth count	Fifth count	Sixth count
P	30	− 4 = 26	26	26	26	26
Q	8	+ 2 = 10	+ 5 = 15	15	15	15
R	3	+ 2 = 5	− 5 = 0	0	0	0
S	20	20	20	+ 9 = 29	− 3 = 26	26
T	9	9	9	− 9 = 0	0	0
U	17	17	17	17	17	17
V	13	13	13	13	13	− 13 = 0
Non-transferable	—	—	—	—	+ 3 = 3	+ 13 = 16

Candidates elected: *P*, *S*, and *U*.

of Table A.3, the LR Droop quota would be 25, but the STV Droop quota is 26.[6]

In the first count, the ballots are arranged according to first preferences. If a candidate has a Droop quota or more of these first preferences, he or she is elected: candidate *P* with 30 votes in the example of Table A.3. In the second count, *P*'s 4 surplus votes are transferred to the next lower preferences, half to *Q* and half to *R*, because the original 30 ballots with *P* as first preference were also split equally between *Q* and *R* as second preferences. Since the second count does not yield another candidate with the Droop quota necessary for election, the weakest candidate (*R*) is eliminated and his or her 5 votes transferred to the next preference on the ballots (*Q*) in the third count. This procedure has to be repeated in the fourth count with the elimination of candidate *T* and the transfer of his or her votes to candidate *S*—who now exceeds the Droop quota and is elected. In the fifth count, *S*'s 3 surplus votes should be transferred to the next preference, but because no further preferences are indicated on the ballots, these votes become non-transferable. In the sixth count, the weakest candidate is again eliminated (candidate *V*); only four candidates are left, and candidate *Q* is next in line for elimination; this means that no further calculations are necessary and that candidate *U* is the third candidate to be elected.

Because STV voters vote for individual candidates, they can vote for candidates of different parties. In order to compare STV with the other PR formulas, we therefore have to make the simplifying assumption that party votes lost by transfers to candidates of other parties are gained back by transfers *from* other parties, or—what is effectively the same assumption, but one that is easier to work with—that voters cast their votes entirely within party lines. (In Malta, most voters actually follow this party-line voting behaviour.) Table A.3 serves to exemplify this situation, too, if we assume that candidates *P*, *Q*, and *R* belong to party *A*, candidates *S* and *T* to party *B*, and candidates *U* and *V* to parties *C* and *D* respectively. The result is obviously very similar to that of LR-Droop: parties *A* and *B* have one full Droop quota and win one seat each, and the third seat goes to party *C* which has the largest remainder of votes.[7]

The most significant exception from party-line voting or offsetting transfers is when parties conclude alliances with each other and encourage their voters to vote for their own candidates first but then turn to the candidates of the allied party or parties. This opportunity, which is an inherent feature of STV, is similar to the possibility of connected lists or *apparentements* that some list PR systems offer. It is examined as a separate variable in Chapter 5.

On the basis of the above arguments, the PR formulas can be classified in three groups: LR-Hare and pure Sainte-Laguë (although the latter is only a theoretical possibility) are the most proportional formulas; the d'Hondt and the two LR-Imperiali formulas are the least proportional; and LR-Droop, STV (which invariably uses the Droop quota, too), and modified Sainte-Laguë are in an intermediate category.[8]

Appendix B

Indices of Disproportionality and Party System Characteristics

THE following list contains the values of the eight basic indices of disproportionality and party system characteristics for the seventy electoral systems analysed in this volume. See Tables 2.1 to 2.8 for an explanation of the notations used to identify the electoral systems and for more information about these systems. LSq is the Gallagher least-squares index of disproportionality, D the Loosemore-Hanby index, I the Rae index, LD the largest-deviation index, ENEP the effective number of elective parties, ENPP the effective number of parliamentary parties, Parl. maj. the frequency of parliamentary majorities, and Manuf. maj. the frequency of manufactured majorities.

Electoral system	LSq	D	I	LD	ENEP	ENPP	Parl maj.	Manuf. maj.
Australia								
AUL1	9.61	13.25	4.26	9.31	2.74	2.40	1.00	1.00
AUL2	8.55	12.29	4.73	8.38	2.76	2.53	0.33	0.33
AUL3	10.24	13.90	5.20	11.13	3.02	2.35	1.00	1.00
Austria								
AUT1	3.61	5.02	2.50	3.35	2.48	2.25	0.25	0.25
AUT2	1.43	2.17	0.78	1.36	2.51	2.42	0.50	0.00
Belgium								
BEL1	3.23	5.98	1.42	3.06	5.18	4.63	0.07	0.07
BEL2E	6.16	11.38	1.65	6.65	7.88	6.86	0.00	0.00
Canada								
CAN	11.33	13.88	5.70	12.76	3.04	2.37	0.60	0.47
Costa Rica								
CR1	3.85	5.44	2.29	3.90	2.84	2.59	0.50	0.00
CR2	4.12	7.20	1.79	4.04	2.76	2.39	0.75	0.50
Denmark								
DEN1	1.81	2.46	0.66	2.24	4.08	3.96	0.00	0.00
DEN2	2.01	2.84	0.75	2.38	3.84	3.66	0.00	0.00
DEN3	1.74	3.34	0.62	1.58	5.22	4.92	0.00	0.00
DEN4E	7.45	14.06	2.83	5.88	6.58	5.13	0.00	0.00

Electoral system	LSq	D	I	LD	ENEP	ENPP	Parl maj.	Manuf. maj.
Finland								
FIN	2.86	5.06	1.14	2.65	5.50	5.03	0.00	0.00
France								
FRA1	3.65	5.42	1.99	3.73	4.59	4.23	0.00	0.00
FRA2	5.48	8.92	2.65	5.56	5.75	5.83	0.00	0.00
FRA3	14.15	20.89	4.89	15.16	4.97	3.50	0.29	0.29
FRA4E	6.07	11.71	2.17	5.37	4.80	3.77	0.33	0.33
FRA5	7.23	12.72	2.47	7.19	4.65	3.90	0.00	0.00
FRA6	11.84	18.68	5.20	10.29	4.40	3.07	0.00	0.00
Germany								
GER1	3.80	8.40	1.15	3.42	5.71	4.65	0.00	0.00
GER2	3.67	7.21	1.27	2.86	4.21	3.63	0.00	0.00
GER3	2.18	3.31	0.96	2.11	3.17	2.95	0.00	0.00
GER4E	4.24	6.67	1.99	4.00	3.18	2.76	0.00	0.00
GER5	0.67	1.35	0.33	0.60	3.56	3.47	0.00	0.00
GER6E	1.91	4.20	0.86	1.58	4.02	3.74	0.00	0.00
Greece								
GRE1	15.79	18.96	7.37	18.96	2.74	1.72	1.00	0.00
GRE2	10.99	16.27	4.75	12.21	3.21	2.22	1.00	1.00
GRE3E	2.70	5.75	1.10	2.29	3.25	3.06	0.00	0.00
GRE4	7.08	9.00	3.40	7.84	2.58	2.15	1.00	1.00
GRE5	4.06	5.85	1.89	3.99	2.64	2.37	0.00	0.00
Iceland								
ICE1	7.49	9.74	3.93	9.09	3.66	3.44	0.00	0.00
ICE2	2.86	3.98	1.39	3.18	4.06	3.84	0.00	0.00
India								
IND1	20.77	29.27	3.54	27.86	4.21	1.79	1.00	1.00
IND2	16.76	23.85	3.27	21.95	4.31	2.27	1.00	1.00
Ireland								
IRE1	3.49	5.22	1.77	3.99	3.10	2.79	0.29	0.21
IRE2E	10.83	16.37	5.93	11.61	4.45	3.43	0.33	0.33
Israel								
ISR1	2.47	5.77	0.71	2.61	5.39	4.73	0.00	0.00
ISR2	0.86	2.39	0.30	0.73	5.10	4.92	0.00	0.00
ISR3	2.61	5.72	0.66	2.58	4.36	3.82	0.00	0.00
Italy								
ITA1	1.56	2.89	0.40	2.03	4.69	4.39	0.00	0.00
ITA2	3.64	5.88	1.31	4.55	3.56	3.06	0.50	0.50
ITA3	2.71	4.69	0.87	3.16	4.08	3.62	0.00	0.00
ITA4E	1.12	2.25	0.33	0.80	4.31	4.42	0.00	0.00

Electoral system	LSq	D	I	LD	ENEP	ENPP	Parl maj.	Manuf. maj.
Japan								
JPN1	5.09	10.67	1.89	6.08	7.78	5.76	0.00	0.00
JPN2	5.77	8.78	2.68	6.56	3.51	2.88	0.65	0.47
Luxembourg								
LUX1	3.11	4.78	1.55	3.04	3.64	3.30	0.00	0.00
LUX2E	13.15	20.20	5.32	14.70	3.93	2.57	0.00	0.00
Malta								
MAL1	3.79	5.15	2.08	3.90	2.97	2.79	0.40	0.00
MAL2	3.73	4.43	2.27	4.24	2.33	2.14	0.80	0.40
MAL3	0.31	0.40	0.29	0.40	2.01	2.00	1.00	0.00
Netherlands								
NET1	1.29	2.70	0.50	1.31	4.89	4.60	0.00	0.00
NET2	1.32	2.96	0.40	1.29	4.92	4.59	0.00	0.00
NET3E	4.79	8.49	1.96	4.52	4.02	3.39	0.00	0.00
New Zealand								
NZ	10.66	12.47	6.96	11.91	2.47	1.95	1.00	0.81
Norway								
NOR1	8.53	10.79	3.29	10.31	3.87	2.92	1.00	1.00
NOR2	4.38	7.07	1.88	4.44	3.77	3.26	0.22	0.22
NOR3	3.65	5.09	1.11	3.91	4.84	4.23	0.00	0.00
Portugal								
POR1	4.25	6.89	1.58	4.98	3.58	3.05	0.43	0.29
POR2E	4.19	8.05	1.59	3.56	4.10	3.47	0.00	0.00
Spain								
SPA1	8.95	15.11	2.38	10.59	3.89	2.72	0.40	0.40
SPA2E	5.41	11.24	1.15	6.07	4.38	3.36	0.00	0.00
Sweden								
SWE1	3.51	5.26	2.09	2.83	3.43	3.06	0.00	0.00
SWE2	2.36	3.41	1.17	2.34	3.30	3.11	0.17	0.00
SWE3	1.67	2.55	0.72	1.81	3.57	3.40	0.00	0.00
Switzerland								
SWI	2.36	5.09	0.78	2.22	5.57	5.10	0.00	0.00
United Kingdom								
UK1	10.55	12.91	5.47	11.61	2.65	2.10	0.92	0.92
UK2E	19.45	23.91	8.46	21.16	2.94	1.85	1.00	0.67
United States								
US	5.41	5.90	5.28	5.90	2.03	1.92	1.00	0.09

Appendix C

Data: Sources, Additions, Corrections, Clarifications

WITH the exceptions to be noted below, the data used for this study can all be found in the following basic and easily accessible sources: Thomas T. Mackie and Richard Rose, *The International Almanac of Electoral History* (3rd edn., London: Macmillan, 1991); Thomas T. Mackie, 'General Elections in Western Nations During 1989', *European Journal of Political Research*, 19 (1991), 157–62; Thomas T. Mackie, 'General Elections in Western Nations During 1990', *European Journal of Political Research*, 21 (1992), 317–32; T. T. Mackie and F. W. S. Craig, *Europe Votes 2: European Parliamentary Election Results 1979–1984* (Chichester, West Sussex: Parliamentary Research Services, 1985); T. T. Mackie, *Europe Votes 3: European Parliamentary Election Results 1989* (Aldershot, Hants: Dartmouth, 1990).

However, several additions, corrections, and clarifications must be noted. I shall organize these by country and by election year. The main additions are the votes and seats data for the ten elections held in Costa Rica from 1953 to 1990 and for the eight elections held in India from 1952 to 1984. (1 December 1990 is the cut-off date for the purpose of this study, which means that the December 1990 elections in Denmark and Germany were excluded. Moreover, the November 1989 election in India had to be excluded because of the lack of comparable data.)

All of the indices used in this study (the indices of bias and the effective numbers of parties) are calculated on the basis of the raw numbers of votes and seats, rather than the vote and seat percentages supplied in the above data sources, because these percentages are given to only a single decimal place—which is not accurate enough for the calculation of the indices. Numbers of votes and seats won by parties are corrected only if they entail substantial errors. Incorrect numbers are presented in square brackets. Small errors in the sources, such as '0' votes or seats which should have been '—' (indicating, for instance, that the party did not participate in the election) or vice versa, are ignored, since they do not influence the calculation of the indices. Where the reported total of 'valid votes' deviates from the total of the votes received by the parties, I used the latter figure. Most of the corrections listed below were supplied by Thomas T. Mackie.

Finally, clarifications are necessary in all cases in which it is not obvious to which particular parties numbers of votes and seats belong, such as when parties present joint lists.

AUSTRALIA

1951–5: I counted only the *contested* seats won by the Labour, Country, and Liberal Parties. Hence the seat totals in these three elections are 118, 114, and 112 respectively.

1975–83: The votes received by the Country-Liberal Party (no. 26 in the *Almanac*) in these four elections were added to those of the National Party (no. 7).

1984: The votes received by the Country-Liberal Party (no. 26) were added to those of the Liberal Party (no. 18).

AUSTRIA

1983: United Greens of Austria (no. 13) 93,798 [93,766] votes; others 9,765 [9,777] votes.

BELGIUM

1946, 1950–8: The votes received by the Liberal/Socialist cartels (no. 5) in these four elections were split equally between the Liberal Party (no. 2) and the Socialist Party (no. 3), as recommended by Keith Hill.[1]

1968: Liberal Party (no. 2) 1,081,079 [—] votes and 47 [—] seats.

1971: The Liberal Party (no. 2) did not split until 1972; hence the Party of Liberty and Progress (no. 21), Francophone Liberals (no. 22), and Brussels Liberal Party (no. 23) were counted as one party receiving 868,842 votes and 34 seats.

1974: I added the 3 seats won by Brussels Liberal Party (no. 23) to the 9 won by the Francophone Democratic Front (no. 14) because they were in an electoral alliance, the votes of which are reported under the latter.

1977: Francophone Liberals (no. 22) 328,567 [328,608] votes; Others 12,375 [12,334] votes.

1978: Communist Party (no. 10) 181,931 [181,921] votes; Flemish Block (no. 29) 76,051 [75,864] votes; Others 26,075 [21,262] votes.

1981: Communist Party (no. 10) 138,526 [138,992] votes; Others 57,309 [57,763] votes.

CANADA

1953 and 1957: Only the *contested* seats won by the Liberal Party and Others were counted; hence the seat totals for these two elections are 261 and 263.

1980: Communist Party (no. 6) 6,022 [6,002] votes.

COSTA RICA[2]

1953: Results of the 26 July 1953 election:

	VOTES	SEATS
National Liberation	114,043	30
Democratic	37,322	11
Independent National Republican	12,696	3
National Union	12,069	1
Total	176,130	45

1958: Results of the 2 February 1958 election:

	VOTES	SEATS
National Liberation	86,081	20
Republican	46,171	11
National Union	44,125	10
Independent Party	20,314	3
Revolutionary Civic Union	6,855	1
Others	2,970	0
Total	206,516	45

1962: Results of the 4 February 1962 election:

	VOTES	SEATS
National Liberation	184,135	29
Republican	126,249	18
National Union	50,021	9
Popular Democratic Action	9,256	1
Solidarity Action	3,358	0
Others	3,918	0
Total	376,937	57

1966: Results of the 6 February 1966 election:

	VOTES	SEATS
National Liberation	202,891	29
National Unification	178,905	26
Revolutionary Civic Union	22,721	2
Democratic	8,543	0
Guanacaste Republican	1,577	0
Total	414,637	57

Appendix C

1970: Results of the 1 February 1970 election:

	VOTES	SEATS
National Liberation	269,038	32
National Unification	190,387	22
Socialist Action	29,133	2
National Front	16,392	0
Christian Democratic	13,489	1
National Union	6,105	0
Costa Rican Renewal Movement	3,279	0
Others	2,602	0
Total	530,425	57

1974: Results of the 3 February 1974 election:

	VOTES	SEATS
National Liberation	271,867	27
National Unification	164,323	16
Independent National	66,222	6
Democratic Renewal	51,082	3
National Republican	32,475	1
Socialist Action	29,310	2
Democratic	14,161	1
Christian Democratic	13,688	0
Cartago Farmers' Union	8,074	1
Costa Rican Socialist	6,032	0
Others	7,730	0
Total	664,964	57

1978: Results of the 5 February 1978 election:

	VOTES	SEATS
Unity Coalition	356,215	27
National Liberation	318,904	25
United People's Coalition	62,865	3
National Unification	25,824	0
Costa Rican Popular Front	12,834	1
Republican Union	8,215	0
Cartago Farmers' Union	7,887	1
Independent National	6,673	0
Independent Party	5,774	0
Socialist Workers' Organization	4,059	0
Others	11,310	0
Total	820,560	57

1982: Result of the 7 February 1982 election:

	VOTES	SEATS
National Liberation	527,231	33
Unity Coalition	277,998	18
United People's Coalition	61,465	4
National Movement	34,437	1
Alajuela Democratic Action	12,486	1
National Democratic	11,575	0
Cartago Farmers' Union	7,235	0
Costa Rican Concord	5,014	0
Independent Party	4,671	0
Others	13,878	0
Total	955,990	57

1986: Result of the 2 February 1986 election:

	VOTES	SEATS
National Liberation	560,694	29
Christian Social Unity	485,860	25
United People's Coalition	31,685	1
Popular Alliance	28,551	1
Christian National Alliance	19,972	0
Cartago Farmers' Union	13,575	1
National Republican	10,598	0
Generaleña Union	4,402	0
Alajuela Democratic Action	4,324	0
Others	12,538	0
Total	1,172,199	57

1990: Results of the 4 February 1990 election:

	VOTES	SEATS
Christian Social Unity	617,478	29
National Liberation	559,632	25
United People's Coalition	44,161	1
Generaleña Union	32,292	1
Christian National Alliance	22,154	0
Cartago Farmers' Union	14,190	1
Independent National	10,643	0
Progress	7,733	0
Alajuela Solidarity	7,330	0
Independent Party	5,566	0
Others	14,993	0
Total	1,336,172	57

DENMARK

1973–7: The seats won by the Schleswig Party (no. 8) in these three elections were added to those of the Centre Democrats (no. 20) since the former's candidates were included in the latter's lists.

GERMANY

1969: Others 71,330 [72,330] votes.
1972: Christian Democratic Union (no. 36) 13,190,837 [16,806,020] votes; Others 27,223 [27,233] votes.
1976: Christian Democratic Union (no. 36) 14,367,302 [18,394,801] votes.
1980: Christian Democratic Union (no. 36) 12,989,200 [16,897,659] votes.
1987: Christian Democratic Union (no. 36) 13,045,745 [16,761,572] votes; Free Democrats (no. 38) 3,440,911 [3,449,686] votes.
1979 European election: Christian Democratic Union (no. 1) 32 [35] seats; Total 78 [81] seats. Note: these adjustments are necessary in order to correct errors in the reported Christian Democratic Union candidates elected and to exclude the 3 indirectly elected Berlin deputies.
1984 European election (excluding the 3 indirectly elected Berlin deputies): Christian Democratic Union (no. 1) 32 [34] seats; Social Democratic Party (no. 2) 32 [33] seats; Total 78 [81] seats.
1989 European election (excluding the 3 indirectly elected Berlin deputies): Social Democratic Party (no. 1) 30 [31] seats; Christian Democratic Union 24 [25] seats; Greens 7 [8] seats; Total 78 [81] seats.

GREECE

1974: The Communist Party (no. 4), United Democratic Left (no. 25), and Communist Party (Interior) (no. 35) were counted as one party, winning 8 seats.
1977: The United Democratic Left (no. 25), Communist Party (Interior) (no. 35), and Christian Democracy (no. 33) were counted as one party, winning 2 seats.

INDIA

The following election results are based on the excellent and extremely detailed data handbook by V. B. Singh and Shankar Bose; I also follow their abbreviations of party names.[3] The results are given separately for all parties that received at least 0.5 per cent of the total valid vote and/ or that won more than one seat. Most of the votes received by 'others' are votes cast not for minor parties but for independent candidates. Only votes cast for, and candidates elected to, contested seats were counted.

(The number of uncontested seats ranged from 1 to 12 in the eight elections, with an average of 4.4.) In 1952, there were 86 two-member districts and one three-member district in which each voter had, respectively, 2 and 3 votes; the votes cast in these districts were divided by 2 (or by 3 in the one three-member district). The same adjustment was made for the 91 two-member districts in the 1957 election.

1952: Result of the 1952 (25 October 1951 to 21 February 1952) election:

	VOTES	SEATS
INC	35,944,791	357
SOC	8,336,515	12
KMPP	4,588,700	8
CPI	2,764,610	16
BJS	2,318,817	3
RRP	1,401,774	3
SCF	1,282,972	2
PDF	939,626	7
HMS	868,893	4
KLP	865,769	1
PWP	736,124	2
SAD	665,031	4
FBM	658,130	1
GP	594,256	5
JKD	512,793	3
TNT	506,374	4
RSP	338,637	3
COMW	266,321	3
LSS	154,970	2
Others	15,627,140	39
Total	79,372,243	479

1957: Result of the 24 February to 9 June 1957 election:

	VOTES	SEATS
INC	43,073,083	359
PSP	9,513,654	19
CPI	8,082,852	27
BJS	5,192,666	4
SCF	1,258,684	6
GP	784,082	7
HMS	728,835	1
PWP	725,301	4
PDF	711,136	2
JKD	610,764	6

FBM	514,854	2
CSJ	414,861	3
Others	18,123,005	42
Total	89,733,777	482

1962: Result of the 16 February to 6 June 1962 election:

	VOTES	SEATS
INC	51,509,084	358
CPI	11,450,037	29
SWA	9,085,252	18
PSP	7,848,345	12
BJS	7,415,170	14
RPI	3,255,985	3
SOC	3,099,397	6
DMK	2,315,610	7
SAD	829,129	3
FBL	826,588	2
HMS	747,861	1
PWP	703,582	0
RRP	688,990	2
JKD	467,338	3
RSP	451,717	2
MUL	417,761	2
GP	342,970	4
LSS	281,755	2
Others	13,432,319	23
Total	115,168,890	491

1967: Result of the 15–28 February 1967 election:

	VOTES	SEATS
INC	59,490,701	279
BJS	13,640,677	35
SWA	12,646,847	44
CPI	7,225,163	23
SSP	7,171,627	23
CPM	6,479,755	19
DMK	5,529,405	25
PSP	4,456,487	13
RPI	3,607,711	1
BAC	1,204,356	5
PWP	1,028,755	2
ADS	968,712	3
FBL	627,910	2

MUL	413,868	2
Others	21,374,536	39
Total	145,866,510	515

1971: Result of the 1–13 March 1971 election:

	VOTES	SEATS
INC	64,040,246	351
NCO	15,279,051	16
BJS	10,786,921	22
CPM	7,510,889	25
CPI	6,935,627	23
DMK	5,622,758	23
SWA	4,498,188	8
SSP	3,554,839	3
BKD	3,190,321	1
TPS	1,873,589	10
PSP	1,526,076	2
SAD	1,279,873	1
UTC	1,053,176	1
FBL	962,971	2
PWP	741,535	0
KEC	542,431	3
RSP	457,815	3
MUL	416,545	2
Others	16,329,425	21
Total	146,602,276	517

1977: Result of the 16–20 March 1977 election:

	VOTES	SEATS
BLD	78,062,828	295
INC	65,211,589	152
CPM	8,113,659	22
ADK	5,579,043	19
CPI	5,322,088	7
NCO	3,252,217	3
DMK	3,224,654	1
SAD	2,373,331	9
PWP	1,030,232	5
RPK	956,072	2
RSP	851,164	4
FBL	633,644	3
MUL	565,007	2
KEC	491,674	2

JKN	483,192	2
Others	12,767,110	12
Total	188,917,504	540

1980: Result of the 3–6 January 1980 election:

	VOTES	SEATS
INCI	84,455,313	353
JNP	37,493,334	31
JNPS	18,611,590	41
CPM	12,156,988	36
INCU	10,450,405	13
CPI	5,122,685	11
ADK	4,674,064	2
DMK	4,236,537	16
SAD	1,396,412	1
RSP	1,285,517	4
FBL	1,011,564	3
JKN	493,143	2
MUL	475,507	2
Others	15,961,215	13
Total	197,824,274	528

1984: Result of the 24–8 December 1984 election:

	VOTES	SEATS
INC	120,108,318	414
BJP	18,466,147	2
JNP	16,630,596	10
CPM	14,287,111	22
LKD	14,095,890	3
TDP	10,132,859	30
CPI	6,733,117	6
DMK	5,695,179	2
ICS	4,035,082	5
ADK	3,968,967	12
SAD	2,577,279	7
AGP	2,505,377	7
ICJ	1,510,900	1
RSP	1,173,869	3
FBL	1,055,556	2
JKN	1,010,243	3
MUL	658,821	2
KCJ	598,113	2
Others	24,636,465	8
Total	249,879,889	541

IRELAND

1948–89: The one uncontested seat (that of the Speaker) was subtracted from the relevant party's seats and from the seat totals in all fourteen elections.
1977: Others 88,482 [88,668] votes.
1979–89 European elections: Independents (no. 8) were regarded as 'Others'.

ISRAEL

1949: Agudat Israel (no. 8), Poalei Agudat Israel (no. 9), Mizrachi (no. 10), and Hapoel Ha'mizrachi (no. 11) were counted as one party (the United Religious Front), winning 16 seats.
1955, 1959, 1973, and 1988: Agudat Israel (no. 8) and Poalei Agudat Israel (no. 9) were counted as one party, winning 6 seats in 1955 and 1959 and 5 seats in 1973 and 1988.
1959: The errors in the votes and seats figures can be corrected, for the purposes of this analysis, by attributing seats to parties as follows: Achdut Ha'avoda (no. 18) 9 [8] seats; Minority Lists (no. 6) 5 [4] seats; Mapam (no. 7) 7 [9] seats.
1961: Minority Lists (no. 6) 35,376 [35,356] votes and 4 [5] seats; Mapam (no. 7) 8 [7] seats.
1977: Others 42,573 [46,969] votes.
1981: Agudat Israel (no. 8) 72,312 [73,312] votes; Others 46,367 [51,535] votes.
1984: Other 56,548 [94,560] votes. Tehiya (no. 40) and Tsomet (no. 46) were counted as one party, winning 5 seats.
1988: Others 55,424 [27,012] votes.

ITALY

1946: Others 595,539 [697,932] votes.
1948: Others 284,081 [—] votes. The Communist Party (no. 11) and the Socialist Party (no. 3) were counted as one party, winning 183 seats.
1976: Liberal Party (no. 19) 478,185 [4,478,185] votes; MSI (no. 24) 2,244,113 [224,113] votes; Others 84,593 [84,553] votes. Proletarian Unity (no. 32), Continuous Struggle (no. 35), and Workers' Vanguard (no. 36) were counted as one party, winning 6 seats.
1979: Proletarian Democracy (no. 37) 294,462 [—] votes; Trieste List (no. 39) 65,937 [65,637] votes; Others 310,897 [605,359] votes.
1983: The Communist Party (no. 11) and Proletarian Unity (no. 32) were counted as one party, winning 198 seats.
1984 European election: Venetian League (no. 12) 0 [1] seat.

JAPAN

1946: Adjusted results of the 10 April 1946 election, based on data provided by Sadafumi Kawato, Faculty of Law, Hokkaido University (votes in districts with 2 votes per voter divided by 2, and in districts with 3 votes per voter divided by 3):

	VOTES	SEATS
Liberal	5,694,321	140
Progressive	4,516,044	94
Socialist	4,187,118	93
Communist	872,879	5
Co-operative	728,698	14
Constitutional Promotion	223,426	0
Hokkaido Alliance	138,992	3
Miyagi Local	102,212	3
Nikko Democratic	101,616	4
Co-operative Democratic	100,993	2
Agricultural	75,050	2
Japan Agricultural	33,507	2
Others (including independents)	6,858,828	102
Total	23,633,684	464

1952: Right-Wing Socialists (no. 40) 4,013,872 [4,103,872] votes.
1980: Others 14 [11] seats.
1983: Democratic Socialist Party (no. 44) 4,129,907 [4,129,747] votes.

LUXEMBOURG

1948 and 1951: The two partial elections held in these years were treated as one regular election.
1989: Liberal Party (no. 14) — [11] seats; Democratic Party (no. 16) 11 [—] seats.

MALTA

1950: Labour Party (no. 3) 29,850 [30,332] votes; Nationalist Party (no. 5) 31,945 [31,431] votes; Jones Party (no. 6) 852 [—] votes; Democratic Action Party (no. 7) 6,329 [6,361] votes; Others 1,953 [2,805] votes.
1951: Constitutional Party (no. 1) 9,150 [9,151] votes; Labour Party (no. 3) 40,208 [40,315] votes; Jones Party (no. 6) 957 [—] votes; Malta Workers' Party (no. 9) 21,158 [21,053] votes; Others 1,206 [2,163] votes.
1953: Constitutional Party (no. 1) 1,374 [1,385] votes; Progressive Constitutional Party (no. 10) 5,128 [5,117] votes.

1966: Christian Workers' Party (no. 11) 8,594 [8,561] votes; Democratic Nationalist Party II (no. 12) 1,845 [1,878] votes.
1971: Labour Party (no. 3) 85,515 [85,448] votes; Nationalist Party (no. 5) 80,686 [80,753] votes.

NETHERLANDS

1979 European election: Labour Party (no. 1) 9 [10] seats; Christian Democratic Appeal (no. 2) 10 [9] seats.
1989 European election: Christian Democratic Appeal (no. 1) 1,813,935 [1,813,035] votes; God With Us (no. 10) 18,854 [28,854] votes.

NORWAY

1949–81: The votes received by the Joint Non-Socialist Lists (no. 13) were allocated to each of the participating parties according to its percentage share (the difference between its total estimated vote percentage and its 'own' vote percentage) as given in Table 19.5b of the Mackie–Rose *International Almanac*.
1953: Farmers'/Centre (no. 7) estimated vote percentage 9.0 per cent [9.9 per cent]
1981: Christian People's Party (no. 10) estimated vote percentage 9.4 per cent [no estimated percentage indicated].

PORTUGAL

1975–87: Since the votes do not include the votes cast by Portuguese citizens residing abroad, the seats won by their representatives must be subtracted from the seat numbers won by the different parties. This reduces the seat totals to 247 [250] in 1975, 259 [263] in 1976, and 246 [250] in the subsequent five elections.
1979 and 1980: The parties belonging to the Democratic Alliance were regarded as one party, winning 125 seats in 1979 and 131 seats in 1980.
1979–85: The parties belonging to the United People's Alliance were regarded as one party, winning 47 seats in 1979, 41 in 1980, 44 in 1983, and 38 in 1985.
1980: The parties belonging to the Republican Socialist Front were regarded as one party, winning 73 seats.
1983: The Popular Democratic Union (no. 7) and the Revolutionary Socialist Party (no. 12) were counted as one party, winning 65,189 votes and 0 seats. Others 42,541 [67,561] votes.
1987: The parties belonging to the United Democratic Coalition were counted as one party, winning 31 seats.

SPAIN

1977: The seat won by the Andalusian Socialists (no. 35) was added to the 5 seats won by the Popular Socialist Party (no. 32) with which it had an alliance (Socialist Unity). The Catalan Centre Party (no. 37) and the Democratic Union of Catalonia (no. 38) were counted as one party, winning 2 seats.

1986: The Popular Alliance (no. 29), Popular Democrats (no. 51), and the Liberal Party (no. 52) were counted as one party (Popular Coalition), winning 105 seats.

1989 European election: Nationalist Coalition (no. 9) 1 [2] seat.

SWEDEN

1985: The Centre Party (no. 7) and the Christian Democratic Union (no. 20) were counted as one party, winning 44 seats.

SWITZERLAND

1947–71, 1979, 1987: Only the *contested* seats were counted in these nine elections, reducing the seat totals by 2 to 7 seats.

1951: Social Democrats (no. 5) 49(2) [49] seats; Total 196(4) [196(2)] seats.

1955: Social Democrats (no. 5) 53(2) [53] seats; Total 196(4) [196(2)] seats.

1963: Christian Democrats (no. 1) 48(1) [48] seats; Social Democrats (no. 5) 53(2) [53(1)] seats; Total 200(6) [200(4)] seats.

1967: Christian Democrats (no. 1) 45(1) [45] seats; Social Democrats (no. 5) 51(3) [51(1)] seats; Total 200(7) [200(4)] seats.

1971: Christian Democrats (no. 1) 44(1) [44] seats; Radical Democrats (no. 4) 49(1) [49] seats; Total 200(2) [200] seats.

1987: Protestant People's Party (no. 8) 37,263 [—] votes.

UNITED KINGDOM

1945: Only the votes cast and candidates elected in the contested 598 single-member and 15 two-member districts were counted, and the results in the 3 uncontested single-member districts and in the 4 STV districts (with a total of 9 seats) were disregarded.

Moreover, the votes cast in the two-member districts, in which each voter had 2 votes, were divided by 2.[4] The results are as follows.

		VOTES	SEATS
1.	Conservative	8,819,150	195
2.	Liberal	2,176,066	12

5.	Independent Labour	46,769	3
6.	Labour	11,551,547	391
7.	United Ireland	92,819	2
10.	Communist	97,945	2
11.	Scottish National	26,707	0
12.	Plaid Cymru	16,017	0
14.	National Liberal	686,652	11
Others		468,179	12
Total		23,981,851	628

1950 and 1951: Only the *contested* seats were counted in these elections, reducing the seats won by the Conservative Party (no. 1) as well as the total number of seats by 2 in 1950 and by 4 in 1951.

1966: Plaid Cymru (no. 12) 61,071 [6,107,199] votes.

1974 (October): Others 114,838 [143,838] votes.

1983 and 1987: The Alliance was counted as one party in these elections, and the separate votes and seats figures for the Liberal Party (no. 3) and the Social Democratic Party (no. 20) were disregarded.

1979–89 European elections: Only the votes cast and seats won in the 78 British single-member districts were counted, and the votes and seats in the Northern Ireland three-member STV district were disregarded.[5] Independent candidates were classified as Others.

1984 European election: The Liberal Party (no. 11) and the Social Democratic Party (no. 14) were counted as one party, winning 2,591,635 votes and 0 seats.

Notes

1. INTRODUCTION: GOALS AND METHODS

1. This basic information is presented in Tables 2.1 to 2.8 in Ch. 2. Douglas W. Rae deserves credit for the first attempt of this kind in the frequently consulted and cited 'Electoral Laws' table in his *The Political Consequences of Electoral Laws* (2nd edn., New Haven, Conn.: Yale University Press, 1971), 42–4. The errors in this table are discussed and corrected in Arend Lijphart, 'The Political Consequences of Electoral Laws, 1945–85: A Critique, Re-Analysis, and Update of Rae's Classic Study', paper presented at the XIVth World Congress of the International Political Science Association, Washington, DC, 1988; and id., 'The Electoral Systems Researcher as Detective: Probing Rae's Suspect Differential Proposition on List Proportional Representation', in Dennis Kavanagh (ed.), *Electoral Politics* (Oxford: Clarendon Press, 1992), 234–46.

2. The interruption of democracy in Greece lasted only seven years, but the complexity of Greek electoral systems and the difficulty of comparing them with those of the other 26 countries is an additional reason for excluding the 1946–64 elections that were held prior to the establishment of the military dictatorship (see Ch. 2).

3. Thomas T. Mackie and Richard Rose, *The International Almanac of Electoral History* (3rd edn., London: Macmillan, 1991).

4. Vernon Bogdanor, 'Direct Elections, Representative Democracy and European Integration', *Electoral Studies*, 8 (1989), 208.

5. Hermann Schmitt, 'The European Elections of June 1989', *West European Politics*, 13 (1990), 116.

6. Rae, *Political Consequences*, esp. 69–86, 185–8.

7. Please write to Arend Lijphart, Department of Political Science (0521), University of California, San Diego, 9500 Gilman Drive, La Jolla, CA 92093–0521, USA.

8. See the first paragraph of App. C for the complete references to these five publications.

2. ELECTORAL SYSTEMS: TYPES, PATTERNS, TRENDS

1. For a review of the dimensions of electoral systems—and of various classifications of electoral systems based on these dimensions—that

have been proposed by scholars in this field, see André Blais, 'The Classification of Electoral Systems', *European Journal of Political Research*, 16 (1988), 99–110; and id., 'The Debate over Electoral Systems', *International Political Science Review*, 12 (1991), 239–60.

2. Douglas W. Rae, *The Political Consequences of Electoral Laws* (New Haven, Conn.: Yale University Press, 1967), 114–25. All future references to Rae's book will be to its revised and enlarged edition published in 1971.

3. James Hogan, *Election and Representation* (Cork: Cork University Press, 1945), 13.

4. George Horwill, *Proportional Representation: Its Dangers and Defects* (London: Allen and Unwin, 1925), 53. In language strikingly similar to Hogan's and Horwill's, Rein Taagepera and Matthew S. Shugart re-emphasize the importance of district magnitude by calling it 'the decisive factor' in their *Seats and Votes: The Effects and Determinants of Electoral Systems* (New Haven, Conn.: Yale University Press, 1989), 112.

5. Douglas W. Rae, *The Political Consequences of Electoral Laws* (2nd edn., New Haven, Conn.: Yale University Press, 1971), 21, 124.

6. Taagepera and Shugart, *Seats and Votes*, 126–41.

7. Rae, *Political Consequences*, 158. His brief discussion of the consequences of assembly size occurs in a new chapter that he added to the first (1967) edition of his book.

8. Rein Taagepera, 'Seats and Votes: A Generalization of the Cube Law of Elections', *Social Science Research*, 2 (1973), 257–75; see also Taagepera and Shugart, *Seats and Votes*, 156–72. The cube law holds that if, in two-party systems and plurality single-member district elections, the votes received by the two parties are divided in a ratio of $a:b$, the seats that they win will be in the ratio of $a^3:b^3$. Taagepera shows that the exponent of 3 applies only under special circumstances, and that it goes up—and hence also that disproportionality increases—as the number of voters increases and/or assembly size decreases. Taagepera's proposition has found striking confirmation in a study of plurality elections to the unusually small legislatures of the Eastern Caribbean countries; see Arend Lijphart, 'Size, Pluralism, and the Westminster Model of Democracy: Implications for the Eastern Caribbean', in Jorge Heine (ed.), *A Revolution Aborted: The Lessons of Grenada* (Pittsburgh: University of Pittsburgh Press, 1990), 324–6.

9. Most changes are increases, but in the few cases of reductions the percentages are calculated as percentages of the lower values. The requirement that elections be successive also deserves special emphasis. For instance, the French 1945–6 and 1986 elections were conducted under very similar PR rules, but they are forty years apart and will therefore be considered different systems. Similarly, the 1958–81

and 1988 double-ballot elections in France will be treated as two different systems because the 1986 PR election intervened; otherwise, the major difference between the two is a 17 per cent increase in assembly size—short of the 20 per cent criterion. (For this purpose, the national legislative and European Parliament elections will be regarded as separate sets of elections; for instance, the Dutch 1956–89 electoral system was not 'interrupted' by the Euro-elections in 1979, 1984, and 1989.) Finally, the 20 per cent criterion is applied to changing characteristics from one electoral system to another, both of which may be averages. This means that, for instance, Luxembourg has only one electoral system for electing its unicameral legislature of 51, 52 (three times), 56 (twice), 59 (twice), 64, and 60 members; the increase in assembly size from 51 to 64 is more than 20 per cent, but there is no way of grouping the ten elections in two or more sets whose averages differ more than 20 per cent.

10. Rae, *Political Consequences*, 126–9.
11. Michael Gallagher, 'Proportionality, Disproportionality and Electoral Systems', *Electoral Studies*, 10 (1991), 43.
12. Matthew S. Shugart, 'Duverger's Rule, District Magnitude, and Presidentialism' (Ph. D. diss., University of California, Irvine, 1988), 17–29, 116–19.
13. Andrew McLaren Carstairs, *A Short History of Electoral Systems in Western Europe* (London: Allen and Unwin, 1980), 23.
14. For discussions of the many other majoritarian formulas, see Hannu Nurmi, *Comparing Voting Systems* (Dordrecht: Reidel, 1987); and Samuel Merrill, *Making Multicandidate Elections More Democratic* (Princeton, NJ: Princeton University Press, 1988).
15. One minor exception is the use of PR in four districts in the 1946 UK election and in one district (Northern Ireland) in the UK election of representatives to the European Parliament—all excluded from the present analysis (see Table 1.1). Another small exception is the rare use of the majority-runoff in US Congressional elections. However, because the American elections are usually preceded by partisan primaries, they also resemble the French two-ballot system in some basic respects.
16. This book is not about presidential elections, but let me briefly note that these exhibit a greater variety of election methods than the majoritarian legislative elections: Costa Rica and Iceland use plurality (although, in the former, a runoff is held if no candidate receives 40 per cent or more of the vote); Ireland uses the alternative vote; and the United States and Finland use indirect elections via electoral colleges (pre-empted in Finland, since 1988, by the outcome of a direct popular election *if* a presidential candidate wins a majority of the votes).

17. In order to distinguish the 'preferential' alternative vote from the other preferential formula—the single transferable vote, which is a PR formula that I shall discuss later in this chapter—the Australian electoral system expert Jack F. H. Wright uses the more precise terms 'majority-preferential' method and 'quota-preferential' method respectively: 'Australian Experience with Majority-Preferential and Quota-Preferential Systems', in Bernard Grofman and Arend Lijphart (eds.), *Electoral Laws and their Political Consequences* (New York: Agathon Press, 1986), 124–38.

18. Another oddity of the US districting system is the occasional use of overlapping districts. For instance, Connecticut had six single-member districts from 1946 to 1962—five small districts and one superimposed state-wide district—in which each voter had two votes, one in the small and one in the state-wide district.

19. Two plurality countries have made special provisions for communal-ethnic minority representation by having reserved seats for these groups. New Zealand has four seats of this kind for its Maori minority. In India, more than a fifth of the seats have been set aside for the 'scheduled castes' and 'scheduled tribes'; in the first two elections, these seats were mainly in two-member districts with one reserved and one unreserved seat. For other examples of securing minority representation without PR, see Arend Lijphart, 'Proportionality by Non-PR Methods: Ethnic Representation in Belgium, Cyprus, Lebanon, New Zealand, West Germany, and Zimbabwe', in Grofman and Lijphart (eds.), *Electoral Laws and their Political Consequences*, 113–23.

20. In situations where the modified Sainte-Laguë formula is applied to parties that have already won one or more seats, as in the upper-tier allocation in Norway and Sweden (NOR3 and SWE3 in Table 2.4), its results are identical to those of the pure form.

21. Throughout this book, I shall use the symbols proposed by Taagepera and Shugart, *Seats and Votes*, pp. xvii–xviii.

22. G. Van den Bergh, *Unity in Diversity: A Systematic Critical Analysis of All Electoral Systems* (London: Batsford, 1955), 68–72. This important property of the d'Hondt formula was also already emphasized by John H. Humphreys, *Proportional Representation: A Study in Methods of Election* (London: Methuen, 1911), 188–9.

23. Several PR countries have had one (Finland, Italy) or a few (Greece, Spain, Switzerland) single-member districts in which, by definition, the electoral formula has to be majoritarian, and is usually the plurality method. The Japanese mainly multi-member SNTV system has also had one single-member district. These exceptions are so minor that they can safely be ignored. Exceptions that appear to be more significant are the large number of plurality single-member districts in

Iceland (1946–59) and Germany, but in both cases plurality is applied in lower-level districts and is overridden by PR at the higher tier (see Table 2.4).

24. Taagepera and Shugart, *Seats and Votes*, 273–5. Another difference is that Taagepera and Shugart prefer to convert thresholds into magnitudes, whereas I prefer to convert in the opposite direction; I believe that the threshold is a clearer and more meaningful measure of the extent to which small parties are disadvantaged.

25. The exact threshold of representation for the d'Hondt formula is $100\%/(M + p - 1)$, and, if we assume that $M = p$, the threshold becomes $100\%/(2M - 1)$. All of the formulas for the upper and lower thresholds for the main PR formulas may be found in Arend Lijphart and Robert W. Gibberd, 'Thresholds and Payoffs in List Systems of Proportional Representation', *European Journal of Political Research*, 5 (1977), 219–30; Markku Laakso, 'Thresholds for Proportional Representation: Reanalyzed and Extended', in Manfred J. Holler (ed.), *The Logic of Multiparty Systems* (Dordrecht: Kluwer Academic Publishers, 1987), 383–90; and Michael Gallagher, 'Comparing Proportional Representation Electoral Systems: Quotas, Thresholds, Paradoxes and Majorities', *British Journal of Political Science*, 22 (1992), 485–91. See also Rein Taagepera, 'Empirical Thresholds of Representation', *Electoral Studies*, 8 (1989), 105–16.

26. The twenty systems in the first group are AUT2, DEN1 to DEN3, FRA4E, the six German systems, ISR2 and ISR3, ITA2 and ITA3, the three Dutch systems, NOR3, and SWE3. In the second group, where the Taagepera–Shugart thresholds cannot be simply calculated from the district magnitudes, the values are as follows: 7.9 per cent for AUT1, 2.0 per cent for BEL1, 16.4 per cent for GRE1, 13.2 per cent for GRE2, 11.2 per cent for GRE4, 6.2 per cent for ICE1, and 4.1 per cent for ICE2.

27. With two of the three alternative indices of disproportionality (the Rae and largest-deviation indices), similar results were obtained.

28. Because, for $M = 1.21$, the effective threshold according to my formula is 43.4 per cent (lower than the 50 per cent for $M = 1$), it may seem to make sense to assign it also a lower threshold than the uniform 35 per cent for all plurality and majority systems. Plurality multi-member districts may indeed attract a relatively greater number of candidates—resulting in a wider scattering of votes and better chances for minority candidates. On the other hand, as argued earlier, for minority parties multi-member plurality districts are less instead of more advantageous than single-member districts, and hence it would be wrong to assume a lower threshold.

29. In a private communication, Rein Taagepera has suggested a

simplification of my T_{eff} formula. First it can be transformed arithmetically to:

$$T_{\text{eff}} = \frac{25\% \left(3 + \dfrac{1}{M}\right)}{M + 1}$$

Second, if the $1/M$ term, which only has an effect at small values of M, is omitted, the result is:

$$T_{\text{eff}} = \frac{75\%}{M + 1}$$

One attractive feature of this streamlined formula is that it yields a reasonable value for single-member district systems: 37.5 per cent. This is remarkably close to the 35 per cent estimated by me. Because my formula (together with the special proviso that $T_{\text{eff}} = 35\%$ for $M = 1$) is so similar to the simplified formula suggested by Taagepera, it makes very little difference which of the two is used. For instance, the use of the streamlined, instead of my, T_{eff} in the regression analyses in Chs. 5 and 6 yields virtually identical results.

30. Moreover, if a small party's support is geographically concentrated, it may be proportionally represented or even overrepresented in spite of failing to reach the effective threshold.

31. For FRA3, the 12 per cent legal threshold is an average of a gradually increasing percentage: 5 per cent of the district vote in the 1958 and 1962 elections, about 13.3 per cent in the three elections from 1967 to 1973 (legally defined as 10 per cent of the eligible voters), and about 16.7 per cent in 1978 and 1981 (12.5 per cent of the eligible voters). For FRA6 (the 1988 election), the threshold remained the same as in 1978 and 1981.

32. For very large magnitudes, the T_{eff} equation tends to yield rather low values because of the assumption that the number of parties (p) is about the same as the district magnitude. For the Israeli case, a more reasonable assumption would be that p is, say, 25. This would yield an effective threshold of about 0.8 per cent.

33. The sum of all remaining votes is divided by the sum of the remaining seats plus 1. This (Droop) quota is divided into the remainders of each party, and parties receive a remaining seat for each full Droop quota; any still remaining seats go to the parties with the largest remainders. This method makes it possible in principle, but unlikely in practice, for a party with a large remainder to win more than one remaining seat. See Panayote Elias Dimitras, *Greek Opinion*, Special Issue (Athens: EURODIM, April 1989), 17.

34. How close actual voter-representative contacts are likely to be also depends on population size: they may be closer in small PR countries

than in large countries that use single-member districts. For instance, the average Swiss district contains about a quarter of a million people compared with more than twice this number in the average single-member district in the United States.

35. The (average) numbers of adjustments seats are: 11 (ICE1), 11.22 (ICE2), 162 (GER1), 245 (GER2), 249.13 (GER3), 249 (GER5), 39.29 (SWE3), 8 (NOR3), 40 (DEN2 and DEN3), 37.50 (DEN1), and 4 (MAL3). Belgium uses a variable number of adjustment seats that equals the seats unallocated by LR-Hare at the lower level. In this respect, it superficially resembles the remainder-transfer systems, but because all votes and seats, not just the remaining ones, are used at the higher level, BEL1 firmly belongs to the adjustment-seats type.

36. GRE5 uses LR-Hare with some additional advantages for very small parties, but it also has a third, national, tier (ignored in Table 2.4 because it has only 12 out of the total of 300 seats) in which the seats are allocated as in a separate mini-assembly—which clearly does not help the very small parties.

37. Remo Zanella, 'The Maltese Electoral System and Its Distorting Effects', *Electoral Studies*, 9 (1990), 205–15. Iceland's lower-tier formula in 1987 is also a rough estimate. The eight districts use quotas that are close to, but slightly lower than, the usual LR quotas: the Droop quota in six districts, the normal Imperiali quota in one district, and something like a doubly reinforced Imperiali quota— $v/(M + 4)$—in the largest district (Reykjavik). The average of these approximates the normal LR-Imperiali formula and, further averaged with the d'Hondt formula in the preceding eight elections, the final average most resembles d'Hondt. In any case, this lower-tier formula is overridden by the d'Hondt formula at the upper tier.

38. Even the large number of adjustment seats in Germany has often not been sufficient—a problem solved by allowing parties to keep their so-called *Überhangmandate*, seats won at the lower tier that a party would not be entitled to according to the proportional allocation at the upper level. I have included these *Überhangmandate*, of which never more than five have been awarded in any election, among the adjustment seats.

39. Taagepera and Shugart, following a different line of reasoning, estimate the effective magnitude for Belgium to be 12 seats, which converts, according to their formula, into an effective threshold of 4.2 per cent—reasonably close to my estimate of 4.8 per cent; see their *Seats and Votes*, 127–8.

40. The general formula for the LV threshold of exclusion is $100v\%/(v + M)$, in which v is the number of votes each voter can cast and M is the district magnitude; see Arend Lijphart, Rafael López Pintor, and Yasunori Sone, 'The Limited Vote and the Single Nontransferable Vote: Lessons from the Japanese and Spanish Examples', in

Grofman and Lijphart (eds.), *Electoral Laws and their Political Consequences*, 157–8. See also Sigeki Nisihira, 'Les Élections générales au Japon depuis la guerre', *Revue française de science politique*, 21 (1971), 772–89.

41. In dichotomous comparisons of the less proportional PR formulas (d'Hondt and LR-Imperiali) with the more proportional PR formulas (all others), LV, SNTV, and STV will all be counted in the latter category. Only if the larger parties nominate the optimal number of candidates and achieve an even distribution of votes among their candidates, does SNTV resemble d'Hondt; see Gary W. Cox, 'SNTV and d'Hondt are "Equivalent"', *Electoral Studies*, 10 (1991), 118–32. Under similar unrealistic assumptions, this also applies to STV; see App. A.

42. The other two Greek electoral systems (GRE3E and GRE5), described in Tables 2.3 and 2.4, are also already systems that are relatively difficult to classify and to compare with the other electoral systems. The seven similarly complex systems used in the 1946–64 elections, prior to the seven-year military dictatorship, were excluded according to the formal criteria stated in Ch. 1. In addition, however, I considered it prudent to exclude them on practical grounds—in order not to give too much weight to these idiosyncratic systems (seven from 1946 to 1964 and five from 1974 to 1990) in the total set of electoral systems examined in this study. Detailed descriptions of the Greek electoral systems since 1926 may be found in Panayote Elias Dimitras, 'Electoral Systems in Greece', paper presented at the XVth World Congress of the International Political Science Association, Buenos Aires, 1991.

43. One of the many special provisions in the Greek electoral laws for the 1974–81 elections was that the 17 per cent threshold was raised to 25 per cent for two-party coalitions and to 30 per cent for coalitions of more than two parties. The term 'coalition' refers to a joint list presented by two or more parties (not to *apparentements*). Whether or not a party was in fact a 'disguised coalition' was a judicial decision. See Phaedo Vegleris, 'Greek Electoral Law', in Howard R. Penniman (ed.), *Greece at the Polls: The National Elections of 1974 and 1977* (Washington, DC: American Enterprise Institute, 1981), 34–5.

44. These estimates are quite close to the actual numbers of seats allocated at the four levels in 1974: 186, 93, 9, and 12; see Richard Clogg, *Parties and Elections in Greece: The Search for Legitimacy* (London: Hurst, 1987), 196–7.

45. This change was partly counteracted by special bonuses for the largest parties at the third tier; hence it may be more accurate to characterize the third-tier formula as a mixture of plurality and d'Hondt. However, this does not change the formula for the whole GRE4 system as one that approximates d'Hondt.

46. The election results at the district level may be found in André Siegfried, *L'Année politique 1951* (Paris: Presses Universitaires de France, 1952), 719–39, and in the corresponding yearbook for 1956, 547–72.
47. With the tiny exception, noted earlier, of a few districts in the United States.
48. The cumulative vote resembles multi-member district plurality in which each voter has as many votes as the district magnitude, but, unlike plurality, the voter is allowed to cumulate his or her vote on one or a few of the candidates.
49. Rae, *Political Consequences*, 134–40.
50. Rein Taagepera, 'The Size of National Assemblies', *Social Science Research*, 1 (1972), 385–401; see also Taagepera and Shugart, *Seats and Votes*, 173–83.
51. As expected, the sizes of the lower or only houses of parliament (in the 1980s) and the sizes of the Euro-delegations of the twelve European Community members are closely correlated: the correlation coefficient is 0.96.
52. Without the reinforced and semi-PR systems, the mean and median thresholds of the other fifty-two PR systems are 5.8 and 5.0 per cent.
53. For the fifty-two unambiguous PR systems, the respective means are 5.5 and 6.2 per cent, and the medians 5.0 and 4.0 per cent.
54. Without the reinforced and semi-PR systems, the mean and median assembly sizes in the PR systems are about 194 and 150 members.
55. For the fifty-two PR systems without the reinforced and semi-PR cases, the respective means (215 and 167) are farther apart, but the medians are again 150 and 152.
56. Dieter Nohlen, 'Changes and Choices in Electoral Systems', in Arend Lijphart and Bernard Grofman (eds.), *Choosing an Electoral System: Issues and Alternatives* (New York: Praeger, 1984), 218.
57. I do not include Greece in this list because, while what may be called its 'effective' assembly size under reinforced PR increased from GRE1 to GRE2 (see Table 2.7), the formal total membership was always 300. France was the only country that substantially *reduced* the size of its legislature—but by less than 20 per cent—in the shift from the Fourth to the Fifth Republic.

3. DISPROPORTIONALITY, MULTIPARTISM, AND MAJORITY VICTORIES

1. Douglas W. Rae, *The Political Consequences of Electoral Laws* (2nd edn., New Haven, Conn.: Yale University Press, 1971), 84–6.
2. Richard S. Katz, *A Theory of Parties and Electoral Systems* (Baltimore: Johns Hopkins University Press, 1980), 140.

3. John Loosemore and Victor J. Hanby, 'The Theoretical Limits of Maximum Distortion: Some Analytic Expressions for Electoral Systems', *British Journal of Political Science*, 1 (1971), 467–77. The index is used in such major works as Rein Taagepera and Matthew S. Shugart, *Seats and Votes: The Effects and Determinants of Electoral Systems* (New Haven, Conn.: Yale University Press, 1989), esp. 104–11, and Thomas T. Mackie and Richard Rose, *The International Almanac of Electoral History* (3rd edn., London: Macmillan, 1991), esp. 510–11. I have also used it myself as the main index of disproportionality in 'The Political Consequences of Electoral Laws, 1945–85', *American Political Science Review*, 84 (1990), 481–96. Instead of using the negative Loosemore–Hanby index in its original form, Mackie and Rose prefer to think more positively in terms of an index of proportionality by subtracting the value of the Loosemore–Hanby index from 100 per cent. For critiques of the Mackie–Rose index and, by implication, the Loosemore–Hanby index, see William P. Irvine, 'Measuring the Effects of Regionalism', *Electoral Studies*, 7 (1988), 15–26; and Vanessa Fry and Iain McLean, 'A Note on Rose's Proportionality Index', *Electoral Studies*, 10 (1991), 52–9.

4. Michael Gallagher, 'Proportionality, Disproportionality and Electoral Systems', *Electoral Studies*, 10 (1991), 38–40.

5. These two indices are illustrated in Arend Lijphart, 'The Field of Electoral Systems Research: A Critical Survey', *Electoral Studies*, 4 (1985), 9–12; see also id., *Democracies: Patterns of Majoritarian and Consensus Government in Twenty-One Countries* (New Haven, Conn.: Yale University Press, 1984), 160–5. For additional indices, see Gallagher, 'Proportionality, Disproportionality', 38–43.

6. Gallagher, 'Proportionality, Disproportionality', 33–51; Gary W. Cox and Matthew S. Shugart, 'Comment on Gallagher's "Proportionality, Disproportionality and Electoral Systems"', *Electoral Studies*, 10 (1991), 348–52.

7. Cox and Shugart, 'Comment', 350 (italics in the original).

8. Since pure Sainte-Laguë is as proportional as LR-Hare (see App. A), an index of proportionality based on its definition would be a good alternative but, for the very reason that its results are so similar to LR-Hare, it is not an alternative that will produce strikingly different values.

9. Cox and Shugart, 'Comment', 350.

10. Rae, *Political Consequences*, 55–6.

11. Markku Laakso and Rein Taagepera, ' "Effective" Number of Parties: A Measure with Application to West Europe', *Comparative Political Studies*, 12 (1979), 3–27.

12. John K. Wildgen, 'The Measurement of Hyperfractionalization', *Comparative Political Studies*, 4 (1971), 233–43; Juan Molinar,

'Counting the Number of Parties: An Alternative Index', *American Political Science Review*, 85 (1991), 1383–91.

13. I am indebted to Rein Taagepera for pointing out this weakness of the Molinar index and for the numerical example.
14. Maurice Duverger, *Political Parties: Their Organization and Activity in the Modern State* (New York: Wiley, 1963), esp. 226; Rae, *Political Consequences*, 67–8.
15. Rae, *Political Consequences*, 74–5.
16. Ibid. 75.
17. In fact, I have done so myself—on the ground that the two parties form a common caucus in the Bundestag; Lijphart, *Democracies*, 115–16. On the other hand, the two parties have clearly separate and independent party organizations.
18. Mackie and Rose, *International Almanac of Electoral History*.
19. The only notable exception is the considerably stronger correlation between the Rae index and the effective number of elective parties in the seventy electoral systems: −0.32 (significant at the 1 per cent level).
20. The extent to which state laws protect the two-party system by discriminating against third parties is detailed in Kay Lawson, 'How State Laws Undermine Parties', in A. James Reichley (ed.), *Elections American Style* (Washington, DC: Brookings, 1987), 243–7.

4. CHANGES IN ELECTION RULES BETWEEN SYSTEMS IN THE SAME COUNTRY

1. Neil J. Smelser, 'Notes on the Methodology of Comparative Analysis of Economic Activity', in *Transactions of the Sixth World Congress of Sociology* (Evian: International Sociological Association, 1967), ii. 113; see also Arend Lijphart, 'The Comparable-Cases Strategy in Comparative Research', *Comparative Political Studies*, 8 (1975), 158–77.
2. As before, only significant (20 per cent or greater) changes in threshold and assembly size were considered.
3. Matthew S. Shugart makes the same operational decision and uses the same justification in his 'Electoral Reform in Systems of Proportional Representation', *European Journal of Political Research*, 21 (1992), 216–17.
4. Giovanni Sartori, 'The Influence of Electoral Systems: Faulty Laws or Faulty Methods?', in Bernard Grofman and Arend Lijphart (eds.), *Electoral Laws and their Political Consequences* (New York: Agathon Press, 1986), 54–5. In an earlier analysis, I unfairly criticized Sartori's distinction by focusing exclusively on the effect of PR systems on

elective multipartism instead of multipartism in parliament; see Arend Lijphart, 'The Political Consequences of Electoral Laws, 1945–85', *American Political Science Review*, 84 (1990), 493.

5. Maurice Duverger, *Political Parties: Their Organization and Activity in the Modern State* (New York: Wiley, 1963), 226.

6. Shugart, 'Electoral Reform', 207–24.

5. BIVARIATE AND MULTIVARIATE ANALYSES

1. André Blais and R. K. Carty, 'The Psychological Impact of Electoral Laws: Measuring Duverger's Elusive Factor', *British Journal of Political Science*, 21 (1991), 79–93.

2. Strictly speaking, there is still a modest incentive to strategic voting in France if a voter is less interested in voting for the candidate he or she sincerely prefers than in influencing which top candidates will remain in the running, given the well-known fact that allied parties frequently agree to withdraw their weaker candidate. Similarly, some disincentive to vote for a favourite but weak party exists in list PR systems, when voters are afraid to waste their votes. Strategic behaviour is completely unnecessary in preferential systems (the alternative vote and STV)—although even here, admittedly only in rare situations, voters can help a more favourite (but not first choice) candidate win against a less favourite one by tactically not voting for either, that is, by truncating their preferences when they fill out their ballots; see Steven J. Brams and Peter C. Fishburn, 'Some Logical Defects of the Single Transferable Vote', in Arend Lijphart and Bernard Grofman (eds.), *Choosing an Electoral System: Issues and Alternatives* (New York: Praeger, 1984), 148–50; and Michael Dummett, *Voting Procedures* (Oxford: Clarendon Press, 1984), 210–30.

3. This finding confirms the conclusions of André Blais and R. K. Carty, 'The Impact of Electoral Formulae on the Creation of Majority Governments', *Electoral Studies*, 6 (1987), 209–18.

4. In addition, the validity and robustness of the regressions reported in Tables 5.9 to 5.11 were checked for the potential disturbing effect of one influential case by replicating the regressions with one case being dropped at a time; these checks all yielded negative results. I am grateful to Nathaniel L. Beck for his assistance with this task; for the procedure used, see Nathaniel L. Beck and Jonathan N. Katz, 'Model Assessment and Choice Via Cross-Validation', paper presented at the Annual Meeting of the American Political Science Association, Chicago, 1992.

5. The complete list of consolidations is as follows: AUL1 to 3; CR1 and 2; DEN1 to 3; FRA1 and 5; FRA3 and 6; GER1 to 3; GRE1, 2, and

4; ICE1 and 2; IND1 and 2; ISR1 and 3; ITA2 and 3; MAL1 and 2; and NET1 and 2.

6. FOUR OTHER POTENTIAL EXPLANATIONS

1. Douglas W. Rae, *The Political Consequences of Electoral Laws* (2nd edn., New Haven, Conn.: Yale University Press, 1971), 126.
2. Ibid. 127.
3. Jürgen Dittberner, *FDP—Partei der zweiten Wahl: Ein Beitrag zur Geschichte der liberalen Partei und ihrer Funktionen im Parteiensystem der Bundesrepublik* (Opladen: Westdeutscher Verlag, 1987); Geoffrey K. Roberts, 'The "Second-Vote" Campaign Strategy of the West German Free Democratic Party', *European Journal of Political Research*, 16 (1988), 317–37.
4. With the usual exception that for the set of all sixty-nine electoral systems, the electoral formula (PR dummy) was excluded because of its strong correlation with the effective threshold.
5. Michael Gallagher, 'Proportionality, Disproportionality and Electoral Systems', *Electoral Studies*, 10 (1991), 45.
6. Ibid.
7. Matthew S. Shugart and John M. Carey, *Presidents and Assemblies: Constitutional Design and Electoral Dynamics* (Cambridge: Cambridge University Press, 1992), 206–58.
8. Maurice Duverger, 'Duverger's Law: Forty Years Later', in Bernard Grofman and Arend Lijphart (eds.), *Electoral Laws and their Political Consequences* (New York: Agathon Press, 1986), 81–2.
9. Martin Harrop and William L. Miller, *Elections and Voters: A Comparative Introduction* (London: Macmillan, 1987), 66.
10. Robert A. Newland, *Comparative Electoral Systems* (London: Arthur McDougall Fund, 1982), 57.
11. Enid Lakeman, *How Democracies Vote: A Study of Electoral Systems* (4th edn., London: Faber and Faber, 1974), 98.
12. In Finland, a 'party alliance' means a joint list and is therefore not an *apparentement*; proposals to allow so-called 'electoral rings', which would be true *apparentements*, have been repeatedly rejected. See Klaus Törnudd, *The Electoral System of Finland* (London: Hugh Evelyn, 1968), 47–9, 141–3.
13. In future analyses, it may be worth trying to make adjustments for how liberal or restrictive the *apparentement* provisions are. For instance, the Swiss rules are very permissive, but the Israeli rules restrict *apparentements* to not more than two parties, and these two parties can benefit only if they independently cross the electoral threshold.

7. ELECTORAL ENGINEERING: LIMITS AND POSSIBILITIES

1. Giovanni Sartori, 'Political Development and Political Engineering', in John D. Montgomery and Albert O. Hirschman (eds.), *Public Policy*, xii (Cambridge, Mass.: Harvard University Press, 1968), 273.
2. In addition to permitting representation of self-identified minorities, PR can also give special favours to predetermined minorities, such as the ethnic minorities whose parties, according to the German electoral law, are exempt from the 5 per cent threshold.
3. Arend Lijphart, 'Constitutional Choices for New Democracies', *Journal of Democracy*, 2 (1991), 72–84.
4. G. Bingham Powell, Jr., 'Constitutional Design and Citizen Electoral Control', *Journal of Theoretical Politics*, 1 (1989), 107–30.
5. See S. E. Finer (ed.), *Adversary Politics and Electoral Reform* (London: Anthony Wigram, 1975); and id., 'Adversary Politics and the Eighties', *Electoral Studies*, 1 (1982), 221–30.
6. The higher-level seats in the multiple-tier system in Greece, used in the first elections after redemocratization, were not adjustment seats (see Chapter 2); however, multiple tiers and adjustment seats were used in several pre-Second World War elections.
7. A valid objection to this proposal for Ireland, where transfers often cross party lines, is that it would count the votes of some small-party supporters twice: these votes may be transferred to, and help elect, a major-party candidate in the district, but also work for the small party itself at the national level.
8. The Maltese arrangement is reminiscent of, but different from, the Scelba Law which was in effect for the 1953 election in Italy but never became operative: it provided that any party or alliance winning more than 50 per cent of the vote would get a huge 'working majority' of almost 65 per cent of the seats; see W. J. M. Mackenzie, *Free Elections: An Elementary Textbook* (London: Allen and Unwin, 1958), 91–2.
9. To my knowledge, the only previous proposal of this kind was made by Ferdinand A. Hermens, 'Representation and Proportional Representation', in Arend Lijphart and Bernard Grofman (eds.), *Choosing an Electoral System: Issues and Alternatives* (New York: Praeger, 1984), 29.
10. An element of arbitrariness obviously remains in that the exact percentage that is selected entails an arbitrary choice. Even when, say, an approximately 4 per cent threshold is generally regarded as fair, should the threshold be exactly 4 per cent, or rather 3.75 or 4.5 per cent, or still another percentage?
11. This suggestion could be extended to all except closed-list PR systems

if, in practice, the voters effectively decide which individual candidates are elected.

12. Donald L. Horowitz, *A Democratic South Africa: Constitutional Engineering in a Divided Society* (Berkeley, Calif.: University of California Press, 1991), 172–3.

APPENDIX A. PROPORTIONAL REPRESENTATION FORMULAS

1. Since this study focuses on the election and representation of parties instead of individual candidates, the divisor–quota contrast is the most important criterion for formally classifying list PR systems. However, an alternative classification, based on the degree of voters' influence on the selection of candidates within lists, contrasts closed-list PR (where the voters cannot change the order of the candidates' names on the list, as in Germany and Israel) with open-list PR (where the election of candidates from a list depends entirely on the voters' expressed preferences, as in Finland) and several intermediate, partly open-list, arrangements (for instance, in Belgium and The Netherlands).

2. A useful short cut, especially for districts with many more than the six seats in this example, is first to award all parties the numbers of seats that equal their Droop quotas (to be explained shortly), and then to continue by using the number of seats already won plus 1 as the next divisor. This procedure is called the Hagenbach-Bischoff method; its results are always identical to those of the d'Hondt formula.

3. This method of calculating the results of LR-Hare is also referred to, especially in Germany, as the Hare–Niemeyer method; see Dieter Nohlen, *Wahlrecht und Parteiensystem: Über die politischen Auswirkungen von Wahlsystemen* (Opladen: Leske, 1990), 84–87.

4. More precisely, the d'Hondt quota is usually not a fixed number but rather any number in the range between the last 'average' to which a seat is awarded and the next 'average' to which the next seat would be awarded (if such a seat were available). In the example of Table A.1, any quota from 13,001 to 13,667 will yield exactly six full d'Hondt quotas to the parties—the same number as the number of seats in the district. In fact, the d'Hondt quota is a fixed number only in the highly unusual situation of two parties being tied for the last seat.

5. The d'Hondt formula's hostility to small parties can also be seen as a consequence of its unique quality (among the list PR formulas in actual use) that its rules never encourage a party to split or to present more than one list as a tactical ploy. For instance, for the same party system as in Tables A.1 and A.2 and a five-member district, LR-Hare yields a seat distribution of 2, 1, 1, and 1. However, if party *B* had presented two separate lists, each receiving 14,500 votes, it would have won an extra seat (at the expense of party *D*). Under d'Hondt a party can never benefit from splitting its vote.

6. In continental Europe, the $v/(s + 1)$ Droop quota is often called the Hagenbach–Bischoff quota. In mass elections, where v is measured in thousands of votes, the difference between the two Droop quotas is so tiny that we can safely ignore it.

7. As Michael Gallagher has pointed out, a large party can achieve a better result if its voters spread their votes evenly among its candidates and if all transferred votes are transferred evenly, too; see his 'Comparing Proportional Representation Electoral Systems: Quotas, Thresholds, Paradoxes and Majorities', *British Journal of Political Science*, 22 (1992), 482. In the example of Table A.3, if party A's candidates P and Q, after receiving R's transfer votes, would have 21 and 20 votes each, they would both be elected (and party C's candidate U would not win). In fact, under the assumption that all of a party's candidates always receive equal support, STV-Droop (or, for that matter, STV-Hare) produces outcomes similar to d'Hondt's, but this is obviously a feat that is very difficult for parties to achieve and hence a rather unrealistic assumption.

8. As noted earlier, this classification cuts across the difference between divisor and quota systems. In one substantive respect, however, the two do differ. All LR formulas suffer from the so-called Alabama paradox—the possibility that when the total number of seats in a district is increased by one, one of the parties may actually lose a seat. In our illustrative four-party and LR-Hare system, this happens to party C when the district magnitude is increased from eight to nine: in the eight-member district it wins 2 seats, but only 1 in a nine-member district. Divisor systems are free from this defect because they award seats sequentially; hence adding a seat to the total of the available seats in a district cannot change the allocation of seats that have already been allocated to the parties in previous steps. The Alabama paradox has received the greatest attention in the context of apportionment, that is, the assignment of legislative seats to districts rather than the allocation of district seats to parties (although the two processes are conceptually identical); see Michel L. Balinski and H. Peyton Young, *Fair Representation: Meeting the Ideal of One Man, One Vote* (New Haven, Conn.: Yale University Press, 1982), 38–42; and Steven J. Brams, *Paradoxes in Politics: An Introduction to the Nonobvious in Political Science* (New York: Free Press, 1976), 137–66.

APPENDIX C. DATA: SOURCES, ADDITIONS, CORRECTIONS, CLARIFICATIONS

1. Keith Hill, 'Belgium: Political Change in a Segmented Society', in Richard Rose (ed.), *Electoral Behavior: A Comparative Handbook* (New York: Free Press, 1974), 101–2. See also Wilfried Dewachter, 'Changes

in a Particratie: The Belgian Party System from 1944 to 1986', in Hans Daalder (ed.), *Party Systems in Denmark, Austria, Switzerland, the Netherlands, and Belgium* (London: Frances Pinter, 1987), 294–5.

2. The results of the ten elections from 1953 to 1990 are based on the seven official volumes of statistics entitled *Computo de votos y declaratorias de elección para Presidente y Vicepresidentes, Diputados a la Asamblea Legislativa, Regidores y Síndicos Municipales* (San José: Tribunal Supremo de Elecciones, República de Costa Rica), published since 1969.

3. V. B. Singh and Shankar Bose, *Elections in India: Data Handbook on Lok Sabha Elections, 1952–85* (New Delhi: Sage, 1986). See also David Butler, Ashok Lahiri, and Prannoy Roy, *India Decides: Elections 1952–1991* (New Delhi: Living Media India, 1991).

4. The adjusted numbers of votes are based on the constituency-level data in F. W. S. Craig (ed.), *British Parliamentary Election Results, 1918–1949* (London: Macmillan, 1977).

5. Since the 1979 European election result as presented in *Europe Votes 2* includes Northern Ireland and since the Northern Ireland votes and seats are not provided separately in this volume, they have to be subtracted on the basis of the Northern Ireland data supplied in F. W. S. Craig and T. T. Mackie, *Europe Votes 1: European Parliamentary Election Results 1979* (Chichester, West Sussex: Parliamentary Research Services, 1980), 126–7.

Bibliography

BALINSKI, MICHEL L., and YOUNG, H. PEYTON, *Fair Representation: Meeting the Ideal of One Man, One Vote* (New Haven, Conn.: Yale University Press, 1982).

BECK, NATHANIEL L., and KATZ, JONATHAN N., 'Model Assessment and Choice Via Cross-Validation', paper presented at the Annual Meeting of the American Political Science Association, Chicago, 1992.

BIRKE, WOLFGANG, *European Elections by Direct Suffrage: A Comparative Study of the Electoral Systems Used in Western Europe and their Utility for the Direct Election of a European Parliament* (Leiden: Sythoff, 1961).

BLAIS, ANDRÉ, 'The Classification of Electoral Systems', *European Journal of Political Research*, 16 (1988), 99–110.

—— 'The Debate over Electoral Systems', *International Political Science Review*, 12 (1991), 239–60.

—— and CARTY, R. K., 'The Impact of Electoral Formulae on the Creation of Majority Governments', *Electoral Studies*, 6 (1987), 209–18.

—— and —— 'The Psychological Impact of Electoral Laws: Measuring Duverger's Elusive Factor', *British Journal of Political Science*, 21 (1991), 79–93.

BOGDANOR, VERNON, 'Direct Elections, Representative Democracy and European Integration', *Electoral Studies*, 8 (1989), 205–16.

—— *What is Proportional Representation? A Guide to the Issues* (Oxford: Martin Robertson, 1984).

—— and BUTLER, DAVID (eds.), *Democracy and Elections: Electoral Systems and their Political Consequences* (Cambridge: Cambridge University Press, 1983).

BRAMS, STEVEN J., *Paradoxes in Politics: An Introduction to the Nonobvious in Political Science* (New York: Free Press, 1976).

—— and FISHBURN, PETER C., 'Some Logical Defects of the Single Transferable Vote', in Arend Lijphart and Bernard Grofman (eds.), *Choosing an Electoral System: Issues and Alternatives* (New York: Praeger, 1984), 147–51.

BRAUNIAS, KARL, *Das parlamentarische Wahlrecht: Ein Handbuch über die Bildung der gesetzgebenden Körperschaften in Europa* (Berlin: De Gruyter, 1932), 2 vols.

BUTLER, DAVID, 'Electoral Systems', in David Butler, Howard R. Penniman, and Austin Ranney (eds.), *Democracy at the Polls: A Comparative*

196 Bibliography

Study of Competitive National Elections (Washington, DC: American Enterprise Institute, 1981), 7–25.

BUTLER, DAVID, PENNIMAN, HOWARD R., and RANNEY, AUSTIN (eds.), *Democracy at the Polls: A Comparative Study of Competitive National Elections* (Washington, DC: American Enterprise Institute, 1981).

—— LAHIRI, ASHOK, and ROY, PRANNOY, *India Decides: Elections 1952–1991* (New Delhi: Living Media India, 1991).

CADART, JACQUES (ed.), *Les Modes de scrutin des dix-huit pays libres de l'Europe occidentale: leurs résultats et leurs effets comparés, élections nationales et européennes* (Paris: Presses Universitaires de France, 1983).

CARSTAIRS, ANDREW MCLAREN, *A Short History of Electoral Systems in Western Europe* (London: Allen and Unwin, 1980).

CLOGG, RICHARD, *Parties and Elections in Greece: The Search for Legitimacy* (London: Hurst, 1987).

COMMONS, JOHN R., *Proportional Representation* (2nd edn., New York: Crowell, 1907).

COTTERET, JEAN-MARIE, and EMERI, CLAUDE, *Les Systèmes électoraux* (4th edn., Paris: Presses Universitaires de France, 1983).

COX, GARY W., 'SNTV and d'Hondt are "Equivalent"', *Electoral Studies*, 10 (1991), 118–32.

—— and SHUGART, MATTHEW S., 'Comment on Gallagher's "Proportionality, Disproportionality and Electoral Systems"', *Electoral Studies*, 10 (1991), 348–52.

—— and NIOU, EMERSON, 'Seat Bonuses Under the Single Non-Transferable Vote System: Evidence from Japan and Taiwan', *Comparative Politics*, 26 (1993), forthcoming.

CRAIG, F. W. S. (ed.), *British Parliamentary Election Results, 1918–1949* (London: Macmillan, 1977).

—— and MACKIE, T. T., *Europe Votes 1: European Parliamentary Election Results 1979* (Chichester, West Sussex: Parliamentary Research Services, 1980).

DEWACHTER, WILFRIED, 'Changes in a Particratie: The Belgian Party System from 1944 to 1986', in Hans Daalder (ed.), *Party Systems in Denmark, Austria, Switzerland, the Netherlands, and Belgium* (London: Frances Pinter, 1987), 285–364.

DIMITRAS, PANAYOTE ELIAS, *Greek Opinion*, Special Issue (Athens: EURODIM, Apr. 1989).

—— 'Electoral Systems in Greece', paper presented at the XVth World Congress of the International Political Science Association, Buenos Aires, 1991.

DITTBERNER, JÜRGEN, *FDP—Partei der zweiten Wahl: Ein Beitrag zur Geschichte der liberalen Partei und ihrer Funktionen im Parteiensystem der Bundesrepublik* (Opladen: Westdeutscher Verlag, 1987).

DUMMETT, MICHAEL, *Voting Procedures* (Oxford: Clarendon Press, 1984).

DUVERGER, MAURICE, *Political Parties: Their Organization and Activity in the Modern State* (New York: Wiley, 1963).

—— 'Duverger's Law: Forty Years Later', in Bernard Grofman and Arend Lijphart (eds.), *Electoral Laws and their Political Consequences* (New York: Agathon Press, 1986), 69–84.

ELKLIT, JØRGEN, 'Simpler than its Reputation: The Electoral System in Denmark since 1920', *Electoral Studies*, 12 (1993), 40–57.

FINER, S. E. (ed.), *Adversary Politics and Electoral Reform* (London: Anthony Wigram, 1975).

—— 'Adversary Politics and the Eighties', *Electoral Studies*, 1 (1982), 221–30.

FRY, VANESSA, and MCLEAN, IAIN, 'A Note on Rose's Proportionality Index', *Electoral Studies*, 10 (1991), 52–9.

GALLAGHER, MICHAEL, 'Proportionality, Disproportionality and Electoral Systems', *Electoral Studies*, 10 (1991), 33–51.

—— 'Comparing Proportional Representation Electoral Systems: Quotas, Thresholds, Paradoxes and Majorities', *British Journal of Political Science*, 22 (1992), 469–96.

GROFMAN, BERNARD, 'A Review of Macro Election Systems', in Rudolf Wildenmann (ed.), *Sozialwissenschaftliches Jahrbuch für Politik* (Munich: Günter Olzog Verlag, 1975), iv. 303–52.

—— and LIJPHART, AREND (eds.), *Electoral Laws and their Political Consequences* (New York: Agathon Press, 1986).

GRUMM, JOHN G., 'Theories of Electoral Systems', *Midwest Journal of Political Science*, 2 (1958), 357–76.

GUDGIN, G., and TAYLOR, P. J., *Seats, Votes, and the Spatial Organisation of Elections* (London: Pion, 1979).

HALLETT, GEORGE H., Jr., *Proportional Representation: The Key to Democracy* (Washington, DC: National Home Library Foundation, 1937).

HAND, GEOFFREY, GEORGEL, JACQUES, and SASSE, CHRISTOPH (eds.), *European Electoral Systems Handbook* (London: Butterworths, 1979).

HARROP, MARTIN, and MILLER, WILLIAM L., *Elections and Voters: A Comparative Introduction* (London: Macmillan, 1987).

HERMENS, FERDINAND A., *Democracy or Anarchy? A Study of Proportional Representation* (Notre Dame, Ind.: University of Notre Dame Press, 1941).

—— 'Representation and Proportional Representation', in Arend Lijphart and Bernard Grofman (eds.), *Choosing an Electoral System: Issues and Alternatives* (New York: Praeger, 1984), 15–30.

HILL, KEITH, 'Belgium: Political Change in a Segmented Society', in Richard Rose (ed.), *Electoral Behavior: A Comparative Handbook* (New York: Free Press, 1974), 29–107.

HOGAN, JAMES, *Election and Representation* (Cork: Cork University Press, 1945).

HOROWITZ, DONALD L., *A Democratic South Africa: Constitutional Engineering in a Divided Society* (Berkeley, Calif.: University of California Press, 1991).

HORWILL, GEORGE, *Proportional Representation: Its Dangers and Defects* (London: Allen and Unwin, 1925).

HUMPHREYS, JOHN H., *Proportional Representation: A Study in Methods of Election* (London: Methuen, 1911).

IRVINE, WILLIAM P., 'Measuring the Effects of Regionalism', *Electoral Studies*, 7 (1988), 15–26.

JANSON, CARL-GUNNAR, *Mandattilldelning och regional röstfördelning* (Stockholm: Idun, 1961).

JESSE, ECKHARD, *Wahlrecht zwischen Kontinuität und Reform: Eine Analyse der Wahlsystemdiskussion und der Wahlrechtsänderungen in der Bundesrepublik Deutschland, 1949–1983* (Düsseldorf: Droste, 1985).

—— *Elections: The Federal Republic of Germany in Comparison* (New York: Berg, 1990).

JOHNSTON, R. J., *Political, Electoral, and Spatial Systems: An Essay in Political Geography* (Oxford: Clarendon Press, 1979).

KATZ, RICHARD S., *A Theory of Parties and Electoral Systems* (Baltimore: Johns Hopkins University Press, 1980).

LAAKSO, MARKKU, 'Thresholds for Proportional Representation: Reanalyzed and Extended', in Manfred J. Holler (ed.), *The Logic of Multiparty Systems* (Dordrecht: Kluwer Academic Publishers, 1987), 383–90.

—— and TAAGEPERA, REIN, ' "Effective" Number of Parties: A Measure with Application to West Europe', *Comparative Political Studies*, 12 (1979), 3–27.

LAKEMAN, ENID, *How Democracies Vote: A Study of Electoral Systems* (4th edn., London: Faber and Faber, 1974).

—— *Power to Elect: The Case for Proportional Representation* (London: Heinemann, 1982).

LANCELOT, MARIE-THÉRÈSE, and LANCELOT, ALAIN, *Atlas des circonscriptions électorales en France depuis 1875* (Paris: Presses de la Fondation Nationale des Sciences Politiques, 1970).

LAWSON, KAY, 'How State Laws Undermine Parties', in A. James Reichley (ed.), *Elections American Style* (Washington, DC: Brookings, 1987), 240–60.

LEONARD, DICK, and NATKIEL, RICHARD, *World Atlas of Elections: Voting Patterns in 39 Democracies* (London: Hodder and Stoughton, 1987).

LIJPHART, AREND, 'The Comparable-Cases Strategy in Comparative Research', *Comparative Political Studies*, 8 (1975), 158–77.

—— *Democracies: Patterns of Majoritarian and Consensus Government in Twenty-One Countries* (New Haven, Conn.: Yale University Press, 1984).

—— 'The Field of Electoral Systems Research: A Critical Survey', *Electoral Studies*, 4 (1985), 3–14.

—— 'Degrees of Proportionality of Proportional Representation Formulas', in Bernard Grofman and id. (eds.), *Electoral Laws and their Political Consequences* (New York: Agathon Press, 1986), 170–9.

—— 'Proportionality by Non-PR Methods: Ethnic Representation in Belgium, Cyprus, Lebanon, New Zealand, West Germany, and Zimbabwe', in Bernard Grofman and id. (eds.), *Electoral Laws and their Political Consequences* (New York: Agathon Press, 1986), 113–23.

—— 'The Political Consequences of Electoral Laws, 1945–85: A Critique, Re-Analysis, and Update of Rae's Classic Study', Paper Presented at the XIVth World Congress of the International Political Science Association, Washington, DC, 1988.

—— 'The Political Consequences of Electoral Laws, 1945–85', *American Political Science Review*, 84 (1990), 481–96.

—— 'Size, Pluralism, and the Westminster Model of Democracy: Implications for the Eastern Caribbean', in Jorge Heine (ed.), *A Revolution Aborted: The Lessons of Grenada* (Pittsburgh: University of Pittsburgh Press, 1990), 321–40.

—— 'Constitutional Choices for New Democracies', *Journal of Democracy*, 2 (1991), 72–84.

—— 'The Electoral Systems Researcher as Detective: Probing Rae's Suspect "Differential Proposition" on List Proportional Representation', in Dennis Kavanagh (ed.), *Electoral Politics* (Oxford: Clarendon Press, 1992), 234–46.

—— and GIBBERD, ROBERT W., 'Thresholds and Payoffs in List Systems of Proportional Representation', *European Journal of Political Research*, 5 (1977), 219–30.

—— and GROFMAN, BERNARD (eds.), *Choosing an Electoral System: Issues and Alternatives* (New York: Praeger, 1984).

—— LÓPEZ PINTOR, RAFAEL, and SONE, YASUNORI, 'The Limited Vote and the Single Nontransferable Vote: Lessons from the Japanese and Spanish Examples', in Bernard Grofman and Arend Lijphart (eds.), *Electoral Laws and their Political Consequences* (New York: Agathon Press, 1986), 154–69.

LOOSEMORE, JOHN, and HANBY, VICTOR J., 'The Theoretical Limits of Maximum Distortion: Some Analytic Expressions for Electoral Systems', *British Journal of Political Science*, 1 (1971), 467–77.

MACKENZIE, W. J. M., *Free Elections: An Elementary Textbook* (London: Allen and Unwin, 1958).

MACKIE, THOMAS T., *Europe Votes 3: European Parliamentary Election Results 1989* (Aldershot, Hants: Dartmouth, 1990).

—— 'General Elections in Western Nations During 1989', *European Journal of Political Research*, 19 (1991), 157–62.

MACKIE, THOMAS T. and CRAIG, F. W. S., *Europe Votes 2: European Parliamentary Election Results 1979–1984* (Chichester, West Sussex: Parliamentary Research Services, 1985).

—— and ROSE, RICHARD, *The International Almanac of Electoral History* (3rd edn., London: Macmillan, 1991).

McDONALD, RONALD H., *Party Systems and Elections in Latin America* (Chicago: Markham, 1971).

MERRILL, SAMUEL, *Making Multicandidate Elections More Democratic* (Princeton, NJ: Princeton University Press, 1988).

MOLINAR, JUAN, 'Counting the Number of Parties: An Alternative Index', *American Political Science Review*, 85 (1991), 1383–91.

MÜLLER, PETER FELIX, *Das Wahlsystem: Neue Wege der Grundlegung und Gestaltung* (Zurich: Polygraphischer Verlag, 1959).

NEWLAND, ROBERT A., *Comparative Electoral Systems* (London: Arthur McDougall Fund, 1982).

NISIHIRA, SIGEKI, 'Les Élections générales au Japon depuis la guerre', *Revue française de science politique*, 21 (1971), 772–89.

NOHLEN, DIETER, *Wahlsysteme der Welt—Daten und Analysen: Ein Handbuch* (Munich: Piper, 1978).

—— 'Changes and Choices in Electoral Systems', in Arend Lijphart and Bernard Grofman (eds.), *Choosing an Electoral System: Issues and Alternatives* (New York: Praeger, 1984), 217–24.

—— *Elections and Electoral Systems* (Bonn: Forschungsinstitut der Friedrich-Ebert-Stiftung, 1984).

—— *Wahlrecht und Parteiensystem: Über die politischen Auswirkungen von Wahlsystemen* (Opladen: Leske und Budrich, 1990).

—— (ed.), *Wahlen und Wahlpolitik in Lateinamerika* (Heidelberg: Esprint, 1984).

NURMI, HANNU, *Comparing Voting Systems* (Dordrecht: Reidel, 1987).

O'LOUGHLIN, J., 'District Size and Party Electoral Strength: A Comparison of Sixteen Democracies', *Environment and Planning A*, 12 (1980), 247–62.

POWELL, G. BINGHAM, Jr., 'Constitutional Design and Citizen Electoral Control', *Journal of Theoretical Politics*, 1 (1989), 107–30.

RAE, DOUGLAS W., *The Political Consequences of Electoral Laws* (New Haven, Conn.: Yale University Press, 1967).

—— *The Political Consequences of Electoral Laws* (2nd edn., New Haven, Conn.: Yale University Press, 1971).

REED, STEVEN R., 'Structure and Behaviour: Extending Duverger's Law to the Japanese Case', *British Journal of Political Science*, 20 (1990), 335–56.

REEVE, ANDREW, and WARE, ALAN, *Electoral Systems: A Comparative and Theoretical Introduction* (London: Routledge, 1992).

ROBERTS, GEOFFREY K., 'The "Second-Vote" Campaign Strategy of the

West German Free Democratic Party', *European Journal of Political Research*, 16 (1988), 317–37.

ROKKAN, STEIN, *Citizens, Elections, Parties: Approaches to the Comparative Study of the Processes of Development* (Oslo: Universitetsforlaget, 1970).

—— and MEYRIAT, JEAN (eds.), *International Guide to Electoral Statistics, i. National Elections in Western Europe* (The Hague: Mouton, 1969).

ROSE, RICHARD, 'Electoral Systems: A Question of Degree or of Principle?', in Arend Lijphart and Bernard Grofman (eds.), *Choosing an Electoral System: Issues and Alternatives* (New York: Praeger, 1984).

RUDDLE, KENNETH, and GILLETTE, PHILIP (eds.), *Latin American Political Statistics: Supplement to the Statistical Abstract of Latin America* (Los Angeles: Latin American Center, University of California, 1972).

SARTORI, GIOVANNI, 'Political Development and Political Engineering', in John D. Montgomery and Albert O. Hirschman (eds.), *Public Policy*, xii (Cambridge, Mass.: Harvard University Press, 1968), 261–98.

—— 'The Influence of Electoral Systems: Faulty Laws or Faulty Methods?', in Bernard Grofman and Arend Lijphart (eds.), *Electoral Laws and their Political Consequences* (New York: Agathon Press, 1986), 43–68.

SCHMITT, HERMANN, 'The European Elections of June 1989', *West European Politics*, 13 (1990), 116–23.

SHUGART, MATTHEW SOBERG, 'Duverger's Rule, District Magnitude, and Presidentialism' (Ph.D. diss., University of California, Irvine, 1988).

—— 'Electoral Reform in Systems of Proportional Representation', *European Journal of Political Research*, 21 (1992), 207–24.

—— and CAREY, JOHN M., *Presidents and Assemblies: Constitutional Design and Electoral Dynamics* (Cambridge: Cambridge University Press, 1992).

SIEGFRIED, ANDRÉ, *L'Année politique 1951* (Paris: Presses Universitaires de France, 1952).

—— *L'Année politique 1956* (Paris: Presses Universitaires de France, 1956).

SINGH, V. B., and BOSE, SHANKAR, *Elections in India: Data Handbook on Lok Sabha Elections, 1952–85* (New Delhi: Sage, 1986).

SMELSER, NEIL J., 'Notes on the Methodology of Comparative Analysis of Economic Activity', in *Transactions of the Sixth World Congress of Sociology* (Evian: International Sociological Association, 1967), ii. 101–17.

STERNBERGER, DOLF, and VOGEL, BERNHARD (eds.), *Die Wahl der Parlamente und anderer Staatsorgane: Ein Handbuch* (Berlin: De Gruyter, 1969), 2 vols.

TAAGEPERA, REIN, 'The Size of National Assemblies', *Social Science Research*, 1 (1972), 385–401.

—— 'Seats and Votes: A Generalization of the Cube Law of Elections', *Social Science Research*, 2 (1973), 257–75.

TAAGEPERA, REIN, 'Empirical Thresholds of Representation', *Electoral Studies*, 8 (1989), 105–16.

—— and SHUGART, MATTHEW S., *Seats and Votes: The Effects and Determinants of Electoral Systems* (New Haven, Conn.: Yale University Press, 1989).

TÖRNUDD, Klaus, *The Electoral System of Finland* (London: Hugh Evelyn, 1968).

Tribunal Supremo de Elecciones, República de Costa Rica, *Computo de votos y declaratorias de elección para Presidente y Vicepresidentes, Diputados a la Asamblea Legislativa, Regidores y Síndicos Municipales: 1953, 1958, 1962, 1966* (San José, 1969).

—— *Computo de votos y declaratorias de elección para Presidente y Vicepresidentes, Diputados a la Asamblea Legislativa, Regidores y Síndicos Municipales: elecciones del 1 de febrero de 1970, y elecciones municipales en los nuevos cantones de Upala, Los Chiles, Guatuso, La Cruz, Talamanca y Matina* (San José, 1970).

—— *Computo de votos y declaratorias de elección para Presidente y Vicepresidentes, Diputados a la Asamblea Legislativa, Regidores y Síndicos Municipales: elecciones del 3 de febrero de 1974, y elecciones municipales en el nuevo cantón de Corredores* (San José, 1974).

—— *Computo de votos y declaratorias de elección para Presidente y Vicepresidentes, Diputados a la Asamblea Legislativa, Regidores y Síndicos Municipales: elecciones del 5 de febrero de 1978* (San José, 1978).

—— *Computo de votos y declaratorias de elección para Presidente y Vicepresidentes, Diputados a la Asamblea Legislativa, Regidores y Síndicos Municipales: elecciones del 7 de febrero de 1982* (San José, 1982).

—— *Computo de votos y declaratorias de elección para Presidente y Vicepresidentes, Diputados a la Asamblea Legislativa, Regidores y Síndicos Municipales: elecciones del 2 de febrero de 1986* (San José, 1986).

—— *Computo de votos y declaratorias de elección para Presidente y Vicepresidentes, Diputados a la Asamblea Legislativa, Regidores y Síndicos Municipales: elecciones del 4 de febrero de 1990* (San José, 1990).

UNKELBACH, HELMUT, *Grundlagen der wahlsystematik: Stabilitätsbedingungen der parlamentarischen Demokratie* (Göttingen: Vandenhoeck und Ruprecht, 1956).

VAN DEN BERGH, G., *Unity in Diversity: A Systematic Critical Analysis of All Electoral Systems* (London: Batsford, 1955).

VEGLERIS, PHAEDO, 'Greek Electoral Law', in Howard R. Penniman (ed.), *Greece at the Polls: The National Elections of 1974 and 1977* (Washington, DC: American Enterprise Institute, 1981), 21–48.

WILDGEN, JOHN K., 'The Measurement of Hyperfractionalization', *Comparative Political Studies*, 4 (1971), 233–43.

—— 'Electoral Formulae and the Number of Parties', *Journal of Politics*, 34 (1972), 943–50.

WRIGHT, JACK F. H., 'Australian Experience with Majority-Preferential and Quota-Preferential Systems', in Bernard Grofman and Arend Lijphart (eds.), *Electoral Laws and their Political Consequences* (New York: Agathon Press, 1986), 124–38.

ZANELLA, REMO, 'The Maltese Electoral System and Its Distorting Effects', *Electoral Studies*, 9 (1990), 205–15.

Index